WHAT IS QUEER FOOD?

ALSO BY JOHN BIRDSALL

The Man Who Ate Too Much:
The Life of James Beard

Hawker Fare: Stories and Recipes from a Refugee Chef's
Isan Thai and Lao Roots (WITH JAMES SYHABOUT)

WHAT IS QUEER FOOD?

How We Served a Revolution

JOHN BIRDSALL

W. W. NORTON & COMPANY

Independent Publishers Since 1923

For information about permission to reproduce selections from
this book, write to Permissions, W. W. Norton & Company, Inc.,
500 Fifth Avenue, New York, NY 10110

For information about special discounts for bulk purchases,
please contact W. W. Norton Special Sales at
specialsales@wwnorton.com or 800-233-4830

Manufacturing by Lakeside Book Company
Book design by Lovedog Studio
Production manager: Julia Druskin

ISBN 978-1-324-07379-6

W. W. Norton & Company, Inc.
500 Fifth Avenue, New York, NY 10110
www.wwnorton.com

W. W. Norton & Company Ltd.
15 Carlisle Street, London W1D 3BS

10 9 8 7 6 5 4 3 2 1

For Perry, love of my life.
What should we have for dinner?

CONTENTS

Part Three:
Cooking in Code
1946–1973

Part Four:
The Rich, Audacious Tang of Liberation
1973–1986

Prologue

THE
ROAD
TO
HUDSON

TWISTED TACKED-UP STRIPS OF INDIGO TULLE AND shimmering holographic vinyl take side-by-side turns down the length of the ceiling, sagging like tattered, stepped-on drag in the pre-dawn y'all-need-to-go-home hour at a club. But it's not yet ten on a Thursday at Lil' Deb's Oasis. Ain't nobody going home.

Not the adorable beardy boys at the high-top deuce, or the barstool camper in thrift-store vintage, a sweater-vest with stripes like Ernie's from *Sesame Street* layered over a smoky sheer shirt. Not even the forty-something in massive, shiny black butterfly-wing eyeglasses, the kind 1970s Cary Grant knew how to work. Lil' Deb's has the beat of a place where anyone who knows they belong has permission to stay.

Ye quaint olde gentrified river port of Hudson is 120 miles north of New York City. A website by a coalition of local business owners calls it "upstate's favorite downtown," which, okay—it's trendy in a comfortable-income kind of way, seducing tourists and escapees from Manhattan and the brownstone belts of Brooklyn with country ham boards, precious takes on Norwegian fishermen's sweaters, antique Shaker pickle crocks, mid-mod Danish chairs. Art galleries: *check*. Twenty-five-dollar cock-tails: *check*. Bougie gays: *check, check,* aaaand *check*.

But all that feels far from Lil' Deb's. The way here has felt like escape.

✳

A FLIGHT DELAY in Tucson made us miss our connection in Chicago. By the time my husband and I touched down in Albany, it was later than it was supposed to be.

Perry and I set off on the forty-five-minute drive to Hudson in a rented Kia, dipping and banking in the dark on roads with scant drivers. New York State Route 23 threads a winding course beneath black silhouettes of what must be sweetgum, beech, and sassafras, past mostly darkened roadhouses and farms, eerie in the blue of our high beams.

Our headlights roused specters of the past. Signs for the Rip Van Winkle Bridge lured us deeper into the woods. I flashed on Ichabod Crane peeping from the one-room schoolhouse that floats his name, and pictured bug-eyed Martin Van Buren glaring at us from the road-side edge of his farm. I was tired, eager for warmth and the comfort of a cocktail. For so many queer and trans people, memorials of the past loom creepy. History, for us, is a nightmare we've only now thrashed awake from, though its grasping fingers reach beyond sleep.

Because after more than fifty years of progress toward LGBTQ-2SAI+ equality—fifty years after the first brick smashed the first pane at Stonewall—being queer in the world is still tenuous, still stubbornly fragile. More than a quarter century after standing up and pledging myself to Perry before witnesses, calling him husband, the word still feels like a fugitive designation. As if any day the arm of straight power could reach in to silence us, the way it kept our queer and trans ancestors mute and unseen. Or as if any second on this dark road, our headlamps lighting up myriad yard signs hyping an anti-woke MAGA crusader in a coming election, some outraged ghost could storm the Kia and snatch *husband* from our mouths.

I've come to Lil' Deb's to find shelter from history. To spend an hour or two in what I want so badly to feel like queer utopia, a space from which enforcing ghouls of the brutal past find themselves permanently eighty-sixed.

I've come to roll the taste of queer deliverance across my tongue.

✳

OUR FRONT-DOOR WELCOME feels assertively free of judgment. I don't know if I can describe exactly how, except to say that Lil' Deb's host, striking in a stretchy maxi sheath and matching black skull cap, radiates the sort of respect you can sense from those who've known its opposite.

We are *received*.

We sit at the back counter, with a view to the hot line through a beaded curtain of purple plastic jewels, sparkling in the light. This might be . . . probably is . . . oh hell, is *for sure* the queerest restaurant in North America, if not the world. Two founders with a collective history of art, design, and cooking premiered Lil' Deb's in 2015, and if it presents, as the *Washington Post* has said, like a gay tiki bar, credit the owners' mix of work-family and blood-family roots in diverse yet similarly humid places: Ecuador, the Yucatan . . . Alabama.

The food is bright and florid, little sure-handed twists on laab, mojarra frita, Goan curry. But it's the look of Lil' Deb's that strikes hardest: too sincere to be camp, too blank of irony to read as kitsch. The neon sign outside the toilets beaming *All the Bodies* into the dimness; the house-merch tee that says *Thank You for Being So Hot!* The sticker with the ultimate Gen Z homo affirmation, *IF U GAY, PERFECT*; the whiteboard fixed to the stainless face of the exhaust hood with DESIRE EXISTS scrawled in caps in orange Sharpie.

Maybe none of this is revolutionary, merely loud and confident, a queer Gen Y–Z mix of affirmation and ragged collectivism. The semi-anarchy of the décor makes it seem as if any second the room could dissolve into chaos, the tape and staples holding everything up suddenly giving out, the ceiling twists and red rope lights dropping like throw streamers; the garland of plastic lemons over the counter and the Savers-esque wall plaque that says *Hospitality* coming down in a crash.

If that did somehow happen, I'm guessing it would feel a bit like the legacy Lil' Deb's is heir to. Because whether anyone here tonight realizes it—the cooks or the host or the cutie in the Ernie sweater—this place is part of a bigger history. Lil' Deb's is the neon and purple-beaded incarnation of a hundred-year struggle to assert a queer sensibility at the table, a joyous expression of desire, connection, and need.

※

It's MORE THAN THREE DECADES since I started seriously thinking about food and the LGBTQ experience. It began with my earliest paid writing gigs, occasional stories for a gay and lesbian weekly, the *San Francisco Sentinel*. (I was cooking in restaurants full-time.) I remember a first epiphany in 1987, when I was getting a piece together on baking pies, dogging my brain to think how a pie recipe could possibly be queer. And then, lingering outside The Stud one night, I noticed one of the bar's window boxes on busy, traffic-strafed Harrison Street had this sprawling rose geranium plant that was unexpectedly thriving. I thought, Holy shit, this is the experience of being gay in a time of AIDS! This neglected hanger-on, devoid of flowers, on an unforgiving block, invisibly harboring an essence of roses.

I picked some leaves and small branches, took them home, and buried them in a jar of sugar so they'd give up their smell. I used it to sweeten an apple pie—to transform it with this sweet, lush perfume: a pie of rebellious survival, of pleasure as defiance. I told *Sentinel* readers to please respect this plant, to take only a few leaves to make sure it went on thriving. I'm not sure anybody even bothered to look for it. It got me started, though: How could food tell a story of gay perseverance? Of deviant joy?

Years later, after I'd left my last cooking job and was trying to sustain a career as a writer, I focused again on the question. In 2009, as a reporter for a San Francisco alternative weekly, I started asking gay and lesbian restaurant chefs if they could articulate a queer culture of the table. No one I talked to seemed comfortable with the question, as if, even in gay mecca, an unkillable stigma clung to queer chefs.

And then, beginning in about 2014, something seemed to change. I wrote a couple more essays about the challenge of expressing queerness in food, this time for *Lucky Peach*, a magazine with national reach, particularly for people in restaurant and media circles. It felt like, for whatever reason—a pent-up group hunger for representations of diversity, let's say—queer people in the industry were demanding to be seen. Queer food fluttered as a collective *idea*, a long-submerged banner of culinary identity, though it seemed more like a swirling vibe, not yet a thing.

Many people, me included, might say this or that dish *felt* queer, because maybe it was brazenly indulgent, liberated from narratives of shame and self-denial. Some chef might trash lingering rules about gendered cooking, or queer dishes from the American canon via bad-ass acts of deconstruction, the way Elizabeth Falkner did in her book *Demolition Desserts*. You could argue that it was a metaphor for dismantling prevailing strictures, if not patriarchy itself.

Still, saying what queer food was on a granular level kept eluding me. Lots of us could say that queer food, like desire, exists, but nobody could definitively point to what it was. There were contenders, of course: drag-brunch crab cakes Benedict, oat-milk iced coffee infused with lavender, Ginger Minj's Drag Queen Muffins (uhhh, cupcakes), anal-friendly chicken biryani from the food for bottoms dude on TikTok, Starbucks' Unicorn Frappuccino, and the dick-on-a-stick from Hot Cookie in San Francisco.

Gay: omg. But you can't feed a movement on stunt snacks alone. All that food wrapped in rainbows reminds me a little of a first-timer at the Folsom Street Fair aiming for a laid-back flex in a brand-new leather chest harness. Without the buffering power of custom over time, cosplay chafes.

It shouldn't have taken as long as it did, but at last I accepted the obvious truth that queer food is not a commodity. There is no essentialized cuisine of queerness, any more than there's one simple answer for what it means to be queer.

I should have been looking harder at queerness: what it is, what it means, and how straight power came to stigmatize it.

NEAR THE CLOSE of the nineteenth century, sexologists forged the modern concept of homosexuality. These were scientists—German, some British—who defined same-gender desire for the most part as a pathology. These men defined homosexuality as an orientation, something baked into a minority of humans from birth rather than a universal, free-floating possibility. Early Victorians tended to regard acts of same-gender sex as optional, often youthful crimes of opportunity instead of as the uncontrollable consequences of the transgressors' essential selves. Sexuality, as a concept, became a thing: a defining attribute, an essential part of your makeup rather than, you know, the innocent fallout from strangers sharing a scarce bed on a cold night. (Hey, Ishmael. Howdy, Queequeg.) It wasn't long before humans would *need* to be classified as either normal or, well . . . queer.

Of course this classification of sick or normal—it happened without the participation of queer people, except as subjects of physical and psychological study. We were observed and analyzed, compelled to "confess"; declared deviants, moral deficients, sick. We were evicted from our apartments, discharged from schools and the military. Fired from our jobs after anonymous tips. Institutionalized, jailed—isolated from "normal" people.

Decades before sexologists coined the word *homosexual* and pathologized queerness, English Victorians took a more nuanced view. Sodomy was technically a crime, though before Oscar Wilde's prosecution in 1895 for gross indecency, authorities tended to look the other way, and rarely enforced the penalties. (Before 1861, they included execution.) Likewise in most other industrialized or industrializing nations—including Japan—where private, consensual acts of same-sex desire elicited mostly shrugs. This was particularly true in countries that adopted the French Penal and Napoleonic Codes, which had decriminalized homosexual acts.

The English-speaking world, meanwhile—that world was a *bitch.*

From the earliest years of white settlement, the land of the free had no stomach for free queer expression, especially among the enslaved. (In Virginia after 1800, for instance, execution persisted for Black residents convicted of sodomy, even after the penalty for whites was eased to lengthy incarceration.) As the twentieth century dawned and homosexuality was understood as deviance explained by science, lawmakers in the states crafted ever more ironclad punishments for queer and trans expression.

Authorities in the UK, the US, and all their vast colonies abroad began monitoring and controlling every aspect of queer lives. What we did; what we wrote or said in public; how we dressed, wore our hair, and gestured, even behind the blacked-out windows of a private club; who we loved and how we lived—these became part of the legitimate interest of the police; of civic, spiritual, and medical authorities; of systems of brutality.

Needless to say, all of this defining who we were, this pathologizing, happened without the consent of queer people.

By now you've noticed that I write about queer people collectively using we/us pronouns; queer people existing across time and generations, variant sexualities, and the myriad constructions of race and gender. A *we* that includes myself, all of us living in places apart from heteronormativity, and manifest the work—the cultural, political, spiritual, intellectual, sexual, and domestic struggle—of embodying dissent, no matter how diverse in means or results. I take an essentialist view of queerness, that yeah, baby, we were born this way; like Gaga says, put your paws up. For those of us who are out, however we define that condition, it means communion in the great LGBTQ2SAI+ project of last century and this one: defining queerness for ourselves, from places of experience; mustering the courage to stress difference in our public identities. *We* is both our queer ancestors, and *us* in our time.

THE YEAR BEFORE I WAS BORN, 1958, saw the publication of *The Problem of Homosexuality,* by prominent psychologists Charles Berg and Clifford Allen. The authors disagree on what to "do" about queerness, and this divergence shows the depth of society's obsession with controlling queer people in the postwar era. Berg argues for compassion: "We are apt to forget that behind the word homosexual there is always a person," he writes in a contemporaneous study. Allen believes in what we call conversion. "If happiness is of any value," he writes, "then homosexuality should be eliminated by every means in our power." And Allen's idea, this "curing" by any means necessary—a medically and psychologically coerced conformity—was considered a form of compassion.

Society seemed to have few, if any, qualms about denying the humanity of people who fell outside the dominant rules of sexuality and gender. In 1962, a restaurant owner in Oakland, California, called in a tip on a customer, a Black trans woman and former waitress, twenty-two-year-old Patricia A. Posten. The responding officer found Posten "unco-operative," according to the *Oakland Tribune*, so the cop yanked off her wig "and won an admission that 'she' actually was a man." Posten was charged with "immoral dress," wearing the skirt, blouse, and heels that thousands of others wore that day in Downtown Oakland—a crime punishable by six months in jail.

The *San Francisco Chronicle* ran a photo of Posten in prison denims, with a deadnamed story and the headline, "Boy Who Doesn't Want to Be One." The African American news magazine *Jet* picked it up, and included photos of Posten posing in cute outfits—shots that, for me, bear a queasy whiff of exploitation. I just hope she got paid.

Popular reports of queer and trans punishment were unquestioning in their cruelty. They strike me now as sport, entertainments devised to remind readers of the consequences of refusing to squeeze within the fixed lines of conduct deemed moral.

Queer people lived underground, or at least kept the deepest parts of themselves. Historian Lillian Faderman describes how in the 1930s it was unthinkable for women to say publicly what it was to be a lesbian, to describe their actual lives, to define themselves. They were "intimidated into speechlessness," Faderman says. "Since they could not speak, . . . the public definitions of them continued to be formulated by those on the outside"—psychologists, politicians, vice squad goons.

But underground, where queer voices cautiously sounded, people sat down together.

We ate.

In the 1950s, amid Senator Joseph McCarthy's Cold War purges of communists and queers from government agencies and the related private sector, a group of lesbians got together every week for dinner in New York. Fear of exposure had kept them from going to bars. "You weren't only afraid if you worked in almost any kind of job," one participant, known simply as Viv, recalls to reporter Sasha Gregory Lewis some twenty-five years later. "You were afraid just to be gay."

They gathered—thirty or forty women every week—at someone's apartment late Sunday afternoons in the early fifties to listen to *The Big Show*, Tallulah Bankhead's variety program on NBC radio. There was a rumor that Bankhead had slept with women. She's glamorous, calls everyone *dahling*, and has the cool of a practiced killer: a man-eater in mink.

Here she is with Groucho Marx, in 1950:

Groucho: What are you doing after the show?
Tallulah: Well, dahling, I'm having a man for dinner.
Groucho: That's the main course. What about after that?

On its surface, the gag is straight: Groucho's hot need to date icy-hearted Tallulah. But the subtext reveals a woman with supreme composure deflecting male power. She's in control of her sexuality, which may or may not include taking women to bed. But just the small possibility that it does, the idea that a star could be tacitly queer and stay visible, was radical enough to anchor hope and a weekly potluck.

I picture a fleet of bowls and pots wrapped in tea towels and old sweaters, cradled in laps on the subway. Some warmed on arrival, lucky to get burner space on the cramped range, a corner of the tiny oven; others gone cold. Ingenious buffets in cramped walk-ups: drop-leaf tables with the leaves hinged up to make as much surface as possible; coffee tables enlisted for food and ashtrays; tray tables extracted from jammed closets; windowsills. Bottles of beer chilling in cold-water bathtubs.

Broccoli–creamed corn casserole; vanilla instant pudding cake; chop suey; molded Jell-O salads; egg-and-pickle-relish sandwiches cut in tri-

angles; Hawaiian meatballs on toothpicks; date bars. The same recipes straight and straight-passing women cook for their husbands and
kids, sparked by the identical cookbooks; the very recipes clipped from
the *Times* and the *Herald.* What makes the food queer is intention: the
obstinacy of survival sealed in gelatin, white bread, Spam. Silent resistance baked into florets, kernels, and fibers. Tallulah Sundays are a
domestic revolution, ordinary recipes feeding a sense of safety; trans-
muting them into queer nurturance.

Care is the focus of a story told by another voice from the potluck
circle. An unnamed woman in the group—"one of the nicest people
around," Viv says—loses her teaching job after a lesbian rumor reaches
the school's director. The woman knows about the queer blacklists,
knows she'll never teach again in the state of New York. Despair makes
her suicidal. "She was on the verge of killing herself," Viv says.

The potluck circle rallies. They make sure someone's always with
her, "keeping an eye out," Viv says. When the woman decides to move
out of state to try and teach again, the circle takes up a collection and
come up with a few hundred bucks—a shitload then—and somebody
has friends in Pennsylvania who invite her to stay until she's back on
her feet. You can bet they eat together every night.

Connecting with food becomes this paradigm for other connections,
shared queer food a hinge for the realization of a queer common purpose. *This is who we are, dahling. This is how we feed our own. This is how
we stay alive.*

Food is part of a queer arc of survival, shared sustenance on the
path that we and others like us kept open so that others could get safely
through. Survival by the oppressed is itself a form of defiance, and the
food that fuels it is a means for resistance. Queer food is ordinary food
transformed by context, part of a narrative of disobedience, to become
something with collective power.

What drives this book is excavation, my almost fevered need to
unearth stories of those who, from the start of the twentieth century
into the middle of the 1980s, used food as self-expression. Stories of
rebels—not the kind with bullhorns and bricks, but ones who defied

ironclad rules of home and family. Stories of those who wrote cook-books filled with language only queer readers could decipher. Of those who opened restaurants that tested limits, and turned the table into a stage for queer performance.

I've worked to restore censored narratives, to pry away the layers of rubble imposed on queer lives so that I might reveal the small details of food and connection they obscured.

"Many things in the world have not been named," Susan Sontag says in *Notes on "Camp"*, "and many things, even if they have been named, have never been described." In the conscious act of naming queer food, this book describes: how a bunch of so-called freaks and deviants built community despite ferocious odds; how we queers defined queerness on our own terms, through hard-won transformations of family, nur-turance, joy, pleasure, and desire. How in doing so we changed how everyone eats; how now we all, queer, not-queer, take food for granted as an essential marker of a culture, a movement, an identity, a dream. You could say it's about how we got to Lil' Deb's, the places we set out from and where we stopped along the way. You could say it's about how we fed that slow-moving revolution.

Part One

THE TASTE
OF WHAT
WE COULD
NOT SAY

1896–1948

Our Cast of Sissies, Freaks, and Exiles

Alice B. Toklas

Hermann Schmidt / Herman Smith

Harry Baker

伍錦霞 / Ng Kam-ha / Esther Eng

Craig Claiborne

Richard Olney

. . . . . .

Plus
Gertrude Stein! Picasso! Lucy, Lady Duff-Gordon!
Mudan Su! Stina! Wai Kim-fong! Betty Crocker!

THE LANGUAGE OF CAKE, PART ONE

[1896]

SURELY THE HANDS OF AN OHIO BOY WILL TURN TO things less salutary than a book of Bible stories after chores. Surely those hands will want to whittle a squirrel from a scrap of buckeye or braid a leather riding harness. Before long, though, this boy will surely run away with friends to chaw tobacco from a nickel plug and study smutty postcards. Surely he'll meander off, air gun in hand, to fire lead at any fencepost not within the gaze of grownup eyes. Boys will be boys, but boyish innocence must find its natural end point in the taking up of manly things. Surely no right-minded young man would elect to spend his idle hours in a kitchen, turning his hand to the baking of delicate things.

Yet this is precisely what thirteen-year-old Harry Baker elects to do—seeks to learn the secrets of making cakes as well as any woman or girl of Allen County.

Perhaps it's the burden of the boy's Christian name, as if some metaphysical being—whether angel or demon is surely grist for neighbors' discussions—stitched a hand for batters, meringues, and arabesques of seven-minute frosting onto the arm of the only son delivered to Mariah "Belle" and Jacob Baker of Lima, Ohio.

Harry's surprising hand begins to reveal itself after one fateful Sunday.

On that day, Harry and his family take in the sermon at Trinity Methodist. On that day, the ladies of the congregation organize a charity baking competition. First prize for cake goes to Clara Butters, whose husband, Frank, is foreman at the local Standard Oil plant.

Harry tastes Clara's entry and is profoundly disappointed. Maybe the layers are dry or greasy. Maybe the flavoring is too light or too heavy. Maybe the icing is grainy. The particulars are lost to time, but from Harry's description of this incident years later, it's clear his disillusionment is a catalyzing moment in his life.

I'm speculating here, but maybe Clara's victory, her crowning that day as Lima's queen of cake, has more to do with standing than skill. Could Frank's position with Standard Oil be the factor that makes Clara's cake unassailable? Is it injustice that picks at young Harry's mind?

He tells his mother he thinks he can do better—that for whatever reason, he believes he can make a cake that might put the ladies of Lima to shame. And Belle and Jacob, following whatever discussions they may have had, allow him to try.

I *see* Harry in this moment, his sleeves rolled up, studying Belle's jottings in the formerly blank pages at the back of what is likely her only recipe book; sense him taking on the lemon-scented Sunshine Cake and delicate Queen, airy with egg whites; achieving the lightest of angel food crumbs; carefully rolling the body of a sponge around a layer of shiny rhubarb jelly, clear and pink; learning the proper movement of the wrist to marble batters of divergent weights and densities. Each has its language, revealing its tender secrets with reluctance, perhaps, and only to the kind of boy with an ear for hearing.

MADDALENA'S PIGEONS

[1908]

A LICE BABETTE TOKLAS, THIRTY-ONE, IS SWEATING IN the heat of a train carriage rattling between Milan and Florence. She's with her childhood friend from San Francisco, Harriet Levy. They turned up in Paris a year ago, expecting to stay only a few months, but it was as if the city refused to let them go, the charm of its flower markets, its caped and starch-capped nannies in the Jardin du Luxembourg, its praline ices as good as San Francisco's. Now, a year later, Gertrude Stein is setting them up for the summer in a rented house in Fiesole, Casa Ricci, perched in the hills above Florence. (Gertrude is bunking nearby at Villa Bardi with her brothers, Mike and Leo, along with Mike's wife, Sarah, and their boy, Allan.)

Before Sarah married Mike Stein, she and Harriet were friends in San Francisco. And it's Sarah, through Harriet, who connects Gertrude and Alice on her first day in Paris.

Alice and Harriet arrived on the boat train, dropped their things at the hotel, and headed right back out to call on the Steins. Gertrude was there, in a brown corduroy suit pinned with this massive coral brooch. She looked incredible to Alice, like nature itself: powerful, sensitive, indestructible. "Large and heavy with delicate small hands," Alice recalled later, "and a beautifully modeled and unique head."

Alice and Gertrude fuse. They go on long walks through the city, often dropping in on Gertrude's friend and alter ego Picasso, to gossip and take in his strange erotic pictures of fractured nudes, amid clutter and smells of dog and paint. Alice takes French lessons with Fernande

Olivier, Picasso's lover and muse, but it's mostly an excuse to talk about fashion, Alice's weakness. Their sessions are packed with talk of silver furs, perfumes, painted nails.

Some who were close to Gertrude before Alice showed up would balk at her presence in Gertrude's life and affections. For Leo Stein, Alice seems a symptom of his sister's self-delusions about her importance as a writer and a genius. Mabel Dodge describes Alice as someone menacing, strange, and hideous: a freak. It's true she has strong looks.

Consider the photos in the Bancroft Library showing Alice and Gertrude in Venice's Piazza San Marco in 1908, among men and pigeons and one especially curious child. Alice looks like a fifteenth-century Florentine adolescent boy with a shaggy bowl cut and a hat that shows like a brimless pillbox. She's paired it with what must be one of her long batik dresses. Her figure reads like the head of a young Medici lord capping a femme-y modern silhouette. Gertrude looks solid, querulous, and hot, but Alice seems to float above gender and history: a strange and beautiful figure haunting a setting of iconic cultural power.

If Alice were somehow to apparate into twenty-first-century urban queerspace, if she showed up hungry to Lil' Deb's Oasis, she'd have the shape of belonging. No doubt in 1908 it was a steeper climb.

Look, I get that antisemitism was probably a convenient and savagely acceptable way to other Alice when, really, almost *everything* about her was too much for some people. Dodge acknowledges Alice's "beautiful gray eyes hung with black lashes," but scorns her "black, folded Hebraic hair" and "half-Oriental get-up. . . . Her barbaric chains and jewels, . . . her melancholy nose."

If I can step in here:

Big fucking deal, Mabel, Alice has a nose. It's the alt centerpiece of Alice's signature beauty, and a kind of symbol, as I see it, of her inborn resistance to conformity. Her looks, her style—I have the feeling she exploits them to assert difference. That she wraps a fierce, uncompromising look around a manner so mild, with what seems like complete deference to Gertrude, "self-obliterating," Dodge says—it messes with some people. Alice is not who women are supposed to be.

She wasn't always this provocative. Was not always so . . . queer.

In San Francisco, Alice squeezed herself into the shape of a house drudge. After her mother died, twenty-year-old Alice took up the burden of looking after her father, grandfather, and younger brother; her uncles and male cousins: consulting with the cook, I imagine, and squinting over household accounts. Alice's friend Annette recalled visiting, and remembered "the stultifying pall that hung over the dining room," the stale funk of cigars the men puffed after pushing their plates away. The smoke seeped into walls and fabrics—everything. Even the wood of the furniture reeked.

Alice did what she was supposed to, mixed, rolled out, baked, and iced the things every upper-middle-class American woman was expected to turn her hand to, de facto displays of subservient femininity: the cocoa-powder cake called Brownstone Front; plain, unsweetened strips of flaky pastry dubbed The Ribbons of Sarah Bernhardt—dull Victorian fancies with dumb names. At home, Alice wore a long, gray dress, like a Quaker. On the street, "she buttoned herself into a severe gray suit and wore a gray cloth turban," biographer Linda Simon says, "seeming, one friend thought, like a nun."

A year in Paris, a year of growing into Gertrude—it's changed Alice.

Though at this moment, en route from Milan with Harriet to join the Steins in Fiesole, Alice surely feels a fierce imperative to *literally* change. The train is stifling, it's become harder and harder to breathe. She must do something or perish.

Alice slips into the dressing room just off the ladies' toilet; opens the front buttons of her frock and un-cinches her suffocating girdle corset of cerise silk, working her fingers into the crisscross ribbon up the back, feeling for the knot that will set her free. She tosses the girdle from the window of the rushing car. She will not wear it again. Not ever.

When she returns to the carriage Harriet says, "What a strange coincidence, I just saw your cherry-colored corset pass by the window." She believes Alice is still wearing the pink girdle she purchased six thousand miles away in San Francisco, while another exactly like it is sailing, miraculously, through the Italian air.

How could Harriet be so thick? Willing to believe an outlandish coincidence rather than the possibility that Alice could be naked under her dress?

Are most of Alice's friends incapable of thinking she'd choose to free herself from the "proper" strangling foundation? Unable ever to know how delicious loose silk can feel in a softly rocking train car; the gentle friction of a camisole skimming liberated nipples, teased as hard and shiny as sugared filberts.

Fiesole proves just as delicious. The hillside roost of stone villas and formal gardens above Florence offers views that urge the eye, says Alice's precious Henry James, into "a hundred gradations of distance." It's a landscape that has sustained artists, cooks, and saints for centuries. It has already begun to coax Alice into a corset-free state of release.

✳

WHAT MAKES THE TUSCAN SUMMER OF 1908 such a rich moment for me is how it begins to germinate the seeds of food's queer future, one that will be ready for harvest in the 1950s, in the pages of Alice's cookbook. To me, the importance of the summer of the flung corset and Alice and Gertrude's steep walks together in the hills above Florence is how it sets the future of their shared domestic life—a life they will not be able to tell the whole truth of, but one in which food and the table become an axis of queer agency.

But first, a wedding.

In the novelette "Didn't Nelly and Lilly Love You," through a cryptic narrative with blurred details and altered pronouns, Gertrude hints at how she and Alice married each other that summer. It's like this:

They're on a long, hot walk and need to rest. They find a garden.

The talk veers delicately, discreetly to the history of Alice's romantic friendships with women.

They admit their attraction, maybe even their desire, for each other. They profess their love.

Gertrude proposes a union, marriage in all respects but official
sanction and public affirmation: a conjugal bond that must be faithful,
exclusive, and last forever. Gertrude promises to be Alice's "husband,"
in the Victorian terms they understand. She will provide for Alice and
be her protector if Alice will be Gertrude's "wife," unstinting of love
and material care. Alice will look to the marketing, the cooking, the
serving of meals. She'll deal with servants, postmen, and laundresses.
Gertrude will be free to write.

They'll share a bed.

Alice cries and says, *I am your bride*: a vow unwitnessed except by the
garden and the birds, the sun, and the hundred gradations of distance
before them.

When they return to Casa Ricci, Harriet, who is not so thick after
all, sees what has happened. Alice is still crying—her happy tears are
endless, Harriet will recall. In the days ahead, there will be no limit to
the handkerchiefs Alice wets with crying.

But for all the evidence of Alice's damp felicity, her marriage to Gertrude has to exist as a promise unknown to the wider world, spoken of
only to each other. It must remain unreported to any taxing authority
or municipal flunky, unacknowledged to blood family, unmarked by
cake or a wedding portrait. *Our future*, Gertrude writes, *would be for
ourselves alone.*

They spend the rest of the summer taking pilgrimage walks, they
call them, visiting sites in the lives of saints Gertrude idolizes, particularly Francis of Assisi. They climb the vertical streets of Gubbio, where
Francis charmed both a wolf and the villagers who wanted it dead.
They tramp to Perugia to see the Fra Angelico altarpiece and to dine
on restaurant dishes graced, for Alice, with an equivalent measure of
artistry: "perfect" renderings of scampi and fritto misto.

The next day they send their luggage ahead and set out on the long
walk to Assisi to visit the church, with its Cimabue frescoes, on the
site of Francis's humble original. The sun is brutal, and though Alice is
wearing a thin cotton dress of Dutch batik, she feels the heat. She asks
Gertrude can they stop. Alice crouches behind bushes to strip off her

stockings, her camisole and bloomers. She finishes the liberation begun on the train with the trashing of her corset. She has stepped out of the life she may once have believed to be inescapable.

There's a photograph from that summer: Alice and Harriet seated on a low wall at the edge of a sloping field of what looks like corn stalks. There are trees, and in the distance the villas of Fiesole cut into the hills. Harriet looks away from the photographer. She looks chewed up by Edwardian vacation clothes (double-breasted blouse, flowing elbow sleeves, embroidered neckline) while trying to balance a ridiculous heap of hat, a sugarloaf carpeted with artificial monkey-faced pansies.

Alice looks straight into the camera: jaw set, smile ambiguous. She's wearing a lace-trimmed shirtwaist, voluminous yes, but she's hatless, her thick hair a deep inverted bowl. Her Mediterranean eyes appear to gaze out from an antiquity that never vanished, that sepia zone of queer imagination where Isadora Duncan and Baron von Gloeden's laurel-crowned shepherds live on.

Harriet looks lost, as if unsure how she got there.

Alice looks found.

✳

PLUCKED FOWLS OF ALL KINDS saturate Tuscany. In Florence, the air of Alice and Gertrude's wedding summer is heavy with the fragrance of chickens sizzling in butter over charcoal. Italians up and down the country lust after winged things, "any and every kind of bird," Elizabeth David will note in the 1950s, "both for the fun of the chase and for the benefit of the table." Yet the fowl they snag are sometimes not the plumpest or most delectable. They need skilled hands in the kitchen.

Casa Ricci's cook, Maddalena, has a talent for preparing runty pigeons. When the little creatures come from the dovecote they are slight and bony, so unlike the "giant luscious birds" Alice has known in California. Maddalena's genius is in defying their smallness; knowing how to make them rich and succulent; how to transcend what might at first look like immovable borders.

First she browns them in olive oil on a stove no doubt fired by charcoal. She covers the pan and nudges them along for an hour over glowing heat; adds salt and pepper and, for each bird, a crushed tooth of garlic. She'll lay out the cooked pigeons side by side in an earthen dish, flock them with Parmesan and bread crumbs, drizzle more oil over the top, and set them in a quick oven to crisp and brown.

The crispness of the birds' new skin, as it were, with a shy kiss of smoke and a brazen kiss of garlic, echoes the crisp little bones underneath. This is the heart of Maddalena's achievement: that a thing assumed to be the pigeons' defect, their scrawniness, a higher-than-usual ratio of bone to flesh, becomes their glory. It's a celebration of the carcass, of beauty beyond the limits of what the world sees as deficient. A beauty of essentials.

Surely Maddalena's pigeons are the reciprocal flavor to a profound revelation, an honest-to-god epiphany: That Alice's desire for women is innate. It is in her bones, the structure of her being. As such it can be neither aberrant nor shameful; it can only ever be who she is.

Alice knew loneliness in San Francisco, the despair from seeing girls she loved choose men, marriage, family. This hot Italian summer has precipitated a stripping of the old burdens, the responsibilities she was told—and believed—that birth as a woman had forged on her. Stepping out of those restraints has brought happinesses once unthinkable. She has transformed from prim gray nun to woman in love, naked under her thin dress.

Of course the truth of her love for Gertrude must go unnoticed by the world, which is to say by fools. Still, this place of perfect calm that Alice has found with Gertrude is so powerful it *will* find voice, though inevitably it must be a voice of silence; of subtle gestures and weighted words, and yes, of food.

Because food is Alice and Gertrude's ineffable language.

Alice knows what it is to be subservient within a family ruled by men: a kind of prison tainted with cigar-stink, under a dreary compulsion to keep house. But her union with Gertrude is a marriage of equals, a mirror reflection. As Gertrude says, *I see you and you see me I reflect you and you reflect me. . . . I love my love and she loves me, I can reflect and so can she.*

Cooking had long been a place of gender inequality, but the queer kitchen was a leveling ground. They see themselves in the closed reflection of a domestic life together. Sitting down together to eat, sharing the sensory details of a meal—these were assertions of queer subjectivity, symbolic of shared pleasure and mutual care.

Not very many are well pleased with other people's ways in having love in them, Gertrude remarks. But ahhhh, she says elsewhere, surely about herself and Alice, *How sweetly we are fed.*

That *we* has all the weight and power of emphasis for me. Is it too much to believe that Gertrude meant it to stretch as far as all queer lovers?

Alice would perhaps never again be so naked, so vulnerable or so open, as she was in Fiesole that summer, but she would turn this secret sweetness into a language—a language of shared tastes, shared impressions, shared pleasures, shared meaning: *Maddalena's redemptive pigeons . . . a de facto wedding feast of scampi and fritto misto . . . the salads composed to look like a cathedral in a pastry shop in Ávila that Alice and Gertrude discover on holiday the summer following Fiesole . . .*

"As a lesbian, Stein lacked a narratable daily life," writes queer scholar Julie Abraham, and of course this is true for Alice. As queer people, we were denied the human imperative of telling stories about ourselves; of paying witness to many of the things we did, saw, thought, and felt. Gertrude turns her lack of a narratable life into history, as in *The Making of Americans.* In *The Autobiography of Alice B. Toklas,* an immediate bestseller when it appears in 1933, Gertrude makes herself and Alice into semi-fictional characters. Not lesbians with nipples and tongues; not women built of joy and desire. They are literature's eccentric companions.

✳

THIS, FROM THE POET KNOWN AS H.D., IN 1919:

Don't you understand
if you today in a crude speech
in a dark land hope to say,
to speak one word of the joy we had
(to people who anyway don't want to understand) . . .
O don't you, don't you understand,
you must count yourself now, now among the dead?

BEFORE LEAVING FLORENCE, Alice buys a table, chairs, and a credenza and has them shipped to Paris. Harriet has bought a Renaissance table for the apartment she will share with Alice. And back in the atelier on the rue de Fleurus, where Gertrude lives with her brother Leo, some elaborately carved Tuscan tables have already caught Alice's eye. Her life seems genuinely packed with heavy wooden pieces. When she eventually moves into the Stein atelier and Leo eventually moves out, one or another of these tables becomes the stage on which she and Gertrude take their meals.

At my most novelistic, I imagine them as redemption for the smoky, man-stained furniture Alice escaped in San Francisco. At my most romantic, I imagine them as the souvenir of the Tuscan summer wedding that cannot be publicly remembered yet finds affirmation every day in the rituals of eating.

The Well of Loneliness, Radclyffe Hall's 1928 novel about the struggle to express lesbian desire in the early twentieth century, ends with the protagonist's anguished plea to God: *Give us also the right to our existence.*

Alice, who perfects the art of being invisible, will someday plot a narrative of her and Gertrude's joy. The story will be broken up and concealed, planted in seemingly innocuous places, buried in recipes and digressive anecdotes.

It's one way Alice will be able to speak about her life with Gertrude, relating anecdotes that may or may not be strictly "true" but they'll be faithful to strict emotional truths. This is how Alice seizes her right to be.

VILE FUGITIVE

[1912]

TWO WEEKS AFTER VICE DETECTIVES IN OREGON showed up at his room to question him, thirty-one-year-old Herman Smith, a.k.a. Hermann Schmidt, is a fugitive in San Francisco, wanted for sodomy and other crimes of an unspeakable nature. Surely Herman is afraid to walk the streets in daylight, risk being spotted in a restaurant or on the streetcar. Is he holed up in the blankest flophouse on the Embarcadero, spending anxious days smoking in bed behind drawn blinds? Is he terrified whenever he hears voices through the transom, and steps in the hall? Does he disguise himself, keeping his face lowered to eat at some near-empty late-night chop suey house at the edge of Chinatown?

It all begins with an unremarkable arrest on a November night in Portland.

Police pick up this nineteen-year-old punk, Benjamin Trout, for swiping petty merchandise. Clearly Trout is scared, and either out of general panic or because he makes a calculated move to distract from his crimes, he volunteers some information at precinct headquarters.

This information is big.

Fucking huge.

Trout says there's this homosexual underground operating in Rose City. He claims firsthand knowledge, having had sexual acts performed on him by local men of respectable standing. He names names. He identifies the places these filthy seductions took place, in upstanding boarding houses and residence hotels. Some of these monsters even approached him in Lownsdale Park, for god's sake, right under the noses of decent people.

Within days, vice detectives round up eleven men, alleged members of an organized ring of sexual inverts: shop clerks, office workers, even a respectable lawyer and a doctor. All *appear* upstanding. They're churchgoers, taxpayers, members of fraternal organizations, the sorts of men who rise to give their seats to ladies on the streetcar. Yet according to a growing log of extracted testimonies, all have been in shocking situations with young men like Trout.

A local paper calls it what many believe it to be: "the ugliest scandal ever brought to light in Portland." And light, the essential disinfectant for vice, is precisely what the police are keen to flood these degenerates with. Because behind closed blinds and in rank bushes, under cloak of darkness, a predatory culture of sexual inverts had festered in one of America's most bucolic and salubrious cities.

To some Portlanders who pick up their newspaper, inky with shouted headlines, it's alarming how easily homosexuals could operate, how invisible they could be. Sex perverts had always been easily identifiable, migrant lowlifes at the dusky edges: hobos riding the rails into town with their "punks"; rough, mostly brown-skinned workers in the logging camps—Chinese, Asian Indian, Greek—at night seducing and corrupting fine young white boys. The men being rounded up now could be their neighbors, brothers, sons—husbands to their sisters! There was no easy way of identifying them, some of whom had mingled invisibly within the china-cup and finger-sandwich stratum of Northwest society.

As detectives hammered suspects under questioning, the list of alleged perverts grew to more than two dozen.

Among them is Herman Smith, a clerk at the Eilers Music House; unmarried, residing at the Cornelius Hotel. When detectives pay a visit to the Cornelius they discover Schmidt has fled, in so much haste, apparently, that he has left most of his things behind. Papers confiscated in Herman's room, what the press identified as letters and "literature," leave no doubt he's been an offender for some time.

A grand jury indicts the absent Herman for "an act," the report lays out, "which grossly injured the person and property of one Fred Rodby, by . . . persuading[,] inducing[,] and causing him, the said Fred Rodby, to expose his private parts in an indecent and scandalous manner and by . . . placing the penis of the said Fred Rodby in the mouth of him, . . . thereby . . . causing a seminal emission from the person of Fred Rodby."

It's criminally indecent to perform fellatio on the twenty-one-year-old Rodby, but prosecutors go a step further. By inducing the emission, they contend, Herman has robbed the victim of his semen. He's not just a deviant. He's also a thief.

In the trials, the defense asks questions suggesting that Herman was also on the invitation list for a homosexual house party, a so-called "drag," where men cavorted in women's gowns. That he has seduced and corrupted respectable young men at the YMCA where he once resided, besmirching its high-minded, wholesome Christian reputation. Was no act too shameless for Herman Smith?

Like Herman, several other men implicated in the scandal flee. The police apprehend a few runaways in Seattle or San Francisco, but Herman's whereabouts remain unknown. The talents Herman deployed for so long to avoid suspicion seem to have helped him slip away. In the eyes of the prosecutor he is a monster in disguise, but because of technicalities in the cases, which surface following the appeals of two of the convicted to the Oregon Supreme Court——including whether oral sex could even be charged as sodomy—prosecutors reluctantly begin dismissing indictments. Ten months after the grand jury's decision of probable cause, the prosecutor drops the charge against Herman.

The semen thief has gotten away.

✳

IT WAS A COLOSSAL FARCE: the untruths screamed from scandal sheets competing for readers' nickels, the conspiracy theories about some pansy cabal, some blind assumption of innocence for "boys" like Benjamin Trout and Fred Rodby.

At the time, historian Peter Boag says, "boy . . . referred to a young man between his late teens and late twenties." As for the so-called victims in the scandal, "All appeared to have willingly participated in sexual relations," Boag says, not only with the accused but with each other. The sex happened in private, between willing parties. If some of the liaisons seemed calculated it probably wasn't because of anything nefarious, only practical necessity. Men in a small city, where anonymity would have been scarce, needed planning. There was no organized ring, no "vice clique," as the *Oregon Journal* has hyped it, just men finding each other, at a time when no meaningful community of queers existed, no social networks that weren't considered criminal. What choice did men have but to slip into shadows?

But hey, sodomy *is* a state crime in 1912. And sodomy is whatever Oregon's prosecutors, judges, and ultimately its legislators say it is: sex of any kind that veered from he/she married missionary. (In the wake of the arrests and convictions, Oregon draws up an expanded list of prohibitions, with a tighter definition of sodomy that includes oral sex.)

The shock of the scandal would leave a mark on one particular nine-year-old in Portland. James Beard already knew he was different, that he liked boys. He knew about the long-distance affair his mother sustained with another woman, an affair that spanned James's childhood and which he understood to be romantic, and his parents' hostility to each other was perpetually on display. James would later recall that she was close to two of the implicated men; surely she knew others. There was an implicit warning for a brash, curious young homosexual eager to feel himself in the world: *be more cautious—hide better.* Make sure your *outside* passes, the way you dress and talk and hold yourself, so you can go on hiding within. So you can retain a measure of freedom.

Of course, with determination and luck, you might be able to get away, physically flee the dangerous world of vice arrests and scandal, of ruined futures. If you didn't have the means to stay gone—the kind of resources Gertrude and Alice had—well, you could always try changing your face, your body, your voice. It's what Herman will try, eventually, though it takes decades. Right now, from his hiding place in San Francisco, Herman has to figure out his next move. Quickly.

Two weeks before Christmas, he secures a berth on the SS *Tenyo Maru*, sailing from San Francisco for Yokohama and Hong Kong, calling at Honolulu, Kobe, Nagasaki, and Shanghai, connecting with steamers for Manila and beyond.

Herman begins his big escape, an eastward race across a map of fear.

HERMANN GEORG LUDWIG SCHMIDT was born in Niles, Michigan, in 1881. Herman, from here on out, is the seventh surviving child born to Friedrich and Anna Schmidt, who immigrated at the time of the US Civil War from a village in Saxony, the geographical heart of modern Germany. Niles is close to the Indiana state line, a land of forests cleared for farming. The Schmidts would appear to have a pretty sizable farm by nineteenth-century standards: multiple cow barns, with apple, pear, and plum orchards sloping to meadows of loamy black soil running for about a mile along the edge of a creek.

Herman's mother dies when he's nine; his father follows less than six years later. Herman's older siblings take up his rearing. It's assumed he'll eventually take up work on the farm, but Herman doesn't seem to be built for farming.

Describing his hometown years later, Herman's most vivid recollections seem to be about flowers: woodbine and wild cucumber, purple asters, old maid's pinks, goldenrod. He seems particularly sensitive to aesthetic beauty.

There's a photo of Herman as a young man, surely a formal senior high school portrait. He lifts his chin for the camera, and the way he bears his head says confidence with a wicked edge. It looks like he tried to bring order to his probably ordinarily untamed hair by imposing a middle part. He flaunts a stiff collar that grips and restrains his neck like a corset; a jacket with gaudy satin lapels. He's serving softness and arrogance, innocence and debauchery—a young man with large, shameless appetites.

After high school, Herman's siblings send him to Chicago for business college, as if knowing how to do the books will make their brother a better manager of the farm when the time comes.

You'd think Chicago would be a place of wonder and sin for a queer kid fresh off the farm, but Herman's locked in the watchful gaze of an older, Scripture-reading couple, friends of the Schmidt family pastor in Niles. "The gay life which went on about us," Herman would recall, "was not for me." I'm not sure how much freight he intended *gay* to carry, but I like to think he's loaded it a tad.

In 1900, Herman's living in Portage, Indiana, with a sister, working as a bookkeeper. Something's not right with his body, though—he feels pain when he breathes deep or twists his torso. Pleurisy, the doctor declares, advising a move to a climate free of lake chill and humidity. A place of fresh, dry, salubrious air.

One of Herman's brothers owns a wheat farm and ranch in the arid high desert of eastern Oregon. So in 1907, the year Alice B. Toklas leaves San Francisco for Paris and her fateful introduction to Gertrude Stein, twenty-six-year-old Herman boards a westbound train. He spends two years in the dusty, parched-grass outback, living on ranch fare. (The Chinese-born cook, John, rustles up Cantonese cowboy improvisations: soy sauce beef stew . . . roast chickens stuffed with rice, pine nuts, and pulverized tangerine peel . . .) Herman is clearly horny for wranglers and rodeo bucks—"These wiry handsome bronzed men . . . in fur-trimmed chaps," he says—they're everywhere. But even with that sort of all-you-can-eat visual feast, the backlands are no place to satisfy Herman's kind of hunger.

The timeline in his memoir doesn't square with the scant trail of documents we have for Herman. In his memoir he claims he leaves the ranch in July 1912, on the death of a sister back in Indiana. He returns home "bronzed . . . by the sun," he says, "so much taller, and entirely well." But from the Portland City Directory of 1910 we see Herman, age twenty-nine, working at a branch of the Eilers Music House, dealer in pianos, organs, and phonographs. This is the Herman who doesn't show up in his memoir, the Herman of the YMCA, invitations to drag parties, and men.

In Portland he registers as a Democrat under the name Herman Smith, as if to make official witness of a clean break, a new identity. But then, November 1912 brings Benjamin Trout, and the indictment, and both Herman's budding independence and his future liberty seem irrevocably sunk. Herman has two qualities that might prove to be his deliverance, though, the first being his charm.

The second is his talent for what seems like endless reinvention.

HE SPENDS ALMOST A YEAR IN FUGITIVE LIMBO on the sea. Scared, obviously; cut off from everyone he knows, obviously. Drifting westward through time zones, longitudes, and hemispheres; sailing at a relentless pace toward the cover of sunsets.

Weeks pass. Months. He gets connecting passage on other steamers. Herman received money from the sale of the Schmidt family home in Niles after his parents died. Was he able to flee San Francisco with a stash of dollars? Does he take small jobs in ports along the way?

Herman lingers at ports of call, cities on whose streets he must never have believed he'd see his shadow.

In *Kitchens Near and Far,* a 1944 cookbook-cum-memoir of his journey (which, of course, skirts the reason for his almost-year of travel), Herman talks about his "strange hunger of the heart and soul." If you read between the lines, though, it's clear Herman enjoys a couple of roaming snacks.

En route to China, Herman gets close to a traveling American, also around thirty, headed to his sister's wedding in Shanghai. This man and Herman end up collaborating on the design for the ceremony. They scour Shanghai, a place Herman calls "gayest city in the Orient," and find humongous silver candlesticks and a white bear rug to frame the couple on the altar. They fill the chapel with a riot of white camellias, lilies, and roses, like some early *style moderne* flowering of drama and elegance.

He chases nightfalls, slipping west through

Shanghai . . .

Manila . . .

Singapore . . .

Colombo . . .

Port Said . . .

Genoa . . .

Gibraltar . . .

And survives to come out at the other end, in New York, city of appetites bigger and more shameless than any Herman could have known.

THE RECORD OF HERMAN'S MOVEMENTS in New York starts out blank. What we know is that probably sometime in or after 1918 he meets the posh English couturier Lucy, Lady Duff-Gordon, famous survivor of the *Titanic* and a celebrity in New York ever since she opened a Manhattan branch of her London house of gowns, Lucile. Herman casually presents her with a single yellow flower. It seems she takes to Herman—after all they've both defied disaster, maybe she feels a flash of something kindred. Anyway, we know Herman's charming and self-assured, and whether or not Lady Duff-Gordon offers him a job on the spot, he does go to work at Lucile. In 1939, Herman tells the syndicated magazine *This Week* that Lady Duff-Gordon made him her manager, though his name doesn't come up in her 1932 book of memoirs, *Discretions and Indiscretions*, detailing much about the history of Lucile in New York.

Which stories can we trust from the shape-shifting Herman?

Lady Duff-Gordon's designs define chic for the moment: svelte, less corseted, ultra-femme silhouettes of layered crepe and lace, with slit skirts and plunging necklines. Florenz Ziegfeld orders costumes from her for his Ziegfeld Follies. She designs for some of the most famous women on Broadway and in the movies, including Mary Pickford.

In 1918, a year into America's involvement in World War I, Herman signs his draft card *Herman Maurice K. Smith:* a frisky new name if not a refashioned identity. He's living in Greenwich Village. In the 1920 Census, Herman's sharing his Village apartment with an actor, Richard Henry Hall—officially Herman's lodger, but they'll live together at various addresses for at least another two decades. (Herman dies in 1951.)

Mismanagement and broken supply chains in the wake of war did what an iceberg could not: they sank Lady Duff-Gordon. With the tanking of Lucile, Herman finds a job at the Famous Players-Lasky movie studio in Astoria, Queens, one of the biggest of the silent pictures era. Again in 1939, he boasts to *This Week* that he was a technical director of costume and color for the studio, "an expert on the lore of precious stones" and "an authority on the history of cosmetics." I mean it's possible.

Still, despite whatever exaggeration Herman may be guilty of, he has a talent for illusion, the possibilities of cosmetics and character design; in the tricks that transform color into nuance on black and white film.

In 1930, in the face of the Great Depression and problems in the movie biz, the studio—renamed Paramount Publix—goes into receivership. Herman's job disappears.

The reason I'm laying out Herman's bio like this is to show how time and again he reinvents himself, time and again adapts. He has this queer knack for survival: from altering his name and tweaking his identity to wrapping himself in stories of who he was, or is. Soon this talent of Herman's to survive, his reliance on fiction, will take the form of food: recipes, and semi-mythical stories of farming and cooking in the American heartland.

It's an expression of queer food in the time of sexual prohibition, crafting fictions around food to mask the daily stories we couldn't tell; a reinvention that let us be in the world, even if we had to wear a mask.

Herman is master of the stage look, crafting beautiful silhouettes, calculating that the audience too far away to notice they're held together with safety pins and tape.

REDEMPTION FUDGE

[1923]

F OR THE BUSYBODIES OF LIMA, WHO FOR YEARS HAD
surely tut-tutted the peculiarity of the Baker boy's penchant for
mixing batters and setting fudge (would he tie himself into one of
Belle's rickrack aprons?), news of Harry's wedding to Mary Fitzwater in Columbus must come as a surprise, if not a relief. Still, a man of
twenty-eight is a teensy bit old to be taking a bride.

It's true Harry had spent part of his youth at Ohio Wesleyan, where
he was no doubt a welcome contributor to the baked bean and cake parties regularly held in the dormitories.

The important thing, I imagine them saying back in Lima, is that
Harry is finally tying the knot, slipping a ring onto Mary's finger—
Mary who, at twenty-six, is nearly as seasoned as her groom. The
important thing was that the happy couple could at last get down to
the business of starting a family.

In 1912, the newlyweds settle in Columbus, where Harry sells insurance for the Mutual Life company. They produce a couple of kids on
a timeline that surely eases lingering doubts back home about Harry's diligence to his divine-sanctioned responsibilities as patriarch. But
Harry's gotta be Harry. As Mary lies in labor at the hospital, giving
birth to a daughter, Harry's home baking a cake.

To relax, he says.

Then, one night, Mary answers a knock and finds a policeman on her
porch. Harry's out—as a roving salesman he's often away in the eve-
nings, either on the road or entertaining clients in his office at Mutual

Life. But the officer says Harry's been arrested—picked up on a morals charge. Maybe that registers in Mary's brain when the policeman says those words; maybe's there's a toddler crying from the kitchen and Mary's hustling a baby on her hip, and a sneer or a look of pity or both on the officer's face, but it eventually sinks in.

Harry's been picked up for performing an indecent act with a young man in a public toilet.

※

SEXUAL VARIANCE IN FARM-BELT OHIO in the 1920s exists on a schizo level of secrecy and denial.

Writer, tattoo artist, and sex researcher Samuel Steward grew up in little old Woodfield, a couple hundred miles from little old Lemon Township. Steward's memoir describes how easy it was, starting in high school, to hook up with men and teen boys who thought of themselves as straight; who carried on conventionally with wives and girlfriends. None of the guys he had sex with, nobody on the football team or from Sunday school, called him out in public—even in some twisted move to save face—as a fairy. Not one of his partners ever implied publicly, that Steward was aware of, that he was a fag, a degenerate, a pansy, or a queer. A parallel life spent rolling around on attic mattresses and wedging into the backseats of parked cars fit so easily—so naturally, it seemed—into the familiar rhythm of Sunday services, homecoming games, and picnic socials.

This was possible because of what Steward says were "breathtaking leaps of illogic" in the strict Christian mind. He separates the thinking into two parts. First, that "people [do] not do such things" (i.e., have gay sex). And second, that owing to the truth of the first part, "such things must [therefore] be nonexistent." Allow nothing, acknowledge nothing.

Queerness is muffled in a paradox so thick it becomes soundless and invisible. The thing that cannot possibly exist fills sweaty stolen half hours, in haymows, garages, and empty Bible study classrooms. It exists in measures of time counted someplace off the normal clock. It makes men temporarily invisible, until they slip back into the stream of standard time, back into their public faces, which are of course masks, but only the wearer is supposed to know that; swab the perspiration from their necks, unwrap a stick of gum, and give the knots of their ties a tug to complete reentry to the visible world.

Being invisible is effortless. But what's the cost to a sensitive man like Harry? What joy can he carry back to the world of his public identity? What's the long-term effect of toggling in and out of time?

Baking had always been Harry's means of expression, cooking of all kinds, really. To charm clients and close deals, set up hotplates in his Mutual Life office; braised Swiss steak in a pressure cooker and baked cakes on a portable tin oven set over the heat—away from Mary's kitchen. For Harry, gay sex must have occurred according to rules as opaque and implacable as the ones regulating the rise of sweet, foamy batters—the lift of self-expression; the boost that comes from self-discovery. Was it also a lifeline rope between worlds for Harry? Something he could pull in the ordinary world to make his way back through the membrane into the queer one, and vice versa?

But then the public toilet in Columbus and the end of everything— except perhaps some relief that the membrane between worlds had at least a tear.

Not long after his arrest Harry leaves Ohio—abandons Mary and the kids. He moves to Los Angeles. Maybe he can reinvent himself, or live as if the old Harry was just a disappointing first try.

Los Angeles is breaking out all around in the 1920s, pushing far beyond the old boundaries, teeming with an influx of new residents from the American Midwest in particular, men and women "influenced," Robert Gottlieb says, "by images of L.A. as a kind of Eden of the imagination." Many others arrived from Mexico, seeking the kind of good jobs that might make Los Angeles seem an Eden of opportunity.

For an insurance salesman from Ohio, the City of Angels had to be the kind of Eden they tell you about in the lesson on Original Sin at Trinity Methodist Sunday school. Thrilling, from the perspective of a man who grew up resigned to the closet, but also dangerous; bristling with temptation and the risk of letting one's mask slip. Visiting LA in the 1920s, writer Hart Crane, a fellow native of Ohio, noted the depth of possibility in the lush bamboo thickets of Pershing Square alone. "The number of faggots cruising around here is legion," he wrote to a friend. In Hollywood, and especially at MGM, the lesbian and gay sub-colony within the growing motion picture community was large and confident, if overtly, *officially* nonexistent.

But Harry Baker is forty. He either can't or doesn't want to try hustling insurance, and maybe he'd have to answer too many questions about Ohio and the family he's left behind.

He isn't estranged from *all* his relations, though. Belle, his widowed mother, visits from Lima and stays in Harry's apartment. She has some kind of unspecified malady. Harry cares for her, and when she dies—still with Harry, in Los Angeles—he lays her to rest. Meanwhile, to make rent Harry has turned to something he's been really good at for a long time.

Harry's been making fudge.

Wilshire Community Kitchen is a restaurant and delicatessen situated between Central LA and Hollywood. Sarah Davidson, who runs the place, is known for her pies and cookies, which she sells for a premium price. Harry notes the mediocrity of the fudge Davidson's selling—at a dollar a pound, no less. He persuades her to sell his superior fudge instead. He mixes up ten-pound batches in his apartment and gets fifty cents a pound for it—enough to live on.

Fudge is only the start. He works on developing a cake: something unique, as light and elegant as angel food or sponge, but rich. He bakes hundreds of trials, prototype on prototype, until at last he comes up with the *one*: baked in a tube pan and glazed: huge, high, light, and sweet, tinted a soft, yolky yellow. And on April 14, 1927, a date etched in Harry's memory, he delivers to Wilshire Community Kitchen the first of what one day, decades later, would be the most famous cake in the world.

NIGHTS AT THE MANDARIN

[1926]

I MAGINE WITH ME THE SPECTACLE OF WHAT MUST FEEL like half of Chinatown packing the Mandarin Theatre to see her: Mudan Su, star of a legendary Chinese women's opera troupe, in her San Francisco premiere. Picture her performance in *Gathering of Zhu-Ai*, which she reprises for two more nights. Think about the debut that continues for two more weeks at the Mandarin: seventeen consecutive nights in all of Mu showing off her vocal and acting skills to a rapt San Francisco.

Now consider the core of her talent, the special alchemy that powers Mu's performances, which is how easily she slips around partitions of gender. She creates illusion with costumes, yes, but mostly she does it with subtle, intangible things. Watch and hear how Mu, using gestures, voice, and attitude, can distill masculinity into a single aria.

She and others on the opera stage can make an audience see a world beyond the one that flickers across the lens of vision, on the vitreous body of the eyes. And that world, the one this woman and a lot of other actors in Chinese opera could make you see: *That* world was more real—closer to some essential truth—than the everyday one.

Surely Esther Eng, though she's only eleven, is in the audience. Surely she shares the collective excitement to see the magic.

The Mandarin Theatre, site of these transformations, is even younger than Esther. This is only its second year as the center of a neighborhood. Together with its nearby rival, the Great China Theater, the Mandarin is communal space: the unofficial village square of Chinatown's culture and ambitions.

"A chattering kind of freedom filled the space," gay writer Wayson Choy recalls of a similar Cantonese opera theater in Vancouver, British Columbia. Every night hazed with smoke from a hundred glowing cigarettes; suffused with the rich smells of dumplings and sweet egg tarts, roasted melon seeds, and tea; of salted plums tucked in a hundred cheeks, sucked slowly. Cymbal clashes from the orchestra every night; every night "pliant notes of the two-string [*huqin*] and the violin" wailing, in Choy's remembering, as if to cast a spell.

"Cantonese opera at night bestowed upon me such a wealth of high drama, of myth," Choy says, "that I lacked for nothing in the ordinary world." Queer kids are accustomed to abstracting particulars of love and desire on stage—maybe opera hits harder with them. Kids who watch shadows on stage, characters either male or female, depending on the story, and translate action into emotional essence. Movies are like that too.

Esther is a girl in love with the movies. A girl *ecstatically* in love with Cantonese opera, its divas, and the China they represent, a country she's never seen. She lives three blocks from the Mandarin and spends as much time there as she's allowed. Before long, as a teen, she'll land a part-time job in the box office. But tonight, surely, she's a spectator, packed into the theater with the rest of Chinatown, impatient for the magic to come—restless for the entrance of Mudan Su.

The Mandarin is a symbol of San Francisco's new Chinatown, lavished with the symbols of the old China. The marquee has the up-curled eaves of a Xieshan roof, poised like the raptor wings of the phoenix. And on the sidewalk in front of the theater's tiled entrance, stands one of Grant Avenue's still-new pagoda-top dragon lampposts.

The Mandarin embodies this sense of modernity, the strength and confidence of second-generation Americans. Chinatown's brash public improvements, like those street lamps, show the prosperity of merchants like Esther's father. There's a sense of optimism here for the new China; for the blossoming of urban culture and progressive ideas after the collapse of the Qing Dynasty in 1911 and the end of repressive imperial rule. Esther came into the world at the dawn of this optimistic future.

She was born Ng Kam-ha in San Francisco in 1914, her grandparents having left Guangdong Province to come to California at the end of the nineteenth century, before the federal Chinese Exclusion Act of 1882. Esther was the fourth of ten surviving children born to Lee-shee and Ng Yu-jat, a second-generation businessman in Chinatown with a successful dry goods business.

Esther and her siblings grow up speaking Cantonese at home; grow up appreciating the two great cultural dynamos in San Francisco's South China diaspora, opera and food.

The Mandarin's programming signals this new age. In the afternoon it screens silent pictures with Cantonese titles. At night, it becomes the chattering town square. A different show almost every night, from seven to midnight, operas elevated on twentieth-century stagecraft, lights and painted backdrops and the smoke and flash of the effects master.

San Francisco, according to actor and film historian Frank Bren, "represented one of the world's great centers of Chinese drama." Together, in a creative rivalry fueled by ambition, the Mandarin and the Great China modernize traditional opera, with its minimal staging, for audiences increasingly wowed at the movies. "Chinese Theater Is Jazzed Up" the *Los Angeles Times* announces in 1925 when the Mandarin stages a pop-up series there, deploying lights and props, elaborate painted backdrops and special effects.

There's arguably some queer resonance here, considering how Chinese opera in the 1920s made an impression on notable queer creatives, including John Cage and Lou Harrison, who "drew from its aesthetics and expression," Nancy Rao says, "to craft modern music, theater, and dance."

Women are at the heart of this theatrical revolution in San Francisco. By the 1920s, actresses from China are free to tour and perform in the US, something previously possible only for men, and this is a major factor of the new Chinese drama. Journalist and scholar Jack Chen says actresses were "the first free, independent professional women to enter this country from China, [and] played an important part in the emancipation of Chinese women."

Through its programming, the Mandarin declares itself "a theater of actresses," historian Nancy Yunhwa Rao says. The owners bring in for residencies the freshest and most talented female stars with auras of glamor they can entice to leave China—as many as the Mandarin's lawyers can persuade US immigration officials to allow in.

This revolving troupe of young divas gracing the Mandarin's stage would make it known for something else, too, something suddenly in vogue at the progressive edges of new Chinese opera: women playing men in stage drag. Not every night; not in every opera. But enough to give the Mandarin a definite flavor—one that nourishes young Esther through a daily diet of high drama and myth; of beautiful, powerful, glamorous women, and the fluid boundaries of gender.

GENDER ILLUSION HAS A LONG HISTORY in Chinese opera. From the thirteenth century till well into the eighteenth, when the emperor banned actresses, women often acted as men onstage. As in Shakespeare's time at the Globe, men and boys stepped in to take on female roles until 1923, when actresses were again allowed to perform.

In Beijing in the 1800s, *huapu,* "flower guides," was a minor literary genre dabbled in by literary daddies. These were small, poetic books that listed, described, and sometimes ranked Beijing's most beautiful and talented teen boy actors, called *dan,* who specialized in female roles: rhapsodic listicles, basically, of drag-performing opera twinks.

In a *huapu* from 1837, the author describes how one such *dan,* called Rain Fragrance, would get ready in his private apartment open to a garden, fresh from a bath, wearing a loosely woven gown "covered in moon shadows reflected from the garden's flowers":

> He would take out his cosmetics box and mirror, ready to
> start applying his makeup for the evening. In a light green
> porcelain box he kept stamens from jasmine flower, from

which he knotted two large butterflies to fix carefully in front of each ear, offset by a shower of fragrant orchids . . .

The author wants you suspended, as he is, in the scene's rippling exoticism, where gender lines soften in the dappled shadows of a flower-scented twilight. The art of the *dan* is transformation: not merely jumping a fence that cleaves the supposed binary, but leading the audience into a place of pure, subjective imagination, where sex and gender dissolve.

"Chinese opera has historically been hella queer," says Amy Sueyoshi, professor of Asian studies and sexuality at San Francisco State University. Opera was "a haven for otherwise gay and trans folks during a time when those labels were not accessible."

Which takes us back to where I started this chapter: the night of April 19, 1926, at the Mandarin Theatre, and the fiercely awaited debut of Mudan Su.

Mu is a great star, the lead of one of China's idolized female troupes. She performed *Gathering at Zhu-Ai* for three straight nights, and headlined the Mandarin for the next fourteen. She was a virtuoso of the art of playing men, whether a warrior with a terrifying pikestaff or a young scholar riding a horse she could make you see with gestures alone. For *Amorous Emperor*, with Mu as the male lead, the Mandarin crew built an elaborate canopied bed with embroidered curtains for its drag-king star to cavort with actresses. "To underscore the intimacy with realism," Nancy Rao says.

But how do you define what was real in a place where even gender—the most basic distinction in the world beyond the street doors of the Mandarin—is mutable? "The collapse of the distinction between the real and the fictional," opera scholar Siu Leung Li says, " . . . reinforced the underlying idea of *becoming* the real through *performing* the real in theater." On stage, in the Mandarin's rarefied atmosphere of dramatic truth, Mu would *actually* transform into a man.

Even when Mu plays women, her way is her own. Instead of singing in the stylized nasal falsetto of operatic femme tradition—a falsetto

perfected by Mei Lanfang, the male actor famous for playing women—
she does so in her natural voice. Even acting as a woman, Mu smudges
the line between "real" and contrived. Between how a woman is supposed to behave and how she acts for real. This *must* be a lesson that
will linger long and slowly comfort Esther, like a salted plum softening
patiently in the cheek.

BAKED IN THE BEDROOM

[1929]

HARRY BAKER LINES UP A SECOND BUYER FOR HIS cakes, and it's a good one: a venue that puts his baking before the eyes and on the tongues of people who know both ambition and maverick genius. The Brown Derby, the bowler-shaped coffee shop across Wilshire Boulevard from the Cocoanut Grove nightclub and the Ambassador Hotel, counts movie stars and studio execs as regulars. Not long after adding Harry's cake to the menu the Derby opens a larger, non-hat-shaped second location on North Vine in Hollywood, near the cluster of studio backlots.

Harry's cake is the first dessert the Brown Derby offers. It exists so modestly on early menus, sometimes as *sponge cake*, at other times as just *cake*. Yet Harry's quiet, necessary creation finds its voice—I'd go so far as to say its power—in the center of movie-colony style and celebrity that the Derby becomes. There's a certain mystery around Harry's cake, a lack of naming that seems of a piece with Harry's own facelessness.

After his cake becomes the lofty, tender darling of Hollywood influencers, Harry turns down the Derby's offer to make him a partner, while taking over production and marketing. Harry refuses to divulge his recipe. He insists on baking at home, even as demand rises.

By 1930, cake rules Harry's entire existence. He lives and bakes in a two-story bungalow on Larchmont, turning out forty-two hefty, golden beauties in each eighteen-hour workday. He mixes the cakes one at a time in the kitchen and bakes in a converted bedroom, set up with a dozen portable tin ovens resting on hot plates, the kind he used in his insurance office back in Columbus. Each oven runs a little different, and thermometers can't be trusted, so Harry uses intuition to judge how each cake swells and browns.

With the money Harry earns from his early success, he commissions an oil portrait of his late mother, Belle. (Harry declares it "more beautiful than *Whistler's Mother.*") After all, she blessed his baking as a boy. Surely he must honor her belief in his unconventional calling.

Forty-six-year-old Harry has a live-in helper: nineteen-year-old Albert Ross McCarney—Mac—a slight kid who never finished high school and likewise fled his family to start fresh in LA. Sally Cobb, who manages the Derbys with her husband, Bob (namesake of the Cobb salad), and, in her former career as a fashion model worked around a ton of gay men, knows you don't need to be Albert Einstein to comprehend the delicate nature of Harry and Mac's relationship. Mac washes pans and makes deliveries, because by now the fame of Harry's cake has spread through the ranks of the Derby elite: actors Corinne Griffith, Barbara Stanwyck, Lily Pons, Marie Dressler (just shy of openly queer), and Dolores del Río (just shy of openly straight). In the realm of cake, Harry is a sort of down-low Adrian, MGM's gay costume designer—creator of Dorothy's ruby slippers for *The Wizard of Oz*— whose couture off-screen, at parties and red carpets, becomes a mark of status for the stars.

The MGM and RKO commissaries have standing orders. First Lady Eleanor Roosevelt, who travels west to manage the risky politics of son Elliott's divorce, swoons over a slice served at a party, and extends a hand for Harry to bring his skills to the White House kitchens. (Maybe because he's a registered Republican, or because he has to keep invisible for all kinds of reasons, Harry declines.) Cary Grant and Randolph Scott, whose romantic and domestic coupling is one of Hollywood's biggest open secrets, are photographed together at the Derby, surrounded by a male studio squad goofing with a fat wedge of what is surely Harry's cake. Gossip columnist Luella Parsons asks for a version of Harry's cake flavored with grapefruit because she's convinced of its slimming powers, and it's here that Harry's cake enters the culture;

becomes a point of aspiration, or a point of expression. The moment
Harry turns his own unexpressed queerness into something others see
themselves in.

※

THE FEVER PARADOX OF AMERICAN FOOD at midcentury was that the
more corporate and impersonal it got, the more human it tried to look;
the more personality it tried to capture: a face, a voice, an accent that
sounded like Rochester, maybe Milwaukee, possibly Omaha: places
most customers for Softasilk flour might have considered cozy, safe,
and relatable: centers of working-class identity and middle-class ideals.
Places where so-called deviance was kept so tightly shuttered it was
plausibly nonexistent, like in St. Paul, Minnesota, at Kirmser's bar—
divergent only after dark—where among the sparse sidewalk traffic
of nighttime downtown, a queer man or woman could slip discreetly
through a door in the blank façade.

Nobody did pretend-face better than the Minneapolis corporation
that became General Mills. In 1921 Washburn Crosby, a milling company that would eventually merge with General Mills, launched a con-
test urging customers of its flours to solve a puzzle by mail and win a
little flour sack–shaped pincushion as a prize. Washburn Crosby had
opened an advertising portal with thousands and thousands of customers (of course almost all were women), and when many of them wrote to
the company with baking questions, the boys in the advertising department passed the letters on to the girls who ran the test kitchen. And
the ad men made up a single fake expert in place of the real ones, and
called her Betty Crocker: *Crocker* in tribute to a retired director of the
company, William G. Crocker, and *Betty* because of how it landed so
effortlessly on the American ear in 1921.

Betty spanned social classes: a generic name for maids and cooks like
the one immortalized in Apple Brown Betty (though that Betty was
brown: mixed race, a *"mulâtresse"* in the old French Creole of New Orleans); but also for the self-assured, fashionable, and very white Betty

Thompson, daughter of a lesser tycoon in the Charles A. Voight comic strip *Betty* that launched in Sunday syndication in 1919. Even though that Betty was well off, still she moved in boxes men controlled; within panels a man literally drew. This male fantasy of domestic order, this woman who baked and cooked tirelessly and existed passively, limned by men to sell sacks of flour and mix, boxes of Bisquick and Crustquick, and the dubious apple pie kit semi-italicized as Pye*quick*—whatever the geniuses in research might forecast an appetite for.

Neysa McMein painted the first official face of Betty Crocker in 1936. The *Women's Home Journal* would describe Betty's face as "an ageless thirty-two." Ruffled white shirt bristling from the collar of her red suit jacket, red bow lips set in an expression that looks like determination, and large, luxurious eyes—as if McMein, a lifelong feminist in an open marriage, gave Betty a stubbornness and a sensuality that registered as a muffled rattling of the domestic order Betty represented.

But by then, Betty already had a voice, and a radio presence. A prim efficiency that seemed unswerveable on the airwaves.

America didn't seem to care that Betty wasn't real. In a tour of the South in 1949, Janette Kelley, head of General Mills' Home Service department, pretty much masquerades as Betty. A story by Sue Scattergood, food editor for the *Birmingham News* in Alabama, straight-up refers to Kelley as Betty for the first three-quarters of the story, as "Betty" drops in on a Black domestic cook, Daisy Lee, to watch her make homemade biscuits (like, not from the Bisquick box). "Betty" asks question after condescending question about mixing, rolling, shaping, and pricking, until Daisy Lee rears up and says, "Miss Betty! Ain't you never eat biscuits like this?"

Which is actually a *read*, since this is supposed to be Betty *fucking* Crocker, sold to America as the expert in all things baking. But she's merely baking's best-known, least-real face.

THE SISSY PROPHET OF ASPARAGUS

[1933]

F ROM HIGH ABOVE, THE MISSISSIPPI DELTA FLOOD-plain looks a little like a dehisced wound. It stretches two hundred miles down the east bank of the Great River south from Memphis, measuring eighty-seven miles across at its gaping middle. Historically, culturally, the Delta is the sticky open tissue of the American South, and thus the United States: a geologic scar shaped by more than just the forceful Mississippi.

It's here, in the town of Indianola, that Raymond Craig Claiborne regularly has the shit beat out of him in junior high school. His ass straight-up kicked: knocked down, his shoulders pinned to the ground, face flattened by palms and fists. Everyone can see he's a weak little pansy. One day Mr. Green, the math teacher at Craig's school, calls him out. He says, "I see we've got a sissy in the class." Says it in front of everybody.

"To this day, in all my life, I have rarely known a more stunning and vivid pain," Craig recalls when he's sixty or so; Craig when he's arguably the most famous restaurant critic in the world, former czar of food coverage at the exalted *New York Times*, editor of the one of the best-selling American cookbooks of all time, loved and feared but mostly loved. He was wealthy enough: living far from the Delta, up north in the Yankee capital. What Craig said about cooking or dining out, the ingredients he liked, the chefs he adored, what appliances he kept on his counter in eastern Long Island—Craig would only have to mention it in print and it would change how you ate or cooked—you, the white, com-

fortably set homeowner in Greenwich, Connecticut, or West Orange,
New Jersey. It changed how you threw a party, how you wore your
French blue-ticking apron from Bloomie's after your guests arrived
because it was the mark of a host who cared about food and hospitality.

Craig showed you how and what to order in a restaurant, or even
how to *think* about food, as part of what he'd convinced you was an
essential part of a quote-unquote *lifestyle*: an intentional existence pad-
ded with aspiration and delightful things, the delicious accessories to
a life lived bold and gracious, fun and fresh! A life incompatible with
ugliness, penury, or trauma. In Craig's byline; in his image, at his
kitchen worktable rocking a Chinese cleaver, dressed in a long-sleeve
shirt with the cuffs folded back, silk scarf at the open neck like a cravat
and a yoke apron tied high at the waist, you could see yourself, the person you always knew you were, a sophisticate with a streak of sass and
an appetite for adventure.

You'd think that nothing could touch the architect of all this; that
Craig would be unassailable. But he was always the boy getting his
face pounded on Indianola pavement. The fear that formed in Mississippi never healed, never faded. Its edges had hardened, but it would
always be raw. Bashing exposes the queer sin of self-hatred. Your
attacker somehow knows the precise location of the exposed vein you
hoped you'd concealed. The pain he inflicts isn't so much physical as
it is psychic: it confirms every fear about your own hideousness, your
incapacity for ever really being loved. The basher becomes faceless.
He disappears behind the blows and your own carefully buried, metic-
ulously rationalized-away self-aversion, reinforced by every ambient
message you ever absorbed, reveals itself as the true assailant. You
become your own basher, and your worst impulses—your every urge
to hide; to lie—loom as your only possible place of solace.

※

CRAIG WAS BORN IN 1920 just north of Indianola, a little town called
Sunflower. Was born in the front bedroom of a house with dormers and

a showy pediment vaunting a street-view display of its own grandilo-
quence, but the Great Depression of 1929 finds the Claibornes scrab-
bling to hold on. Craig's father, Lewis, did some rash speculating in
land and cotton. He's lost everything. The family moves to a larger
town where Craig's mother, Miss Kathleen, can take in boarders. The
dive in fortunes only intensifies young Craig's sense of worthlessness.

Miss Kathleen, whose family name is Craig, would prefer her son
forgetting he's a Claiborne. "She would admonish me daily: 'Never forget . . . that you are a Craig,'" he says, and he complies. He strips off
his first name, Raymond, to represent as a Craig, with the aristocratic
power of the white Southern male. He cinches tightly the stifling belts
and straps of straight tradition.

Yet he crushes on brainy boys and jocks. Gordon, son of Indianola's
mayor, picks Craig up in the family Chrysler. They drive endlessly on
weekends, round and round the town, out into the country. Gordon
likes comic books and girls and Craig is cold to both, but they find a
mutual liking for sleeping together in Gordon's bed on Friday and Saturday nights. "Innocently," Craig would recall, though innocence can
appear a nuanced thing against the sheets.

I say that because, from early in the Depression, at a young age,
Craig shares a bed with his daddy, spooning him nightly in a situation
that strains any simple take on innocence. The official rationale for this
is that the Claibornes need all available beds for paying boarders, and
anyway Lewis and Miss Kathleen had long ago ended any pretense of
sleeping together. It would be years later, after years of psychotherapy,
that Craig would make a messy public confession of this most Gothic
arrangement in a childhood racked by fear and Southern ghosts.

For all its institutional homophobia, queer love burns in the Delta—
anyway, queer *desire* does. It flames up under oaks and in abandoned
sheds. In cars parked off the main road after nightfall, beyond the last
few shacks out where town ends. Queerness flourishes in silence, "quietly accommodated with a prevailing pretense of ignorance," says historian John Howard. Furtive, sweaty explorations by teens is "tacitly
condoned," Howard says, until the so-called innocent perpetrators

reach an age when marriage is expected to wash away the sweat and memory of those desires.

For adults, queer sex is "clandestine but common," Howard says. Eyes with the weight of recognition might lock at a church social or family reunion; in the click of a light borrowed from a traveling man taking the air in the courthouse square after dark, or above the open pages of the *Jackson Daily News* in a station waiting lounge. Most know better than to say the words that could shatter any plausible pretense of ignorance. Disavowal is the key to survival.

In his 1948 novel *The Welcome*, Mississippi-born Hubert Creekmore writes about Don Mason, a young gay man who escaped to New York City, but amid the disruptions of the Great Depression moves back to his boyhood town in the Magnolia State. Don carved out a happy queer life up north, but Jim Furlow, his lover on the down-low through high school and college, stayed behind in Mississippi, got married, and went to work at his daddy's country law firm. Jim faces an arid future with a woman he hates and who despises him, and Don's unexpected return splinters Jim's equilibrium: the way he numbed his heart when Don left; the way he sealed his eyes to desire.

Forced to reckon, Jim feels the chill of eternal disavowal. "Fright. Fright," he realizes at the critical point of revelation. "Always fright. That's what it's been, all the time, all my life . . . " Don works out a way to stay in Mississippi—to "belong," i.e. qualify for membership in small-town white society, while not completely betraying his queer-ness or surrendering his identity, but Jim is trapped in the agony of denial. (This made Creekmore's novel groundbreaking in 1948, and no doubt shocking to many—a protagonist who wasn't tragic for having merely been born a homosexual and who didn't have to die to atone for it. In *The Welcome* it's *denial* of queerness, not acceptance, that proves catastrophic.)

Still, for most people born queer in Mississippi, dissembling is a lingering flavor, a taste edged with a tang of fear that never leaves the mouth. Turning fright into something transcendent, though, without having to publicly reveal your sexuality—if *that* were somehow possible, couldn't it make up for the trauma? Couldn't it make the taste go away?

✳

CRAIG IS A YOUNG MAN living with the fright of his own desires. Rather, *not* living with them—avoiding them the best he can; steering clear of the treacherous well of queer desire. If you read his 1982 memoir, it's easy to guess that the rawest edge of Craig's fearful longing growing up was Black men working for the Claibornes as servants—the "help."

Take Albert.

Young Craig idolizes Albert, a "handsome, mahogany-colored man with a strong physique and hair the color of white ash cotton." One day in Sunflower after Christmas, Albert is refinishing the Claiborne floors. In the living room, he leaves a pail of varnish untended.

Craig had found sparklers in his Christmas stocking. He waves a lit one, wandering from room to room. He sees the pail of unknown liquid in the empty living room and dips his sparkler in, and of course the bucket erupts, shooting flames that probably should destroy the house but don't (adults rush in, the fire is smothered). The incident results in no catastrophic damage, though you can bet Albert was punished. But Craig is left with an indelible mark in the shape of a moral: That any time an innocent drops his spark into an irresistible well of dangerous opacity, chances are the ceiling comes down in flames. Brazen acts of transgression spark disaster.

This puts a gay spin on an old racist narrative in America, a myth based on what Wesley Morris calls *the national terror of Black sexuality.* Part of that terror is white awe of Black bodies; the fear and fascination attached since long before Emancipation to the mythical Black penis. No doubt: Craig regards Black sexuality as a special source of fright, a force so powerful it might lure him out of the closet.

Consider the case of the Black maid Dora, who gets her kicks by inviting unspecified girls to the Claiborne house for playdate "sessions": i.e., the invited showing schoolboy Craig "theirs" in return for a look at "his." (These sexually curious young guests—are they girls Dora knows and has recruited? Are they schoolmates Craig's invited over, only to be corrupted by Dora?) He registers this as a double violation, an assault on his innocence, his sexuality. This is ugly: Craig going all in on the myth of Black hypersexuality and the corruption of white purity, some curdled reverse fantasy of the plantation master compelling his human chattel to breed, but again there's a queer twist. Dora is trying to humiliate Craig, whom she knows is gay, with these "sessions." Craig implies though that Dora deploys these mysterious girls as a form of conversion therapy, a way of seducing him straight.

This makes it even more imperative for Craig to hide his sexuality—to sublimate it by recasting it as something benign, something with the untaintedness Craig has never known, since being queer, his little crushes on Gordon and Albert, have convinced him he's fundamentally damaged. If there was a cloak to screen his dangerous desires, the dirtiness he keeps to himself, he might appear almost normal from the outside.

Someday, that cloak will be food. Food is Craig's redemptive *somewhere*, the place he devises to hold his terrifying queerness captive, unseen by the callous, the bullies eager to grind his face in the pavement.

He grows up sensitive to what Miss Kathleen and Blanche, the Claiborne family cook, placed on the table. Learns the resonance of food at her table; to parse the meaning and gravity of a dish; to feel the social nuances of the table.

Asparagus has a special resonance.

As a first course for the boarders' Sunday dinner, the richest most luxurious meal of the week in Miss Kathleen's house, it might figure as a mantle for toast points: spears of white asparagus from the can—an extravagance—overlaid with a tangy cheddar cheese sauce, decorated with strips of pimiento.

I imagine this dish as a model for Craig as he learns to transform the raw edge of queerness into something safe; something socially acceptable.

You think of the erotic resonance of asparagus in its natural state; recall Proust in the first volume of *À la recherche du temps perdu*, which arrives in English translation not long after Craig is born. Proust's narrator describes ivory asparagus newly cut from the garden, the stalks still feral. "Tinged with ultramarine and rosy pink which ran from their heads, finely stippled in mauve and azure, through a series of imperceptible changes to their white feet, still stained a little by the soil of their garden-bed: a rainbow-loveliness that was not of this world."

The asparagus is priapic in its unprepped state, before the spirit's been processed from it: engorged via pink and purple veins, filthy at the cut lines, touched by Himeros, god of desire.

It's ecstatic, earthy, poetic. In the original French that "rainbow-loveliness . . . not of this world" is *des irisations qui ne sont pas de la terre*: Proust's queering of asparagus; his reveal for us of its iridescent fairy light.

But canning kills its stippled rainbow colors. The asparagus on Miss Kathleen's Sunday table has been bled of phallic possibility: over-manipulated, pumped with canning brine till soft and flabby. Laid out on toast points, white bread trimmed of crust (another nod to extravagance); cosmeticized with cheese sauce and pimiento.

Craig is still a sissy; he will always be one. But this is how he will persevere: by bending desire into innocence. How long would he last as the one angling for traveling men's eyes Sundays in the courthouse square? How would he survive?

Instead he has Miss Kathleen's three-layered salad on Sundays: lime gelatin on the bottom, cream cheese in the middle, tomato aspic on top. Cut in cubes, adorned with lettuce, topped with dabs of mayonnaise. It represents triumph over anything crudely, vulgarly itself; anything with seeds and skins; juices that drip down a wrist. Craig adores dishes that civilize nature—creamy dishes, sweetened ones. Food with the coarseness leached out.

Yet the highlight of young Craig's emotional life features his nurse, a Black woman he knows only as Aunt Catherine. On the back porch in Sunflower, in view of walnut trees, the bantam chickens and guinea hens that roam and peck, and the wooden shanties where Aunt Catherine and Albert live. On that porch Aunt Catherine works the plunger in the ancient wooden churn to make the butter "come," in the language of the old Southern work song: *Peter at the gate, a-waitin' for the butter cake, come, butter, come.*

This is a ways distant from lime gelatin and tomato aspic, yet it's the center of Craig's being.

As a boy his longed-for tidbit is the thickened sour milk called clabber, churning's byproduct: poured in bowls to set, chilled in the icebox, and dredged with sugar. When he can, he eats it cradled in Aunt Catherine's lap, carried along in the movement of her porch rocker, out of sight of the house.

Because the truest, deepest pleasures are inevitably the ones that hide.

PAPER CHICKEN FOR DIVAS

[1934]

O N A FEBRUARY NIGHT, A REPORTER FOR THE *SAN Francisco Chronicle* gets to look around backstage at the Mandarin Theatre. Katherine Hill's guide, Charlie Gee, leads her up steep wooden alley stairs to the stage door, down a narrow hallway and into the crowded, cavernous backstage space, a combination green room, conference room, open dressing room. She describes a jumble of wardrobe trunks and people: stock performers, dressers, stagehands, loads of unidentified others. Kids, older ladies, teens. "Coatless, preoccupied men wove a sure course among the various groups, fetching costumes from lacquered trunks and bulging cardboard boxes," or hustling through the wings to deliver a prop to the actors on stage.

Eating happens everywhere backstage, Hill says. A cluster of teens scarfing rice, the tinkle of chopsticks on bowls. (Surely there's a burner somewhere among the trunks, hot rice perpetually ready from a pot with carbon-blacked sides.) Hatless fetch boys in blue denim overalls, running trays of food up the alley stairs from a nearby restaurant and hauling down empties. Hill doesn't name the restaurant—maybe Tai Sam Yuen next door? The sign out front says Chop Suey, but that's for tourists, of course. The Mandarin boys haul up pork boiled noodles, fried chicken wings, braised bitter melon, mustard green soup: rich proteins, restorative broths, bracing tannins. Perhaps one of the resident divas might be tempted to try the paper chicken? It's the priciest thing on the menu, next to roast duck and chicken salads. Fried envelopes of delicate glassine containing one pure-flesh bite of chicken, a piece of dried mushroom perhaps, with a dab of hoisin sauce, essences and aromas sealed in the paper.

The reveal's a surprise: a flash of steam, a small sensory rush. The perfect theatrical morsels to tempt masters of spectacle and surprise.

Hill's an outsider backstage. "They don't like sightseers much," she says, and describes how Charlie Gee translates, with a polite smile, how one of the crew has questioned Hill's being here. The Mandarin feels like sprawling family with ragged edges, the actors and musicians and crew and many assorted others. And as with any family, food shapes and nurtures the lines of connection. It keeps everybody more or less cohesive. This journalist from a newspaper, especially one that consistently depicts the residents of Chinatown as a foreign enclave—members of a separate colony—simply doesn't belong.

Hill notices a girl. She has "a sports hat," i.e. baseball cap, "drawn over her face. . . . snatching a nap in a steamer chair."

It's possible that this is twenty-year-old Esther. She's always read younger than her age. She'd definitely feel comfortable enough to doze off, even amid the chaos of the evening performances. Esther grew up backstage. It's her home.

She attends high school at a public girls' academy far from the confines of Chinatown. She's spent countless hours not only at the Mandarin, but in the city's growing profusion of Chinese-language movie theaters—she loves cinema.

While still in high school, she landed a box office job. She's part of the theater family under the monitoring eye of the backstage aunties who press food and cups of tea on everyone; part of the fights and flirtations, the generosity, petty bitchiness, and humor; connected to the brilliance of individual performances and the genius of the collective.

Food is something that holds together this diverse circle of performers, stagehands, and designers, a family in which queerness is both ordinary and singular: one circuit in the grid powering the Mandarin's shine. Theater family is not *exactly* the same as queer family. Still, it shows what's possible when the idea of kinship, connection, and the embrace of care, spread beyond genetic circumstance.

No doubt because of her father's prominence, Esther was always able to meet the visiting actresses, women whose glamour shimmered and spirit swirled like the clouds that cut across San Francisco's western sky at sunset. The constant thrill of seeing international stars helps Esther imagine life beyond the invisible, immovable walls of Chinatown.

By eighteen, Esther had settled on the style she'd be faithful to for the rest of her life: trousers, masc tailored jackets, short hair—a contrast to the body-hugging, slit-leg, cap-sleeved cheongsam dresses that fashion dictated for young women. Being an Ng keeps Esther in the public eye, and at least in the community press, her unconventional presentation wins praise. A 1933 item in San Francisco's *Chinese Digest* about fashions in hair praises Esther's "sleek boyish bob . . . worn with one very slight wave at the left side, which breaks the straightness." Esther's look challenges straightness, alright.

Amid the nightly hustle of the Mandarin, Esther meets the beautiful Wai Kim-fong, an actress in residence. It's not clear when they become lovers, but they're inseparable. Soon, Fong will become Esther's artistic muse and creative partner.

The form this will take is motion pictures. About the time in 1934 that the *Chronicle* reporter spots the maybe-Esther snoozing on a lounge chair backstage, the for-real Esther tells her father she wants to make movies.

She might just as well have told him she wants to run for governor of California, the idea is so preposterous. Technically it's *possible.* Another San Franciscan, Dorothy Arzner—another lesbian, who keeps her hair short and wears the sort of suits men do—is directing pictures in Hollywood for Paramount and RKO. But a woman from Chinatown?

The early 1930s see a surge of American interest in China. Published in 1931, Pearl S. Buck's novel *The Good Earth* remains on the bestseller list for two years; Buck takes home the 1932 Pulitzer Prize for fiction. After Japan invades Manchuria in September 1931 and reveals its hunger for further conquest, US popular opinion regards Chinese resistance as heroic. Surely Esther's father senses opportunity.

Perhaps anticipating a market for Chinese films, in 1935 Yu-jat launches a studio from the Ng family home on Washington Street: the Kwong Ngai Talking Pictures Company. He names Esther co-producer of its first film project, a musical drama intended for the Chinese-language market in the US and for audiences in China. Kwong Ngai, which changes its name to Cathay Pictures Ltd., rents studio space in Hollywood. Esther and director Frank Tang shoot the aviation-themed picture partially in color. It's released in January 1936 as *Sum Hun* ("*Heartaches*"), starring Fong, opposite male lead Beal Wong. It's billed as the "First Cantonese Singing-Talking Picture in Technicolor."

It's the launch of Esther's career. Some time later, a reporter asks Esther if she was scared making her first picture with zero experience. "I just went ahead and I wasn't afraid or anything," Esther says. "It just came to me. I don't know why."

What sticks with me is where Esther stays while she's working on the film. Cathay Pictures lists an address on Fountain Avenue as its Hollywood base. This appears to be an apartment in a large, two-story Spanish-style complex on a residential street. I suppose it's where the San Francisco–based cast and crew huddle up: Esther and Fong in the bedrooms, everyone else kipped on couches, piles of blankets on the floor.

What sticks with me is the food that must have come out of the apartment kitchen to feed everyone early and late: cabbage soup, congee, corned beef hash, shaggy bean sprout omelets, fried rice, stir-fried beef with tomato and egg. It's a taste of the Mandarin, a.k.a. home. And in a way, it would be another beginning for Esther, a taste of her future in New York City, as a restaurateur in the 1950s and '60s, conjuring the queer family vibe of a vanished backstage world.

THE LONELINESS OF
RHUBARB

[1932–1942]

T HREE YEARS INTO THE GREAT DEPRESSION, HERMAN
Smith is ravaged. He has no steady work, whatever modest invest-
ments he had have all gone to crap, and magazine editors are passing
on his story pitches. His partner, Dick, isn't landing acting gigs. They
moved on up from the Village to an apartment on the sixteenth floor
of the new, vast London Terrace complex in Chelsea, and even though
they've rented out a room to a couple of guys, rent is still a bitch.

Once more, a woman to the rescue.

Like Lady Duff-Gordon before her, Juliana Force sees something in
Herman Smith. It's not clear how they meet. Force is the first director of the Whitney Museum of Art, under the aegis of founder Gertrude Vanderbilt Whitney. She's also the New York administrator for
the Public Works of Art Project, the New Deal artists' relief program.
She owns a circa-1810 farmhouse in South Salem, New York, fifty miles
northeast of the city, a place she visits only occasionally. It houses her
collection of choice Shaker antiques.

At the end of 1932 she asks Herman and Dick to take over from
the previous caretaker, to move in and open the house as a semipublic
restaurant and inn. Dick is butler, waiter, footman, caretaker. Herman
cooks and tends the garden. He calls it Shaker Hollow.

A small item about automobile day trips from Manhattan in *The
Observer* describes Shaker Hollow and other inns like it, "quaint";
"suavely conscious of the advantages of their leisurely country pace,

their traditional atmosphere and furnishings, and their fresh-from-the-garden table delicacies."

For three years Herman cooks spoon bread, country hams baked in biscuit dough, and an unusual burnt-sugar custard dessert called crème brûlée. Until, in 1936, Juliana Force sells her main home in Pennsylvania and moves to Shaker Hollow. Herman and Dick move to Ridgefield, Connecticut, to an old farmhouse known as the Rectory.

Herman is fifty-eight in 1936. He collects recipes and putters in his herb garden. For *The American Home* magazine he writes articles with recipes; with tips on throwing parties. In a letter to a friend, he says he's writing a book about his earliest experiences with food.

That same year, the publisher Little, Brown scores a hit with a gentle food and farm memoir titled *The Country Kitchen* by Della T. Lutes, author of books on etiquette, needlework, and children's Bible stories. *The Country Kitchen* evokes the Lutes's strawberry-shortcake girlhood on a Michigan farm a hundred miles from Herman's family home.

Seven years into the Great Depression, an America getting by on hash and starchy gravy seems hungry for every bite of what *The Country Kitchen*'s taffy-pull nostalgia, its reductive tableaus of country life sweetened with Christian morals. Little Della, the book's narrator, hits the same spot as Hollywood's sprinkle-faced muffin, Shirley Temple. In a 1935 screening of Shirley's *The Little Colonel*, the audience applauded for eleven seconds after the final fade-out, persuading the skeptical movie critic of the *New York Times* to declare that the picture "ought to bring out the best in every one who sees it." *The Country Kitchen* likewise rides that lane, through similar scenery flocked with warm fuzzies.

Across the country, women's civic groups were buying copies of *The Country Kitchen* for their local libraries, bookshops were recommending it, and at least one chapter of the Daughters of the American Revolution presented it to members as a must-read.

Does *The Country Kitchen*'s success eat at Herman as he thinks about his next incarnation? Does he contrive to dress Michigan country corn in something more radiant—frame it in elements more poignant and wordly—than Della's gingham and oilcloth? I mean, darling: Why not make it art?

Herman's butter-churn memoir would conjure a stern but kindly woman with mysterious origins and a single name; a brilliant cook (aging, still vigorous) from far away, who's known tragedy and exile. A survivor both finding and bestowing redemption through food.

As the mounting possibility of war in Europe stokes anxiety, Herman is poised to make his latest queer metamorphosis. He's gone from being a man indicted for sexual perversion, a fugitive, a couturier's assistant, movie makeup master, innkeeper, chef.

He's ready to take on Stina.

✳

TOWARD THE END OF 1942, months after a US at war decrees food rationing, a brief, enthusiastic book review appears in the *New York Times*. *Stina: The Story of a Cook* is half memoir, half cookbook, offering a taste of lush kitchen nostalgia. *Stina* charms Jane Holt, the *Times* reviewer. It's seductive, the way it teases you away from the drab reality of ration books "to a pleasant time and place, when thick yellow cream and fresh eggs, chickens and hams and great roasts were plentiful."

The pleasant place of this fantasy of wholesome, old-fashioned excess: farm-country Michigan.

The time: the late 1800s.

The author: Herman Smith. The *Detroit Free Press* calls him a worthy successor to Della Lutes, but *Stina* is more than Midwest farm nostalgia. It's a book in which Herman conducts his final, and perhaps his greatest, act of reinvention: a performance of redemption.

In *Stina*, Herman would live in a state of immortal innocence in an Edenic landscape. He exists in a perennial state of virginal rapture: skinny-dipping in the pond; feeling the joy and heartache of his first (heterosexual) crush; being fed on ample suppers and Golden Rule morality by the stern yet gentle family cook, Stina: a French-speaking Alsatian refugee from the Franco-Prussian War.

Stina is already in late middle age when she begins working for the Schmidts, Herman's six siblings plus their delicately ailing mother and a stiff yet benevolent father. She cooks French dishes from the abundant produce of an American farm—perhaps, in 1942, a mythologized one, an orderly Grant Wood composition, eerie in its perfection, of split-rail fences, cornfields, cattails, and haymows. You sense Herman's time in movie production bleeding through the page.

"Small, almost elfin," Herman says of Stina, "with the brightest, blackest, wisest eyes I have ever seen." She dispenses tough love, and at the same is a cook, he says, "deserving of the cordon bleu." She sleeps in a "small cold immaculate chamber not far from mine," Herman notes—a kind of nun's cell, I guess—"but all her waking hours were spent in the kitchen which was her pride." She's not quite flesh in Herman's descriptions, but rather a caricature of the good widow: devout—celibate. Her only concern seems to be working to a state of noble exhaustion for a family under a benevolent patriarch in the fecund, faithful heart of a nation blessed by God.

Is Stina short for Christina? What about Ernestina, Faustina, Lustina? Without a surname she's just . . . Stina, which to my ears has the ring of midcentury drag magnificence, an echo of real-life queens Guilda and Lestra.

A headline in the November 20, 1942, features pages of the *Evening Star* newspaper in Washington DC conjured resurrection: "Stina Lives Again in Charming Book."

Did she ever, though? Live, I mean.

In 2008 Craig Jacobs, a reporter for the *Niles Daily Star,* Herman's hometown daily, goes on a quest to find the historical Stina. He enlists a town librarian who's researched the history of Niles and genealogies of some of its residents.

Jacobs and the librarian sift through available records but come up with nothing: no death record for anyone who could plausibly have gone by Stina; no obits; no headstone in the local cemetery, where Herman describes, in his 1944 follow-up to *Stina,* how forget-me-nots bloomed on her grave. In the US Census of 1880, no servant who could be Stina is recorded for the Schmidt household. (Fire destroyed the Census documents for 1890.) Herman doesn't talk about Stina in 1947, in a speech he delivers at a big community picnic. He lists all the famous people he's known from Niles, and even names the town's "magnificent cooks," without a peep about Stina. Even Herman's great-great nephew, an unofficial Schmidt family archivist, hadn't found a trace of Stina in the surviving documents. It's more than likely that Herman invented Stina from his own psyche; mined an old source like *Tante Marie's la veritable cuisine de famille* (Stina's sole cookbook, he says, and claims to have inherited) to call up the cuisine bourgeoise world of the nineteenth century.

Can I prove that Stina is an invention, a fake? I can't, even if all the signs point there.

She's simply not plausible, for one thing. She's supposed to be in her sixties, but singlehandedly cooks massive Christmas feasts for a couple dozen Schmidts. There are heaps of cookies, cakes, pains d'épices; prune tarts, baba au rhum. A daylong parade of pâtés, rabbit casseroles, a stuffed goose, homemade sausage, wine soup with potato dumplings. Surely all of that would kill a modern-day thirty-year-old kitchen boss bitch with sleeve tattoos, stepping out every twenty for a smoke break.

In my reading, Stina *is* Herman—the other half of the fictional boy narrator. A Victorian Mrs. Doubtfire, the drag alter ego who has come not to disrupt but to reaffirm the power of traditional family. He becomes Stina to restore equilibrium to a situation in which Herman's queerness is actually a threat to the stability of the blood-family unit.

As the boy narrator, Herman is pure innocence. Stina takes on the grinding work of sustaining the patriarchy, creeping out of her cell at dawn to sustain a family that isn't even hers, but a family at the mythical heart of the conservative order. In my reading Herman tried to convince the world he's good by becoming a woman who is selfless, and beyond any need for sex.

At least twice after the book is published, Herman inscribes copies as both himself *and* Stina. He writes, *With Stina's blessing and the best wishes* [or *deep affection*] *of Stina's boy.* It's as if his hand literally embodies this duality of Stina/Herman.

Could this be anything other than a play for redemption? Herman's rewriting of the culture's caricature of homosexuals as predators and moral deficients.

To survive in a world that criminalizes joy and prosecutes pleasure as the Biblical crime of sodomy, Herman *has* to become Stina.

Queerness can't speak in its own voice in 1942. It needs an intermediary who can pass in the straight world. Stina is wise and nurturing, but Herman's made her life one of tragedy and displacement. She's transient, solitary—the beloved stranger, a perennial outsider. Is she a manifestation of Herman's regret for his outlaw past, his path to survival?

Queerness manifests as nurturing in Herman's world, and Stina is his avatar of care, his nurturing heart of food. Food from the hand of someone who knows what it's like to be uprooted; knows what isolation and estrangement feel like; knows loss.

Herman/Stina reminds me of the Māhū people in native Hawaiian culture who combine traditional traits from male and female. They have a special role as cultural caretakers, healers, and guardians of sacred traditions. Stina's wisdom is food: the French, Alsatian, and German dishes she's brought to the American Midwest, a symbolic planting of old rootstock in new soil. She uses her foreignness—her kitchen skills, her experienced palate—to plant in a landscape of virtuous fertility.

There's this lonely mournfulness in some of Stina's recipes, an odd mood of almost grief. Of rhubarb, Herman says, "Although this succulent plant was alien to Stina she appreciated its virtues and, artist that she was, made use of it in many ways not known to native cooks." She's the outsider, bringing humane wisdom to a world that runs on cruelty and ignorance.

For Rhubarb en Captivité, you cut the stalks into four-inch sticks, coat with sweet batter and deep-fry "until the color of old honey." To serve, you flood a flat glass bowl with "a lake of rhubarb and red cherry sauce," then surround it with a fence of the fried rhubarb, stacked zigzag like split rails, "with drifts of powdered sugar" like blanketing snow. Herman says he finds this particularly interesting, which seems about right. It is, after all, a small, poetic queer tableau of estrangement. An ode to the probable incarceration Herman had avoided as a young man, and that he'd never really managed to escape, no matter how long or how far he ran.

BOOK OF SECRETS

[1938]

R ICHARD NATHAN OLNEY'S AN ODD BOY: QUIET AND slight, brown-haired and brown-eyed, closer to animals than to other children; devoted to plants and flowers, even at age eleven. He's the eldest of nine surviving children born to banker-lawyer Norris and Doris Olney. They keep a crowded coexistence in a virtuous white-frame house in northwest Iowa, in a village of just under six hundred called Marathon.

Norris keeps a sober Christian tone at home. He is worshipful, proudly patriarchal in his recitals of grace. But Richard seems to have an absolute belief in sensuality. He stirs up jugs of Kool-Aid and pops corn to sell at a little summer stand, but heaps the popcorn into sacks large enough to hold five pounds of potatoes and sells it for only three cents the bag—an act of profligacy combined with an incitement to gluttony that offends his parents' biblical virtues. It gives them cause for worry.

Richard helps with the family cooking, lends a hand to his mother, Doris, when she fries chicken for supper; makes pot roast and apple pies. Well, Doris isn't much of a cook. Surely she appreciates the help.

He takes on the mashed potatoes, though it takes a lot to yield enough to spoon onto eleven plates, but Richard is diligent. Picture the pile of russets he pulls from the burlap sack (on special at Mohr's in Albert City, a hundred pounds for $1.29), the wet brown peels pored like football pigskin; the peeler's wooden handle, slick

from starch, slipping in the boy's hand. The mound of peels grows,
soaking the newsprint spread out on the kitchen table to spare it.

In 1941, the year Richard turns fourteen, Crown publishes *The Escoffier Cook Book: A Guide to the Fine Art of Cookery for Connoisseurs, Chefs, Epicures.* Almost three thousand recipes, printed on the kind of stock used for Bibles; paper your index finger glides across as it physically traces the steps for composing a Mousse of Crayfish or Poivrade Sauce for Venison. Richard has seen the book in a shop. It costs three dollars, which is a heavy outlay, but what price can you put on a source so mysterious and so profound?

This book of secrets wrapped in a dust jacket bearing a fleur-de-lis surrounded by a raspberry-pink aura that seems to glow. This American conversion of Escoffier's 1903 *Guide culinaire,* the master's comprehensive manual for chefs, such a grand and useless book for an Iowa country teen to covet—except if you think of it as a gay boy's talisman: a charm to ward off the soul-killing cruelty of imposing an ordinary life on boys who read secrets in the flowers.

And when you're the banker's son in a place where everyone relies on loans to level the stress of growing crops, you can walk around with your queer French book and no farmer's kid unwilling to feel the fury of his father's hand is going to kick your ass.

Doris has to see that *something* is different about Richard.

The owner of a nursery greenhouse in Sioux Rapids gives Richard an unpaid summer job potting plants and fertilizing shrubs. The young man rides the train ten miles each morning and back each night, sometimes hauling plants the owner lets him take to grow in his mother's yard. One day Doris drops in on the greenhouse man to make sure her son's story is legit, as if she senses something quietly, dangerously transgressive in Richard's essence.

Without telling anyone, Richard orders multiple plants. He starts digging holes in the yard for where they need to be planted, following his deeply intuitive sense, I have to believe from what I know of Richard, of where those plants should be.

When Doris notices his digging she scolds him: Richard! You can't just dig up the yard without consulting anyone! Some day you'll have a wife and you'll need to respect her wishes.

Richard says, Then I'll never get married.

Years later, after Richard still hasn't taken a wife, Doris thinks that perhaps she, having put it like that, is partly to blame for his resistance. Though of course nobody was going to make Richard compromise, or persuade him to ignore the truth of things revealed.

"THE MAN AMONG THE WOMEN"

[1939]

I N 1936, WAI KIM-FONG AND ESTHER ENG SAIL TO HONG Kong to premiere *Heartaches*.

The film is a success.

"Still only twenty-two," film historian Frank Bren writes, "she was no doubt unaware of the fact that she was already unique in world cinema—China's premier Movie Brat." Historian Christianne A. Gadd calls Esther a "gender rebel."

Fong and Esther put off returning to California. They decide to stick around Hong Kong for a while.

The local press hails Esther as a celebrity. Several articles call her China's first woman director. Technically she's never directed a picture. That changes after Nanyang, Hong Kong's biggest film studio, invites her to helm a feature. In the next three years, as the Chinese war of resistance against an encroaching Japan rages on the mainland, Esther makes five films in Hong Kong, including *It's a Women's World* (1939), featuring an all-woman cast of thirty-six.

Esther is publicly more visible than ever, appearing at premieres and parties with Fong and other women actors with the dom physicality of the Hollywood auteur. She smiles for the cameras with her arm around Fong, the way Orson Welles lays a possessive arm on Rita Hayworth.

As a famous foreigner, Esther would have options for socializing with other queer people, out of sight of the public. "There were no exclusive spaces for homosexuals," Hong Kong historian Travis S. K.

Kong says. "Only . . . secret parties or boat cruises catering for mainly the gay and lesbian middle-class, celebrities, and expatriates." But Esther's public presentation, her clothes and hair and manner, make an unmistakable assertion of her sexuality. It's as if Esther has absorbed the old lessons of the Mandarin, of gender as a public role, a costume, a field of expression, an attitude.

Most press reports look away or shrug. They describe Esther as "the man among the women," and her female companions as "good sisters" or "bosom friends." But a male entertainment reporter for Hong Kong's *Sing Tao Daily* claps back on the gender rebel those around her, using Esther's given name, call Brother Ha:

> We used to call Fong Esther's "bosom friend," but this is not quite right. Lover, have you ever heard anything stranger? . . . [Fong] and Esther were living proof that "same-sex love" exists in this world. Man or woman, old or young, everyone called her Brother Ha . . . Esther herself liked to be called Big Brother. As sure as I am that she's a woman, it makes me terrified to call her Brother!

Homophobes can write all the shit they want about Esther, but they can't deny she *is* a legend. Along with Dorothy Arzner, and before Ida Lupino in the 1950s, Esther is "the only woman directing commercial American feature films," notes Frank Bren. And she's one of probably only two women (possibly besides Xie Caizhen in Shanghai in the 1920s) making feature films in early Chinese cinema.

And there's no denying that Esther *is* Brother Ha, a queer badass. She seems to carry a certain protective aura that shields her from the kind of public homophobia she'd experience in the States. This speaks to China's openness in this period.

Granted, as a British Crown colony that criminalized what it branded "buggery," Hong Kong civil society demanded complete queer discretion, if not absolute invisibility. But the scene in the literate urban mainland was open to queerness as a flavor of human possibility, despite lesbians going unseen, thanks to misogyny. Still, "the Chinese indigenous concept of homosexual liking, *hao nanse*, is basically neutral," historian Tze-lan D. Sang says. "The term carries no negative value judgment, no comparison of homosexual taste to either disease or the perversion of an aim-specific, originary 'normal' erotic drive."

European sexology would eventually convince China that homosexuality was disordered, and of course after 1949 the Chinese Communist Party would brutally prosecute queer expression. But Brother Ha has three productive, super-queer, cinematically historic years in Hong Kong, until, in 1939, as Japanese troops surround the Territories, she finally heeds her parents' warnings to flee.

Back in San Francisco, Esther directs *Golden Gate Girl*, released in 1941, filmed on location around the city. It opens with a brief shot of the main character as a baby girl, played by three-month-old Lee Jun-fan, a.k.a. Bruce Lee—like, the future *Fist of Fury* Bruce Lee. (Bruce's father, Lee Hoi-chuen, was a Cantonese opera singer from Hong Kong, on tour in SF with Bruce's mother, Grace Ho, when Bruce was born.) I mean, if Brother Ha can transform Bruce Lee into a girl, she might be capable of anything.

But Esther's power and brilliance would be all but forgotten. Nine of the eleven films she directed, co-directed, or produced would end up lost, including the five she made in Hong Kong, a fact of erasure both tragic and shocking. Were her Hong Kong pictures collateral damage amid the violence and chaos of invasion? The Japanese military reportedly confiscated a print of *Heartaches*, presumably because of its theme of Chinese resistance against an unnamed foreign aggressor (clearly Japan), and no other prints have surfaced. Could censorship explain other losses? Did Japanese authorities destroy Esther's films because of her public queer identity?

If Esther is remembered today, it's partly due to Craig Claiborne, who brought attention to her in the *New York Times* as a Manhattan restaurateur with a striking personal style. It's due to eminent queer historian Jonathan Ned Katz, who elevated Esther to the status of lesbian hero. But it's primarily due to S. Louisa Wei, a film scholar in

Hong Kong, whose 2013 documentary *Golden Gate Girls* (with Law Kar) mourned Esther's inexplicable erasure from cinema history, and surfaced a rich cache of archival material—hundreds of salvaged photos discovered by chance in a dumpster south of San Francisco.

To me, the key to unlocking the full power of Brother Ha's achievement is to be discovered somewhere in the gender-fluid memory of the Mandarin, nurtured by the backstage rituals of eating together. It's in that packed Hollywood apartment during the making of *Heartaches*, in the queer chi swirling through rooms filled with joy, the promise of the future, and a smell of something always cooking.

INGREDIENT X

[1948]

T HE ONLY PHOTOS OF I'VE SEEN OF HIM, MAYBE THE only ones known to exist, are of Harry Baker at sixty-four: retired from baking, spilling the secret he'd kept for twenty years.

The news photographer's lights leave a shine in his hair waves; catch the immaculately pressed shirt, dark tie, yoke straps on his plain apron, as he mixes batter for the cake. The look is correct—you imagine this is how Harry grooms himself for church, minus the apron. Assuming Harry *goes* to church, because there's this dissonance in the cocktail ring on the wedding finger of Harry's left hand, a large, princess-cut square of some dark stone or glass that hints at a thirst for the baroque, more carnal than holy, a passion for the kind of opulence studios serve in costume pictures. (After all, Hollywood had made his cake locally famous.)

It's Harry's smile that gets me in these images, the expressive centerpiece in a carefully molded mask of affability. It even dwarfs the extravagant cake, its skin troubled by fine cracks, swollen above the enormous tube pan's rim.

The paper teased the story all week, and on Sunday the Minneapolis *Star Tribune* published the pictures: Harry, pulling a cake from the kind of cheap, portable oven he'd packed into his converted bedroom in LA. The accompanying feature pivots on a newsy revelation.

"This is the story of 'Ingredient X,'" *Tribune* food editor Mary Hart announces, "the 'mystery' ingredient which has resulted in a brand new kind of cake, the first new major type in 100 years. Today, the mystery is ended."

The spilling of Harry's tale coincides with a major launch by General Mills, the flour and cake-mix corporation with Minneapolis headquarters that boast a sprawling test kitchen. Harry's cake, now no longer his, has been dubbed "chiffon"—a name cooked up in General Mills' marketing department. As part of the launch, they've released a chiffon recipe booklet under its Betty Crocker brand, hyping the unique power of its Gold Medal flour to produce the perfect cake. They call it "the cake discovery of the century."

The company's invested heavily: bought Harry's original recipe along with the ownership rights; spent months altering Harry's proportions and technique, streamlining the method, rejiggering the oven temp and time. And they've sunk a shitload into marketing, with the hook being chiffon's mystery addition: Ingredient X, the secret Harry's kept, with near-paranoia, for twenty years.

It turns out Ingredient X is oil in the batter, used instead of butter. Plain old Mazola vegetable oil, the kind for frying chicken. Cheap and neutral-tasting. Luxurious in the way it adds sheen to the face of a cut slice; for the delicacy it gives the crumb.

Chiffon would prove epically popular for Betty Crocker. In its booklet, and in the mega-selling *Betty Crocker' Picture Cook Book* of 1950, with a sub-chapter on chiffon, Harry Baker isn't mentioned. Chiffon belongs to Betty, and, apart from the *Star Tribune*, it's her image, not Harry's, that becomes the face of chiffon. And, rather than ending the mystery of Harry's cake, this is for me where the mystery of Harry's cake begins—the mystery of how something that is the product of queer experience can become so thoroughly wiped of its original meaning. How queerness is completely effaced.

I look at the story of the long-kept secret of chiffon cake as a convenient distraction, a marketing gimmick, and a diversion from the *true* story of Harry's cake, a story inseparable from the compromises, the accommodations, and the untruths that were an essential part of gay and lesbian experience.

The way it reduces Harry's story to a recipe, a formula that twists on half a cup of common salad oil; the way it commodifies the notion of perfection—the story of Ingredient X is a de-queering narrative.

Cakes made with oil instead of butter were hardly new in 1947, when Harry sells his recipe to General Mills—or even in 1927, when he says he perfected his recipe. James Beard notes how salad-oil cakes experienced "terrific popularity" during the 1930s, and says some cooks would substitute clarified butter for the oil, genoise-style. In the 1920s Mazola, the corn oil brand Harry uses, published several recipes for oil-based cakes. A full-page ad in the *Ladies' Home Journal* of June 1924 has the headline, "Accidentally She Discovered It," about an unnamed, no doubt made-up "housewife" who finds herself out of butter and Crisco on cake-baking day and turns instead to Mazola.

The ad includes a recipe (also available in a booklet you could get for free by dropping Mazola a request). It looks plausibly like it could be the recipe Harry begins from, tweaking the proportions of sugar and flour and water, but mostly, it's about eggs. Because the innovation in Harry's cake isn't the oil, it's the extravagance of eggs—depending on their size, seven or eight to make a single cake. Yolks added with the oil and other liquids, whites whipped stiff and folded delicately into the base as if assembling a soufflé. This volume gives Harry's cake an exuberance that at last makes good on his promise to make a cake superior to Clara Butters's homely, disillusioning Ohio church-fair winner.

It's this robustness of foam within the yellow, sticky, oleaginous base of the batter that pushes Harry's cake into an arguably queer state. His merging of yellow cake and angel sponge ignores the American tradition of what seemed an inescapable binary, either yolk-rich butter or fluffy white sponge.

Harry's cake shows the expansion of pleasure that is possible in the defiance of limits.

※

HARRY SELLS HIS CAKES to anyone in the know, anyone willing to come up with the sobering price of two bucks. He leaves a cake for you on his front porch; you follow the posted instructions and stuff your two dollars into the mail slot and split. You don't ring the bell. You don't see anybody, except maybe by accident: a glimpse of Harry through a gap in the blinds, a flash of Mac's face through the window of his delivery van turning onto Larchmont.

Harry doesn't answer the phone, for fear, he says, of losing his concentration and spoiling his cakes. He conceals the Mazola empties in his trash, fearing his batter formula's secret will tip into the open. Harry's identity has become fused with his work. Both exist in the closet, the exuberant product of a clandestine life. It's that mystery helps lend Harry's cakes their aura: quirky, invisible, exclusive. Hollywood *does* love a mystery.

You could argue for the queerness of cakes baked in a bedroom, surrounded by all the intimacy that room provides, all it implies—cakes that rise, that find their shape and complex aromas in a place kept private to allow desire its space to blossom. There's queer magic in a cake based on common salad oil that transforms on billows of egg whites—like Stanley Kowalski's harsh exposé of the cheap charms spun by Blanche DuBois in Tennessee Williams's *A Streetcar Named Desire*: transforming herself from brokenness and disgrace, with the help of a little cheap powder and perfume and the glow from a paper-lanterned light bulb into the Queen of the Nile.

The myth of the recipe is Harry's illusion. It's the performance of baking and selling his cakes—alchemizing flour into glitter—that transforms the closet into a site of magic.

And both Hollywood and the authors and publishers of cookbooks in the repressed and proscribed West—the Calvinist political, social, and cultural theocracy of America and Anglo-Teutonic Europe, with its belief in total depravity and limited atonement—need the closet. *Need* the closet as the place where passion and sensuality find expression; the place where transgressive pleasure can be bought as cheaply as a twenty-cent slice of Harry's cake, without tarnishing anyone's manifestly righteous public image.

The face of American food was fake. Something queer in the food survived: an enlargement of the accepted limits of sensuality. But this was something that had to be contained within straight narratives; translated into acceptable fictions of family, faith, and comfort. Of course queer people participated in these fabrications—what else was possible?

Especially after 1945, and with the hardening of a conservative social and cultural order, nonconformity scares the hell out of people: the fine, churchgoing, Commie-hating ones with family rooms and television consoles, new refrigerator-freezers and electric ranges. American writers had long found narrative power in homoerotic subtexts: *Billy Budd,* *Huckleberry Finn, The Great Gatsby.* Themes of innocence and corruption, secrecy and disclosure—what Eve Kosofsky Sedgwick calls binarisms in a literature of the crises of self-discovery and self-revelation. And Hollywood, bound in the self-imposed straitjacket of the Hays Code's gay and lesbian censoring, worked out its own shrouded queer narrative language.

In the early 1940s, this vulnerable moment in a world at war, the pioneers of queer food are forced to give up subjectivity; to cede power to a straightness that co-opts the power of queer food while disguising its source in queerness. It pretends, like the citizens of Samuel Steward's Ohio, that queerness can't exist so doesn't. But it takes the delicious products of queerness and puts a new face to them.

Harry's swapped one life of concealment for another, from Ohio to the bungalow on Larchmont: working in virtual seclusion at strange hours, keeping watch over his ovens, unloading Mazola empties to the trash when nobody's around. He's left pain and probably trauma in the wake of abandoning Mary and their kids. If he's guilty of cruelty, it's the cruelty of a queer-hating world he was compelled to enact.

As compensation, he brings a cake into the world—a cake with an intensity of joy only Harry is capable of giving birth to.

This should be the moment when Harry rises. Instead it's where the arc of his story begins to collapse.

The title for the Larchmont house becomes tangled in litigation, and in 1945 Harry learns he has to leave. That's not all that's eating

at Harry. Though he's only in his early sixties, he makes an allusion a
couple of years later, as he recalls his decision to try to sell his recipe,
to his creeping fear of memory loss. This suggests Harry's never written down his recipe; that he's kept it secret, perhaps to protect it. This
suggests that the formula for the world's perfect cake exists only in
Harry's head; that the language of cake is as yet uncoded.

And look, he's been mixing batter and trotting to the bedroom for
eighteen years. Surely he's tired. Maybe Harry feels starting over in a
new place, having to reconstruct his particular cage of secrecy, is more
than he can cope with. Mac may already have moved on. By 1950, he's
an out-of-work jewelry store clerk married to a woman named Leslie
Jean; they have a daughter and live with Leslie Jean's mother in the San
Fernando Valley.

Harry spends the next year trying to interest General Mills in
his formula for cake. You have to figure he uses all his old salesman's
skills to frame his recipe as a revolution in the world of cake; that
he builds the sales pitch General Mills later adopts, that his secret
recipe is the first major innovation in cake in a hundred years, cake's
Manhattan Project.

Setting aside Ingredient X, it's egg white foam that forms the real
magic of Harry's cake. Is it part of a reclaimed architecture after a
war that imposed heavy restrictions on sugar and eggs? Soufflés and
meringues, whipped cream cakes—they represent a quiet new optimism of the kitchen, kindred in spirit to Christian Dior's New Look
fashions of 1947, a flowering of femininity in an extravagance of fabric.

Harry pitches with relentless purpose. He declines to meet with
directors in the regional offices in Northern California. Instead he
holds out for a meeting at headquarters in Minneapolis and gets it. To
prepare, Harry wrangles time in a test kitchen in the offices of the local
gas company, essentially re-creating the sequestered conditions of his
Larchmont bungalow with a similar level of paranoia about revealing
his cake's secret. He bakes dozens of cakes for General Mills execu-
tives and test kitchen staff to taste and pick apart. Two members of the
test kitchen ask to watch him mix and bake his cake and he lets them,

except he adds the salad oil, his mystery ingredient, from a blind container and doesn't tell them what it is.

It works. In the early months of 1947, the company makes Harry an offer for his recipe and the rights to his cake.

We don't know what the price was. Some say twenty-five grand (something like $340,000 in 2023 dollars); others say fifty. An astronomical payout feeds the myth of Harry's cake, something General Mills has every incentive to feed, but does it make objective sense?

General Mills was a mammoth corporation with lawyers and leverage and a hundred home economists capable of reverse-engineering cake samples to guess Harry's ingredients, his method of mixing and baking. I bet if they agreed on $5,000 it would've been a major coup for Harry.

After all, Harry's main value to General Mills is the *story* of his cake—the recipe guarded for years by its perfectionist creator, the glamor of Hollywood and the celebrity aura of the Brown Derby—but the narrative's details are problematic to a corporation. The official story of Harry's cake can only be a partial one. His murky Ohio past, his reason for settling in LA, his absent wife and kids—Harry is a sordid challenge to the tightly controlled image of Betty Crocker as a feminine icon of home and family. Harry's carefully filtered story, a Minneapolis *Star Tribune* exclusive surely shaped by General Mills as part of its chiffon rollout, is as much of the truth as the world is ever going to know.

Because the irony is that the actual secret of Harry's cake is the one neither he nor General Mills can or would want to tell. The real Ingredient X isn't salad oil but queerness. And both Harry and General Mills are committed to keeping *that* secret locked in an almost indecipherable code. Harry needs to disappear—get out of the way so his queer cake can be altered; sanitized in a process of home-ec reinvention.

General Mills spends a year wiping Harry's fingerprints from his cake. A General Mills home economist bakes four hundred cakes with minor variations, searching for the perfect commercial recipe. She beats the egg whites stiffer; adapts the proportions to different brands of General Mills flours; streamlines the mixing of the batter. Harry's cake becomes efficient, above all replicable. It gets indelibly stamped with the face of Betty Crocker and picks up a name: *chiffon*, anodyne and marketable. (The name is technically an appropriation of an existing cake, already sold by some bakeries in the mid-forties: a chiffon made with creamed shortening, suggestive of tenderness and fluff. Even some whipped cream–topped pies advertised by bakeries were called chiffon.)

The General Mills marketing department drives its hook in deep: The first new cake in a hundred years! With the implication, amid the Cold War ethos that asserts industrial capitalism as a moral good, that chiffon isn't just cake: It's evolutionary progress.

But in the inevitable flattening that comes with commercial exploitation, has Harry's cake been obliterated?

Where Harry's was silk bouffant, Betty's is a pouf of spun nylon, foolproof, adaptable to myriad flavors, tints, and icings; suitable for birthdays and bridge parties and teen-girl sleepovers.

By the time Harry's cake makes it to a cookbook—General Mills' heavy, spiral-bound *Betty Crocker's Picture Cook Book* of 1950—it's both subtly and dramatically changed: a catch for selling Gold Medal and Softasilk flours, with recipe booklets free for the taking at the market or tucked inside bags of flour. "WARNING," begins the recipe for Betty Crocker Sunburst Chiffon Cake. "Do not use any flour except Gold Medal with this recipe. . . . Do not risk a food-wasting baking failure—use Gold Medal." I mean, when you put it like *that*.

With his fifty grand or five or whatever, Harry gets lost. Maybe he travels. "He was heard to remark," the *Star Tribune* tells its readers, "how nice it might be to travel around the world." There's a rumor he's in South America. His name appears to slip from LA city directories. His family back in Ohio hires a private eye to find him. (Did they read about the payoff from General Mils? Are they seeking a slice?) The hunt leads nowhere. Harry's erased himself, leaving only the heavily redacted story of a cake with the queerness expunged.

Harry, it seems, was in LA, all along. The 1950 Census shows him living alone in what appears to be a building of modest apartments on

South Flower Street, close to where Frank Gehry's stainless steel–clad Walt Disney Concert Hall now heaves and ripples in the California sun. A 1974 death notice confirms Harry had been living downtown, apparently unnoticed.

It's unlikely that news of the passing of the man who created chiffon cake would stoke much public interest in '74. In a year when carrot cake was the sexiest dessert in America—in a decade when tastes had turned to macramé rustic, chiffon would seem the obsession of a vanished time: the dingy rayon day-dress of a quarter century ago, forgotten in the closet.

Harry had become a ghost long before, and with him the cake that once told a story of queer survival. Queerness, queer happiness, a growing imperative to express desire through resistance, for public visibility at the table—they've only begun the radical act of living in daylight.

Part Two

TABLES UNDER A PARTIAL SKY

1948–1961

Our Cast of the Hungry, the Shameless, and the Kindred

James "Jimmy" Baldwin

John Bulica, a.k.a. John Bulecca,
a.k.a. Johnny Nicholson

Karl Bissinger

Edna Lewis

Richard Olney

Esther Eng / Brother Ha

. . . . .
. . . . .

Plus
Arnold! Mary Painter! Lucien Happersberger!
Beauford Delaney! Bernard Hassell! Scott Peacock!
Clementine Paddleford!

HUNGRY IN PARIS

[1948]

A S HIS PLANE SHUDDERS ONTO FRENCH GROUND, Jimmy's starving: an empty gut below a wrung-out heart, a spirit starved for sanity, purpose, and queer emancipation. In New York they feed you the latest flavor of derangement and call it American progress, but it's the same old starvation diet of fear and reaction, the same old poverty of love.

Jimmy believes Paris will be his refuge. Believes it as far as hope is possible.

He flew on a one-way ticket, bought with the last of the fellowship award money he got for pitching a book, a collaboration with a photographer on Harlem churches: *James Baldwin, twenty-four, from whom we expect the twentieth century's second Negro renaissance.* But with the book unfinished and the money all but gone only a penurious kind of promise remains. He feels the guilt of leaving his mother Berdis and all his young brothers and little sisters behind in Harlem; mixed up with the joy of starting fresh with his last forty dollars and the panic of where's the cash going to come from to eat. And a November evening in Paris, he discovers on his descent to the tarmac, can be every bit as freezing as one in New York.

Saint-Germain-des-Prés on the Left Bank, the bohemian heart of postwar Paris, is a quarter of expensive, shitty rooms in cold-water hotels, bleak rather than romantic, where an animated collection of the displaced and expatriate live in states of discomfort. There are the ambitious in exile like would-be-novelist Jimmy, mixed up with the aimless young; those trying to escape the despair of a world in which 60 or 70 million could so easily perish, and Why? For what? Desperate to leave an America still drunk from its so-called victory over fascism. An America where a Black man on a subway platform can get the life damn near beat from him as dozens look on, just for standing with a white woman—for *standing*. And where, after being thrown together in combat zones of busted towns and makeshift barracks, men who willingly, eagerly had sex with other men find they cannot take the truth of what they did. An America of men who cannot live with the possibility of queer desire swimming in their blood, or that it could again rise to the surface. An America of men so panicked to admit even the possibility of desire for other men that, instead of facing it, they get to work killing themselves with booze or smack.

In Paris, to be a Black American so soon after the war has ceased, is to be spectacularly alone in a city with "no doughnuts," Jimmy writes, "no milk shakes, no Coca-Cola, no dry Martinis." America got its national identity not through some ancient codified system of cuisine like in France but via sugar water: cloying, carbonated with fizz so harsh it just about lacerates the throat, endlessly advertised in images of extreme heterosexual whiteness: the college quarterback taking a break with a frosty bottle of pop as his cheerleader gal looks on in rapture; the young blond wife toting that same bottle streaked with beads of condensation to her handsome husband, who has abandoned his lawn mower for the backyard hammock.

For Jimmy, America lurks somewhere in the fry vat, the drugstore DrinkMaster, the cocktail shaker; in the corner tavern, at the lunch counter and hamburger stand, all segregated. America is a nation that forged its identity at tables apart. In France, though he sometimes dreams of Berdis's fried chicken back in Harlem, Jimmy will have to stitch a life around food from meals provided by better-off friends, and from wisps and pickings underground.

The rare times he has a few coins jangling around his pocket he might catch something to eat Chez Rafi, an Algerian café. He might slurp cheap tripe or onion soup at dawn at Les Halles, the sprawling late-night/early-morning food market where those who drank till the bars closed fortify themselves before slumping off to bed. Other times he scrambles for sustenance, often through the generosity of friends. Once he barters a plate of fried chicken for belting out "The Man I Love" at Inez Cavanaugh's jangling club and soul food parlor in the shadow of the Sorbonne. Mostly, however, Jimmy finds himself hungry in Paris.

But there's freedom in want; dignity in being thirsty for the Coke and the milkshake if the price of them is your humanity.

Paris tempts with hope of remedy—a cure for the sickness of New York City after the war, a time of what Jimmy calls "the most terrifying personal anarchy." The American refugees of Paris hold out hope for a kinship of the waked up. People refusing the lives they were expected to slip into at home, obediently, the way you submit to wearing an embroidered apron from your bridal trousseau or take on the heaviness of a hand-me-down church robe. Instead, the self-exiled in Saint-Germain spend long hours on café terraces, draining bottles of cheap Cognac that burns and ragged Algerian wine. They get drunk every night; stoned on kif; high on themselves: the novels they'll write, the pictures they fantasize about painting.

Jimmy can afford no room of his own sometimes and crashes with whoever is left standing in the predawn. He moves in an almost all-white circle. "No thoughts of color in early Paris and our own liberation time," writes a white friend whose bed Jimmy has shared. *No thoughts of color* is fine to say if you're white, but Jimmy has thoughts—oh, he has thoughts. To be Black and queer in France weigh heavier on your mind than *vin Algérien* sits in your stomach. Liberation time can go fuck itself.

Eventually, a friend finagles a room for him at the eighteenth-century Hôtel Verneuil, its tapered facade mooring an intersection of narrow streets in the Seventh Arrondissement. The Corsican family who manages it, the Dumonts, live on the ground floor; the five stories above have twenty-seven rooms and no baths, only a single squat toilet for sharing. Room No. 1 goes by the hour, for couples seeking a quick bang and a toweling off, if they dropped the extra coins for a towel; the others are occupied by writers. Jimmy's circle is white and straight: Otto Friedrich, Herbert Gold, George Solomos (a.k.a. Themistocles Hoetis). They come together as a kind of family, where everything is communal: "food, a room, a coat, a typewriter, money, alcohol, hashish," Jimmy biographer David Leeming says. "It was for all to share."

Food is not something to obsess over or covet for Jimmy, not like a Piaget watch or Longchamp wallet; not a magic cookbook you can haul around. It's not even an object of epicurean desire, as it is for so many white American tourists swarming Paris starting in 1950, looking for "authentic" versions of the unpronounceable *homard à l'Américaine* and *blanquette de veau* they knew searingly expensive versions of in thickly brocaded restaurants in Dallas or Detroit. "It's pork chops, baby," Jimmy likes to say—no matter how elevated, how esoteric, how unrecognizable on the American tongue. Food is coalition to Jimmy: a way of keeping everyone around you, everyone you care about—your empathy circle—alive. Food is an act of figuring out where you live, in the emotional sense, the place where you belong. Jimmy articulates a queer ethic of nurturance. It's not the food that matters, per se—it's all pork chops, baby—it's the context that queers it. The intention that queers it; how it comes to the table; who's at the table.

He knows this, he's seen it in New York. He's felt it.

BEFORE PARIS, Jimmy was known to drop in on Frank and Dorcas Neal's weekend salon in Midtown, midnight gatherings of artists, writers, actors, and composers, mostly queer but not exclusively so; mostly Black but not exclusively so: Billy Strayhorn, Talley Beatty, Lou Harrison, Brock Peters, Charles Sebree, John Cage, with straight comrades Harry Belafonte, Felrath Hines, Eartha Kitt. "For those in the group who were Black and gay," Dorcas Neal told Strayhorn biographer David Hajdu, "it meant the world just to see that there were others like them in the arts."

Food is central to the experience of the Neal Salon: "a pot of chicken and rice or ham and beans," Hajdu says, "plus a plate of sandwiches on the table." Things typically break up at five or six in the morning, and continue sometimes right through to breakfast. Food defines the salon as a place of sanctuary: a self-sustaining cocoon packed with comforting things to eat; where the nighttime city—a place of danger for queers, especially Black queers—can have no purchase.

No need to go outside, baby. Not until the sun obtrudes.

Billy Strayhorn—Duke Ellington's arranger and musical collaborator, gay and Black, the composer of "Lush Life" and "Take the A Train"—eventually orchestrates another salon, one centered even more than the Neals' around food and the shared performance of cooking. Saturday afternoons, Billy shows up at the Upper West Side brownstone of Marian and Arthur C. Logan, the celebrity physician whose patients include Ellington and the Reverend Dr. Martin Luther King Jr. Billy hauls in a couple of grocery bags from the fancy food department in Macy's basement, packed with all the fixins for paella. Billy calls the dish his "pot." Within months, Billy's Saturday paella party at the Logans' is a virtual salon of Billy's friends and the Logans' friends—gay, straight—where everybody, including a few of the Neal regulars, just shows up.

Billy orchestrates everybody to prep for the Saturday pot: chopping vegetables, peeling garlic, scrubbing clams, excising the nasties from shrimp—all while flying high on cocktails. If the Neal Salon is all about inflating a bubble of queer safety around dishes already prepared, Billy's Pot is a shared act of transformation: cooking as a joyful staging of Black queer creation.

Both are descendants of the great Harlem literary and visual art salons of the 1920s, especially A'Lelia Walker's Dark Tower, in her townhouse west of Lenox Avenue, and Wallace Thurman's gatherings a few blocks west, in his flat with walls given over to homoerotic murals by Bruce Nugent.

The lingering flavor of these has somehow made its way onto Jimmy's tongue.

THE SHAPE OF BOHEMIA

[1949]

W HAT CAN WE TAKE FROM JIMMY? THAT QUEERNESS is contingency? That it has meaning only in opposition to the notion of heterosexuality, especially a heterosexuality that is considered the human default? So by extension, queer food must be contingent on occasion and spirit—in the intention of the cooks and the collective eaters, a willingness, actually a determination, to elevate difference and perform acts of defiance at the table. *We hereby declare in the sharing of this food that we are all both masc and femme, Black and white, butch and faggot; that we are all a little bit of everything mixed.*

What about where the table sits?

THEY'RE STRICTLY FROM THE NEW BOHEMIA
Old-guard society mixes with workers in the
arts at New York's gay parties

THE MARCH 1950 REPORT by Rhea Talley, correspondent for the *Courier-Journal* of Louisville, Kentucky, describes a newborn social scene in New York City. The undisguised meaning of "gay" is light-hearted, carefree, but a kind of linguistic smirk telegraphs the coded subject of Talley's *actual* story: artsy parties where brash and reckless young gays mix with circumspect older ones, a generational shift. For James Baldwin, self-exile in Paris was essential for expressing desire the way he needed to, but these young bitches were letting it fly in New York, for god's sake, and before the eye of columnists and photographers.

Southern novelists Speed Lampkin and Truman Capote, with pale, elfin faces suggesting corrupted prep-school boys; lyricist John Latouche, sharing a joke with *Mademoiselle*'s Leo Lerman. They mix with weathered scene queens Cecil Beaton and Carl Van Vechten, and the usual crowd of camera-thirsty straight eccentrics who always make a soirée feel gayer: Salvador Dali, Carol Channing, Isadora Duncan's brother Raymond, showing out in signature toga and strappy shepherd's sandals.

The implication of *bohemian* was obvious in 1950. At a moment of broad consensus on the existential importance to society of conforming, it meant dressing up deviant appetites to look like artistic or literary taste; a socially acceptable marker for brash, different . . . queer.

Talley reports that the headquarters for this curious squad of aesthetes is Café Nicholson on East Fifty-Eighth Street, "a tiny place decorated in the style of an old apothecary shop. This sounds 'just too quaint,' but the cafe has, possibly because one of the owners is a *Flair* and *Vogue* photographer, a sophisticated style. Everybody seems to know everybody else[,] in the European coffee-shop tradition."

That photographer is Karl Bissinger. Café Nicholson had been officially open less than six months when Talley's piece appeared— "officially" because the restaurant was operating without a license since at least May of 1949.

Karl, thirty-five, and his boyfriend, thirty-three-year-old Johnny Nicholson, signed an application for a business certificate in September 1949. What the document fails to capture is that Karl and Johnny have a partner for Café Nicholson, a chef: Edna Lewis, also thirty-three.

By the time the restaurant is legitimately, legally open for business, it's already becoming what John T. Edge calls "a canteen for the creative class." And already, with its foraged urban bric-a-brac, was articulating a backward-looking boho aesthetic for New York, the postwar world's most forward-looking metropolis. Karl, Johnny, and Edna decorate the café with discards from the nineteenth century: iron grilles, gas lamps, Victorian Gothic window frames, garden statuary—the apothecary's vibe Rhea Talley touches on. Karl, Johnny, and Edna reclaim this urban junk, and in that act of reclamation they make it queer—queer in the broadest sense.

Look at Karl's now-famous photo from 1949, used for the February 1950 issue of *Flair* magazine. We see the backyard at Café Nicholson in daylight, under a canopy of trees in the full leaf of summer. A long table cluttered with wine glasses and a couple of straw-sheathed chianti bottles. It recedes from the camera's eye toward the out of focus back door and a smiling Virginia Reed, thirty-six, a Black server bearing a teapot on a tray.

The five white people at the table have reached fame or are stalking it. Tennessee Williams, thirty-eight, whose *A Streetcar Named Desire* is still in first run on Broadway, consolidated his status as legendary by bagging a Pulitzer the year before. There's Gore Vidal, twenty-three, author of an instantly notorious gay novel, *The City and the Pillar*; painter Buffie Johnson, also thirty-seven, who lives across the street; playwright Donald Windham, on the cusp of twenty-nine, whose first novel would appear in the coming year; and dancer Tanaquil Le Clercq—Tanny—nineteen, prodigy and future wife of choreographer George Balanchine.

The image Karl recorded that stifling day is saturated with the flavor of change, the formerly unrepresentable, the forbidden—because everyone at the table is gay or bi (except for Tanny, as far as I can say). Even Virginia Reed (listed as unmarried in the 1950 US Census, living in the Bronx), before she came to Café Nicholson, was the personal domestic of Spivy (a.k.a. Madame Spivy, a.k.a. Spivy LeVoe, a.k.a. Bertha Levine), the lesbian cabaret singer, songwriter, and actor with outsized wit who owned a swish nightclub, Spivy's Roof, on the ninth floor at East Fifty-Seventh Street and Lexington Avenue. For sure Virginia's seen some things. She's maybe *done* some things.

Words and words have been filed about this image: about the historical moment it captures, the racial stratification. "It is, in effect, a class picture of the young and the talented in the American arts, more than ready for their close-ups." (William Grimes, in Karl Bissinger's *New York Times* obit.) Gore Vidal, writing in 2007, talks about the optimism of a world briefly at peace, heady and hopeful under a Pax Americana, before US howitzers start blasting the Korean Peninsula.

I think Karl wants us to see New York as a revolutionary place, a city of smart iconoclasts under forty. Here they are with chianti and a reviving cup of tea in the drowsy afternoon, taking a break from the intellectual grind of making the culture. I see it as a queer artifact: a souvenir of a moment when those whose lives were defined, or shaped by sexual variance had a growing sense of confidence in public. A souvenir of a budding queer generation, to paraphrase Grimes, rehearsing for its closeup.

In the months after World War II is declared done, in the frenzy of remaking, before regimes of social conservatism harden with the Cold War, there's a queer push to break out of our straitjackets of invisibility. Café Nicholson is perhaps the only public restaurant in 1949 where queer people can gather out of doors in New York City to look at each other. To just . . . *be*.

In the cautious, coded, circumscribed atmosphere of the postwar decade, it must feel incredible, the freedom to gather around a table at a public establishment under a wide-open sky. The porch at the A-House in Provincetown, or Duffy's bar at the beach in Cherry Grove, Fire Island—the places for queer public sociability outdoors are rare, if you don't count risky cruising zones, the outlaw gay underground. The weight of pent-up desire to eat and drink in the open is real—an alternative to windowless bars; house parties with drawn blinds. Even the gay and bohemian San Remo Café on Bleecker Street in the Village, semi-open to the street, established a certain flow with the sidewalk. There's an urgency to breathe in the open—to become like Alice B. Toklas, un-cinching old fears during her Fiesole summer with Gertrude Stein. But the postwar defiance toward old strictures is no longer individual, no longer private; it's becoming shared. The communal urge to carry tables outside, a growing imperative to be *seen*.

This is an early glimmer of a liberation movement.

And yet, readers of *Flair* magazine in 1950 are kept from glimpsing it. Karl's photo in the backyard of Café Nicholson accompanies an essay by Charles J. Rolo called "The New Bohemia," a rambling, pretentious precursor to Rhea Talley's story in the *Courier-Journal*. But the image is altered. The figures around the table are silhouetted to erase the background: the restaurant, the trees—even Virginia Reed. And the caption—"A dinner party," full stop—is at best misleading, and at worst a lie.

The queer freedom that Karl's unmanipulated image represents, will have to remain unseen; what's left is a picture with the latency stripped out. The openness of Johnny's garden under a partial sky and the raw, unmediated pleasure of Edna's cooking—these must wait to have their closeups.

THE BANQUETTE
REVOLUTION

[1947+]

ARGUABLY THE FIRST QUEER RESTAURANT IN AMERICA sat appropriately twisted on and yet not of Union Street in San Francisco, close to Washington Square and its spiky Catholic cathedral. The door to The Paper Doll stood obliquely off Union, around the corner on a narrow dead-end alley called Cadell Place. If you didn't know, you might think it only a bar: nocturnal, sequestered; a façade hung with a low striped awning like curtain bangs, blind to the street. But The Paper Doll pushed beyond the limits of the postwar queer bar to become something more: a space that sheltered and nourished; that let anyone in, but demanded respect for lesbians, gays, and those whose dress and presentation might challenge the strict gender rules of the street.

It opens in 1944, and from the start attracts a sexually variable mix of seamen, tourists, and blue-collar locals. In 1947, The Paper Doll's heterosexual owner, Thomas Arbulich, reaches out to Mona Sargent, the straight proprietor of SF's foundational lesbian bar Mona's, to become a partner and working manager.

"She just sort of turned it on as a gay bar," a one-time regular recalled.

Mona's and a handful of other gay and lesbian bars in San Francisco have a dual identity. They're both queer gathering places, and tourist stops for straight visitors (well, *allegedly* straight) to gawk at drag shows and the clientele. Gender-blurring bars and nightclubs are legendary draws in SF. Places with the lingering flavor of the old Barbary Coast. Places to marvel about back home, in the right company. Places a man in town on shore leave or for a business convention could slip away to and find available sex workers in a range of genders.

The Paper Doll is different. "It offered sanctuary from the tourism which had grown to include Grayline tour stops," explained the legendary activist Phyllis Lyon, "providing a budding community as an alternative where [lesbians and gays] could eat, talk, and gather."

It looks more or less like a standard supper club, but queer customers can hang out in the open, with a cocktail and a plate of chicken. At Café Nicholson the mix is weighted to the straight and, as its reputation spreads, to the famous. The Paper Doll feels radical by contrast: a queer bar without the defensive infrastructure and paranoia of queer bars, the screen of dim lighting, the bartenders enforcing rules on touching and butch or nelly language. The Paper Doll is an establishment without the usual defenses of discretion.

The clientele is of mixed gender. Gay men cluster at the long bar, queer women crowd into the booths opposite. In 1949 college undergrad Susan Sontag crosses the bay from Berkeley to see the lounge acts. There are, she notes in her diary, "several attractive women who served drinks—all in men's clothes." Poet Thom Gunn, who came from England in 1954 to study at Stanford, becomes a regular. So does Samuel Steward, protégé of Gertrude and Alice. Future political activist and cabaret artist José Sarria likes to go in makeup and jewelry, accompanied by his mother.

"They had these big booths and you'd get there, there'd be two in a booth," recalls Charlotte Coleman, a regular. "And then all of a sudden they'd push people in and push people in with you. So after you went there every Friday night, you got to know everybody because everybody had to sit with each other. There wasn't any other seats."

This is how community roots, and how it spreads.

There's an art studio behind the barroom; regular exhibitions in the dining room. Emmy Lou Packard, a friend of Frida Kahlo's and assistant to Diego Rivera in San Francisco in 1940, designs the space: a cabana-stripe awning covering the long bar, and a plastic cutout collage of backlit figures for the inside face of the blacked-out picture window. Robert Pearson McChesney, the abstract expressionist painter, contributes a mural that references Balinese stick puppets.

The menu's built around prime rib and roast chicken, and it's the excellence of the kitchen that helps define The Paper Doll, makes it a night out for queers who want to feel fine in a room full of queers. Because Arbulich pays off the police, the vice squad making trouble in Tenderloin bars stay away. It's artsy, sociable, discreet. It queers the American bar and grill. Though the menu's limited, the food's about the same as the food in one of the big, brash dinner houses on Van Ness Avenue, but here you're jammed in a booth with random lesbians and a boy in makeup with his mom.

The kitchen's reputation spreads, the lounge acts get better. Nat King Cole plays for a week in 1952; Carmen McRae is a frequent headliner. Straight people crowd in, but they enter on queer terms. Patrons have to mind their own business, not gawk or laugh at the queer ones. The prime house rule is respect, and as long as they abide by that, straight patrons are free to enjoy a plate of queer prime rib, with a queer baked potato, a queer dinner roll, and a queer pat of butter.

Though it would have its battles with the cops and the State Alcoholic Control Board for "immoral activities" (in one police report, a man was seen cupping the buttocks of another for a full fifteen seconds), The Paper Doll inspires the successive generations of queer and queer-owned restaurants.

That includes San Francisco's Brasserie, opened in the 1970s by a trans woman, Alexis Muir, grandniece of naturalist John Muir. (In 1966, she helped create the culture-shifting Stud bar.) Alexis riffs off the queer model set at The Paper Doll: a kitchen that can execute, in a place with live entertainment, tangy servers, and artsy decor, including, at the Brasserie, walls and ceiling painted to look like leather. The restaurant critic R. B. Read declares it "gay from the core outwards," as if the queer restaurant had managed at last to scrape the paint from its windows.

RICHARD ~~FUCKS UP~~
TELLS THE TRUTH

[1951]

RICHARD OLNEY'S IN AMES, STUDYING PAINTING AT the university. (This is in 1944.) As he turns eighteen, he faces an interview with the draft board in Iowa City. The psychiatrist asks the standard question: Do you like girls? Some queer boys lie; others choose to take it literally, answering without prevarication that yeah, they *like* girls (platonically). Anyone answering *no* risks catastrophe. To answer no is unthinkable, but occasionally guys do the unthinkable.

Richard does the unthinkable. Richard says he likes boys.

Sometimes catastrophe is in no particular hurry. Sometimes it sneaks up sly and slow.

The army never calls Richard up for service. I bet he thinks nobody in the government's screening bureaucracy could give a damn about who this arrogant little art student has wet dreams for.

So now it's 1951, six or seven years after his brush with Selective Service. Richard's twenty-four and living in New York, waiting tables in Greenwich Village. He gets a letter from the Fulbright Commission letting him know he's been selected to study art in France on a scholarship. Richard is ecstatic, until months later, when another official letter arrives, informing him that his Fulbright scholarship has been revoked, no reason given.

It turns out (duh) that Richard's official file with the State Department listed his mental state as "psycho-neurotic": shrink-speak for queer.

Richard is crushed. He's forced to explain it to his mortified parents. But they believe in Richard's talent. He must go to Paris to realize his gift.

Norris says that for a year, he'll wire Richard an allowance of a hundred bucks a month to study painting, all on his own. And in 1951, almost exactly five years before the first weekend of the Paris queer salon that will change him, he arrives. He finds a room at Hôtel Verneuil, the same place Jimmy lived as a greenling. Richard finds his place, his friends: filmmaker Kenneth Anger, painter John Craxton, film critic Elliott Stein. And everybody—*every*body—says he has to meet Jimmy Baldwin.

THE SALVAGE QUEEN OF FIFTY-EIGHTH STREET

[1949]

NOBODY FIGHTS FOR QUEER RESTAURANT TABLES under the open sky as doggedly or as elegantly as Johnny.

He has dark Coptic eyes that seem too large for his smooth face. In an iconic portrait by Karl Bissinger, Johnny's boyfriend, those eyes show a model's knack for ambivalence, a fifty-fifty mix of boredom and seduction.

Seated at a marble cafe table at Café Nicholson, amid the greenhouse canopy of potted palms, a faïence plinth, and statues of maidens frozen in the kitteny gestures of belle époque soft-porn, Johnny seems to know exactly what he's serving Karl's lens. His body language registers a coded message of occupying gayspace: legs folded, torso turned slightly toward the camera, forearm resting on the back of a Thonet hairpin chair. The wrist registers as limp if you're inclined to see limpness; or it could simply be Johnny gripping the chair's back in a gesture of turning. Those eyes, though; hair cut short above the high forehead; suggestively open dress shirt with French cuffs and slacks that look like sailors' flap pants, with buttons sited sideways across the crotch for ease of access. Though it's gray old Fifty-Eighth Street, with car horns and the rumble of trucks going to and emerging from the double-decker Queensboro Bridge that must echo in the restaurant, Johnny's giving Havana.

He's giving Barcelona.

He's giving motherfucking Cap d'An*tibes*, with a twist of *Darling, I'm here.*

✳

"Here," for Johnny, was once Carroll Street in St. Louis.

He was little John Bulica: born in 1916 to Constance and Nick Bulica, a.k.a. Nicola Bulecea. Johnny's father was born in a small town in what would become Albania, never went to school, couldn't read or write. He marries Constance, and they immigrate to the US in 1903. He manages this old-school restaurant and gentlemen's bar in downtown St. Louis, Caesar's Club, and after it shutters decades later, he open his own tavern—Vicki's Bar—across from Lafayette Park, in a formerly flush but long-battered neighborhood. Vicki's is a family effort: Johnny's older sister waits tables, her husband's the cook. Little Johnny washes dishes starting at age six. He can probably picture a drab future slinging beers to drunks, swabbing the pisser after closing, far from where fabulous is.

He leaves school after eighth grade and gigs as a boy-of-all-work, i.e. flunky, at a department store downtown. He spends as much time as he can in the furniture department, soaking in the decorators' tricks.

He has relatives in New York City. He makes as many trips as he can, hitching when he can't swing train fare. In 1940, after the US implements the Selective Training and Service Act, Johnny registers for a possible call-up in the future. He's drafted in St. Louis in 1941, but exempted after the screening psychiatrist recognizes him as a notorious truant he'd seen years before at a children's psych center (and maybe the shrink also pegs Johnny as queer, though this is a guess). With seventy-five dollars in his wallet he heads to New York, this time for good.

He's already affected the surname Nicholson—a fantasy rerouting of Johnny's ancestry, it strikes me, across the tongue of stately olde England, while still (and this is total speculation) acknowledging being Nicola's son. The reborn Johnny Nicholson is landing Christmas-season work at Lord & Taylor, the luxe Manhattan department store. He works his way onto the window display staff, learning the visual merchandising ropes.

Meanwhile, he's learning the *ropes*.

At the movies, he watches a man in the aisles cruising sailors. He realizes he knows this man: it's Tommy Carabina. Tommy dated Johnny's sister back in St. Louis, now he's a hairdresser on Fifth Avenue. Johnny becomes Tommy's ingenue, his *project*. He gives Johnny a taste of gay life in Greenwich Village.

At the same time, Johnny's working as a flunky under Lord & Taylor's master of window display, Henry Callahan, while stitching together a typical New York patchwork of gigs: bending chicken wire into mannequins' bodies for store displays, hawking his designs for perfume bottles. At Lord & Taylor, he meets Karl, a student at the Art Students League who's also picking up window work. They became inseparable.

Karl and Johnny share a one-bedroom flat with a shared toilet down the hall and no heat on East Fifty-Ninth, in the constant roar of traffic entering and leaving the Queensboro Bridge. They jump to a better place: a big street-level commercial space on East Fifty-Eighth.

Johnny's a natural collector. He has an eye for evocative castoffs on the street: outmoded furniture with classic bones, scraps of architectural salvage in a city with little patience for the past. After Karl lands a job as prop boy in the photo department of *Vogue*, they transform the Fifty-Eighth Street space, by now crammed with Johnny's finds, into a prop shop, renting out pieces for editorial shoots. (A cluster of important photographers have their studios two blocks away, on Fifty-Sixth Street.)

In 1948, Karl and Johnny spend six months in Europe, Johnny's first time abroad. In Rome he's gagged by Caffè Greco, which opened its doors in 1760 and never closed: a space with the accidental stylishness of fixtures and pieces persisting from the past; the freshness of urban excavation.

In Paris, Johnny gets a frisson from the tasteful modern rehabbing of old, old things: menus illustrated by queer artist and filmmaker Jean Cocteau at the revived brasserie Le Grand Vefour (where Cocteau and the glorious Colette reign as regulars); Cocteau's fluid murals at another restaurant, La Méditerranée. Years later, Johnny would recall the lightning strikes these places delivered, revelations that a restaurant or a café could exist as a kinetic work of art. In a postwar West hurtling to remake itself as a sleek and efficient machine for amassing capital, there's this countercultural urge to open up spaces washed in old patinas as stages for new identities; spaces with a dynamic mix of art and performance, showing out as bohemian, a.k.a. queer. Spaces where masks could slip.

This at a time when a US at peace is losing its mind, shifting politically and culturally to the right, frantically trying to slam shut whatever gaps in cultural oppression the war pushed opened: forcing women out of the work force, blasting progressive policies as Commie conspiracies, and beginning to mobilize political support for a massive purge of lesbian and gay workers from civil service.

In Paris, Karl's camera witnesses a kind of coming out of old queer culture and new. He shoots portraits of Colette; of Cocteau and his muse, Jean Marais; and twenty-three-year-old Truman Capote, the original demon twink, posing in a wicker chair under pitched garret panes with the city's rooftops beyond. At least in France, queerness shows its feathers without fear under a semi-open sky.

Back in New York, Johnny incubates a new project.

"When we came back in 1948, New York was the dreariest place you can imagine," Johnny would recall many years later. "And the city was worn out. After six months in Europe I really didn't want to come back. I was very, very unhappy about [not being able to sit] in a café very leisurely. So that gave me the inspiration to open Café Nicholson." A friend hires him to design the interior of a new restaurant, Daniel's on East Fifty-Fourth. It leaves Johnny thirsty for more.

He secures a cheap month-to-month rental on a storefront across Fifty-Eighth Street from the prop shop, a space with a rear garden canopied in summer with ornamental plums and the annual lushness of Trees of Heaven but otherwise open to the sky. One day he runs into Edna Lewis, a friend of his and Karl's in the broke bohemian artist and window-display gig-work circle, and tells her he and Karl are planning to open a Caffè Greco–style hangout with coffee and sweet rolls. Edna says forget about a café, aim for something with meat on its bones and blood in its veins. Open a real restaurant. She says she'll do the food.

This is Johnny's story of Café Nicholson's genesis. Edna remembered it differently: How one weekend, at one of their frequent get-togethers, Johnny, announced that he was going to open a restaurant. "Turning to me," Edna recalled, "he said, 'You're going to be the cook of my restaurant.'"

However it began, this is how it starts.

THE QUEER EDUCATION OF MISS LEWIS

[1949]

I CLAIM NO KNOWLEDGE OF EDNA LEWIS'S ROMANTIC leanings, no insight into her desires. I cannot name the people she shared a bed with or compile a list of those she lusted after or loved. Edna's intimacies are outside the scope of this book. What concerns me is unraveling *queer* to mean something more comprehensive than romantic or physical longing. My focus here, as I trace the rise of a culture of food that challenges power, is the queerness of the outsider.

Seeing Edna through a prism of queerness—it takes us closer to bell hooks's notion of queerness as something bigger and more inclusive than the clapping of flesh and the rustling of sheets. hooks renders herself "queer-pas-gay": queer in opposition to gay, a state of disidentification with coercive homosexual orthodoxy. She distills queerness this way: As "the self . . . at odds with everything around it," the self that has to "invent and create and find a place to speak and to thrive and to live."

Queerness is a reach for authenticity; the work of cutting through coercive norms—even those cemented by gay power—to descend to truer and truer places. Queerness is a life of inner ferment, the endlessly repeated birth of the self into a world that despises difference and would starve it, and it's the quest for shelter, for sustenance. Queerness is making peace with estrangement, a digging in and making do where the alternative—the smothering imperatives of the dominant world—is what makes *making do* feel like joy.

Within the encoded gayness of Café Nicholson, with its insinuations of *bohemian*, Edna finds ground to root her outsider talent. She's a woman with no restaurant training or experience, suddenly cooking at a high level in the spare idiom of true luxury. She shops in Italian markets downtown, sources bread from an Italian baker, makes do with the available tools—limited, janky—to manifest elegance. And she's persuasive: the idiom Edna will apply at Café Nicholson lives after her time there; goes on to help define a queer language of food that flows beyond the lines and edges of that particular restaurant.

It's a language I first took in at Miss Ollie's, a restaurant chef Sarah Kirnon launched in Oakland, California, in 2012. Not long after opening, Kirnon hung a John T. Hill photo portrait of Edna above the pass, next to one of her grandmother, Miss Ollie—a tribute, Kirnon tells me, to Edna's work and dedication; to the delicacy of her flavors; her touch. To me, out in Kirnon's dining room, it signaled Edna's status as mother, muse, and conscience in a restaurant where queerness roamed like an animating spirit. With the image of Kirnon and her cooks through the pass, under a sort of photographic retablo of Edna and her candescent smile, I started to see how some queer essence of food and hospitality could be another piece of Edna's legacy.

Later in life Edna's close to Scott Peacock, a white man nearly fifty years her junior, a chef originally from Alabama. He is at various times her working partner, domestic support, roommate, and collaborator on the 2003 book, *The Gift of Southern Cooking*.

When they met, in 1988, Scott was a chef at the Georgia governor's mansion, just twenty-five years old, keen on living and cooking in Italy. He was struggling with his sexuality. "It was something I fought with for such a long time," Scott says.

After Edna died, Scott revealed how she gave him support to come to terms with who he was—helped him embrace the simple food of the Deep South he'd spurned as a young cook *and*, as he implies in the documentary *Fried Chicken and Sweet Potato Pie*, helped him come out. "What I didn't realize for the longest time," Scott says, "was that as Miss Lewis was teaching me to accept Southern food and seeing the uniqueness and to celebrate the wonderful things about that, it's a way of accepting yourself. When you accept those parts of yourself that are on the outside and you began to see grits as something to be proud of, and equal, then you began to see those things about yourself. . . . It's a lot bigger than cooking." Edna helped Scott clear a path to biscuits and self-acceptance.

They met about the time of Edna's third cookbook, *In Pursuit of Flavor*. And while she was respected among chefs and aficionados of so-called New American cuisine and of fine Southern cooking, she was hardly the icon she'd become in death. (Especially after January 2017, when an Edna Lewis elimination challenge on Season 14 of *Top Chef* propelled Edna's 1976 book, *A Taste of Country Cooking*, to the heights of the Amazon Best Sellers list.)

Novelist Chang-Rae Lee, visiting for a 2001 piece in *Gourmet* magazine, says Edna and Scott share a place twenty minutes from Atlanta, in what Lee describes as a "patch of low-rise, older brick apartments . . . not by any means awful, but the landscaping is tired, and it all seems plain and unspecial, like a small college dormitory." Lee characterizes their banter and good-natured ribbing as "girl talk." Scott calls Edna "mother." He's painted the bathroom a shade Lee names "Day-Glo pretty-in-pink."

Edna and Scott are allies anchoring marginal space, carving out their own place of creation and mutual understanding. And mother let me tell you: It is queer as hell.

I can't tell if this is a throwback for Edna to her friendship with Karl and Johnny, or if creative gay solidarity was somehow a constant in her career. What I know is that Café Nicholson was for a brief moment this inclusive, ego-driven, transformative, way-too-much, colossally queer experiment in creative expression.

EDNA REGENA LEWIS was born on a farm in 1916, one of eight children, to a place known as Freetown in Orange County, Virginia, a community founded by the formerly enslaved, including Edna's grandfather.

She begins to learn by watching her mother, Daisy, and others cook. She takes on more and more of the cooking at home.

When Edna's twelve, during the Great Depression, her father dies. At fourteen she's already employed as a servant, and at fifteen leaves Virginia to work as a cook for a family in Washington, DC. At sixteen she joins two other young women headed to New York City.

Like Johnny, Edna seems determined to not be stuck.

After false starts, including an ironing job at a Brooklyn laundry from which she was canned three hours after she started, Edna lands a job with the Communist Party as a typist. Have her fingers ever touched a typewriter's keys? It doesn't seem to matter. Edna just . . . takes things on.

Again like Johnny, Edna seems to find in New York City a mecca of independence, a place that affords the sort of liberation impossible in Freetown. She's political, takes classes taught by the party, attends discussions. She campaigns for FDR. She's inclined to resist rules that reinforce exclusion: of course racism, but also anti-unionizing, and voter suppression. They were the only ones, she says, referring to the Communist Party, "the only ones who encouraged the Blacks to be aggressive, and to participate." She gets a job with the Communist paper the *Daily Worker*, printing subscription labels.

You figure that with her interest in cooking, she might save up enough to dine at a restaurant above the level of cafeterias and the Automat. Despite New York's lack of formal Jim Crow laws, discrimination against Black diners is common. Below Harlem, a customer who looks like Edna can count on being shown a shitty table behind a partition, or around a corner, near the kitchen or the toilets—hidden, exposed to rude service. It doesn't matter if you're famous. In 1951, Josephine Baker publicly blasts Manhattan's Stork Club after her white companions are served expeditiously while she waits and waits for a steak that never arrives. In the 1980s, Edna becomes chef of Brooklyn's cherrywood-arched and brass-chandeliered Gage & Tollner restaurant, but four decades earlier, trying to eat there would likely have resulted in humiliation and frustration. In a time before the open kitchen, Black and brown workers were kept on the side of the porthole swing door unseen by the public.

I DON'T KNOW EXACTLY WHEN Edna meets Karl Bissinger. It's sometime in the 1930s though, in the years before the war changes a lot of things in New York.

"Edna and Karl were both part of a bohemian crowd, and Communist-adjacent," Phyllis Eckhaus, friend to both Johnny and Karl, says. Though really, *adjacent* seems to better describe Karl, scion of a wealthy Cincinnati family that built its fortune on candy. His childhood was painful. He came to New York and enrolled in the Art Students League. His circle of friends, including Edna, had come to the city to shed strained or difficult pasts. "We were bohemians to escape our backgrounds," Karl once said. They came to New York be free.

Eckhaus guesses that Edna would have met Johnny through Karl.

"We all went to the same parties," Edna told the writer Susanna Cuyler. "Karl had a lot of records, but usually we'd talk."

Besides Karl and Johnny—boyfriends sharing a cold-water walk-up near the Third Avenue El, the elevated railway running north and south through Manhattan to and from the Bronx—Edna spends her social hours with artsy boys and girls connected to the Art Students League. It's a bohemian group, some queer, and all with futures. There's painter and sculptor Jeanne Owens, who's also Karl and Johnny's roommate; photographer Richard Avedon; textile and fashion designer Ken Scott; and painter and fashion illustrator Sylvia Braverman." ("Sylvia's mother had a thrift shop," Edna recalled, "and we'd get dresses there.")

There's a lot of drinking at these dinners and parties—you'd need the whole next day to recover—but the food is terrible unless Edna's cooking. She does simple country dishes, cheap by necessity. Does she make biscuits? Deviled eggs and pickled cucumbers? Sugar cookies and Apple Brown Betty? She gets a reputation as a cook.

Owens, who's also a competitive swimmer attending international meets, goes to Paris and carries back a jar of gazpacho for Edna to taste. She describes to Edna seeing whole pigs roasted in South America.

For a party, Scott displays different kinds of cookies on a high shelf, a plate rail that runs around a room in his apartment. It makes such an impression on Edna, this outré blending of food and aesthetics, that she'll recall it in conversation some four decades later.

By the late 1930s Edna's sewing dresses at home for a New York fashion house. Through a friend of Johnny's, she gets gigs working on department store windows starting with the big Christmas displays. She's building chicken-wire forms, sewing satin backdrops and covering them with sparkly stones and peacock feathers.

Edna's surrounded by progressive politics and Black activism. She's getting jobs as a seamstress, sewing her own clothes, and she finds new employment, ironically, working in the most frivolously sybaritic centers of Manhattan capitalism: the luxury department stores along Fifth Avenue. She picks up gigs assisting the window dressers at Bonwit Teller, surely one of the queerest occupations in the city.

At Bonwit, Edna surely works for Gene Moore, the window artist who came to work for Bonwit in 1945. Moore's signature was a spare, rigorously narrative style. (He would become legendary in coming decades for his work at Tiffany on Fifth Avenue. In fact, it's Moore's low-sheen spangled windows that Audrey Hepburn, as Holly Golightly, munching a cruller and sipping a coffee, gazes into—and through which we gaze at her—for the opening credits of *Breakfast at Tiffany's*.)

Meanwhile, Johnny's work on the windows at Lord & Taylor was ruled by another master of the form, Henry Callahan.

Both Moore and Callahan lean on dramatic light and shadow to focus the gaze. Windows by both men show an affinity with the eye of George Platt Lynes, the queer photographer of dancers and male nudes. They seem to quote the surrealist photographs of queer British photographer Angus McBean. They sometimes slip in wacky elements, as in Moore's two-headed mannequin for a Bonwit hat display; the heightened stories in the staging of mannequins and props recalls the magic realist tableaus of the painter Paul Cadmus, where narratives of men about to hook up weigh as heavy in the air as muggy weather.

Look at the female mannequins in a 1947 Bonwit window, in a series featuring art on loan from the Guggenheim, known then as the Museum of Non-Objective Painting. The window shows two stylish women (one somewhat older, the other young, fresh, sassy) in an art gallery before a huge Rolph Scarlett painting, captured in the moment of discovering they're both wearing B. H. Wragge dresses in different styles but sewn from the same print fabric. The mannequins' body language shows surprise, peevishness, but also a kind of shared attraction, as if showing off their figures to each other. As if demanding, "Who wears it better?" As if signaling that halfway through a pitcher of martinis in the older mannequin's apartment, those dresses are coming *off*.

For me it's an easy jump from Gene Moore's strict visual editing to Edna's later pared-down yet luxurious culinary style. In Edna and Johnny's creative and cultural education, sexual desire is an invisible engine driving a compulsion to buy a smart new peplum jacket or pair of long evening gloves. Longing that cannot show itself in daylight becomes an urgency for other experiences, including taste: meeting sensuality in rich, delicious things.

Toward the end of 1947, thirty-one-year-old Edna marries Stephen Kingston, an ex–merchant seaman who'd apparently worked as a cook for a company of Marines stationed in San Francisco. He's a Communist Party leader in Brooklyn's Stuyvesant Heights neighborhood, working with the party's African American coalition on labor and civil rights. He's also on the local council of the National Negro Congress, fighting employment discrimination in Brooklyn. Earlier, Kingston was part of the Communist Party's vigorous defense of the Scottsboro Boys in Alabama, and authored a 1941 pamphlet on abolitionist Frederick Douglass.

I imagine Edna's life feels like slipping in and out of two parties happening at the same time in side-by-side apartments. In one she's hooting and drinking and (I am sure) hearing every scandalous detail with unfiltered queer boys like Johnny. Next door in the other she's talking race and class oppression with earnest heterosexual comrades. (Well, *publicly* heterosexual—the American Communist Party denounced homosexuality in 1938 as a sickness of the bourgeoisie, denying membership to any and all known queers.) I mean, Karl and no doubt other gay friends of Edna's were communists, but sort of—I don't know, secular commies, without the orthodoxy that must have reigned in the offices of the *Daily Worker.*

Still, what's consistent in Edna's life, and Johnny's and Karl's too, is resisting the sort of life that kills expression. What's consistent is a commitment, if you'll indulge me in calling it this, to queerness.

SOUFFLÉS IN SOUP CUPS

[1951]

C LEMENTINE PADDLEFORD, THE *NEW YORK HERALD'S*
plucky food columnist, shows up at Café Nicholson.

The entrance is a strip of hallway, the walls of Gothic paneling. Look through the cut-out spaces to your left, a peep
show into Edna Lewis' kitchen. . . . Ten steps along here's
the dining room. On one side, the fixtures of an old time
soda fountain and candy store picked up on Canal Street,
the place dating back to 1854. Lay an admiring eye on the
fountain bar, baskets of brown eggs, of white eggs; bowls of
fresh fruit, whole cheeses, old time candy jars holding chutney which accompany the curry on curry day.

Edna's cooking is like nothing else in New York. The menu doesn't
really change. Edna grills beef filet over charcoal and serves it with a
béarnaise sauce mounted with enough butter to make it pile like soft
whipped cream. There's a chicken flavored with fresh herbs and baked
till the skin crisps and turns extra dark. A weekly Malaysian curry
with coconut, served with apple chutney Edna's husband Steve makes
from a recipe he learned as a seaman. A simple salad of Boston lettuce dressed with lemon, garlic, herbs, and olive oil goes out with the
entrees. There's no liquor license; you have to bring your own bottle in
a paper sack or order out from a nearby bottle shop.

Paddleford especially likes Edna's chocolate soufflé, "coming scented to glory of hot sugar and chocolate, risen to ethereal lightness, caramelized by the oven's heat to a confection that one cannot glimpse without delight, cannot taste without ecstasy." She spots Edna peeking out from the kitchen to gauge what Paddleford thinks.

The food inspires wonder, but the space, the way it barely operates as a conventional restaurant—it's like nothing else in New York.

Paddleford interviews Johnny. Why doesn't he have a liquor license? He tells her it's because they don't have a lease from the landlord; that to get one, they'd have to add a mandatory second toilet.

Could it also be that applying for a license would put Café Nicholson under the hard gaze of the State Liquor Authority, New York's frontline agency for ensuring bars and restaurants aren't gathering places for homosexuals? The prime engine for the suppression of queer public life? Before the late 1960s, gays and lesbians in the state of New York have, as historian John D'Emilio says, "no legal right to assemble and be served in places providing liquor."

And of course Café Nicholson's unspoken mission is to create queer space in the open—to *hold* space.

Paddleford asks Johnny if he plans to put a cover over the "fine little garden" at the back to seat more guests when there's risk of a downpour. "Heaven forbid," he tells her. "We refuse to have one of those awnings screwed down like a lid over our bit of sky; we keep the garden wide open to the moon and the stars and the rain."

I realize that thinking of Café Nicholson as a 1949 queer oasis flirts with presentism: the fallacy of regarding the past through the lens of the present. Couldn't something like the opposite be true? That the lens of the present is inadequate for capturing crucial subtleties of the past? I believe Café Nicholson's queerness was a subtle read; and that to think of gay and lesbian couples touching or kissing under Johnny's open sky is a modern fantasy.

"Stephen Reynolds" is the pseudonym of a gay man interviewed in Charles Kaiser's *The Gay Metropolis*, a study of New York gay social history from 1940 to 1996. He tells Kaiser about going out in the Village in the 1950s, and in a discrete club one floor up from the street, seeing a famous male interior designer dance with another man. "I nearly fainted," Reynolds says. "We had never seen such a thing as that."

Public expression happened in gestures, Reynolds implies: clear polished fingernails on a man, or an "outré" shirt—the kinds of things Johnny may have flaunted. "We were just who we were," Karl Bissinger tells documentary producer Catherine Johnson. "You were gay. It never crossed your mind that if the other people didn't put up with you you never talked to them again, you never saw them again." Karl and Johnny referred to each other as *companions*: "In those days that's the word we used," Karl says. "You know, your gay . . . *companion*."

Café Nicholson was a place, especially at the beginning, where one's discretely gay behind could settle comfortably into one of Johnny's Thonet chairs, the way the subjects in Karl's backyard photo for *Flair*, Tenn and Gore and Buffie and Donald, seem so at ease despite the stifling afternoon.

"I think people felt safe being who they wanted to be there," Johnson says, adding a caveat that Café Nicholson wasn't a place where you could flaunt obvious difference or desire. And in fact the first customers are from Karl, Johnny, and Edna's art and photography worlds: fashion models, editors from *Harper's Bazaar*.

After that, after word spreads, everybody in New York who's pretty much anybody comes.

EDNA COOKS WITH SEMI-IMPROVISATIONAL FURY.

"Until Café Nicholson there were only two kinds of restaurants in New York," fashion editor Babs Simpson tells *Vanity Fair* in 1999. "Checked-tablecloth places serving spaghetti and meatballs or velvet-banquette places like Le Pavillon." In the first, the ingredients were basic; in the second, rich meats went to die under an inventory of expensive canned imports from France.

Edna's cooking is polished with the kind of shine that comes from an impulse to cook good ingredients correctly with a limited range of enhancements. Maybe she honed this amid the necessary economy of cooking in the rural South. Maybe she honed her editing skills, how to achieve simple, powerful narratives from a few marquee elements in the gay school of New York window display. I think both possibilities are likely.

Edna cooks from a place of ingenuity, where deprivation becomes pleasure; where limits sanction joy. This is where Blackness and queerness coexist in Edna.

"We were all doing things that we were not trained for," Edna told Susanna Cuyler. "Just bold young people with new ideas."

One day at Café Nicholson, they decide they need a temp to wait on a table of union leaders at lunch. Johnny hires a young woman he meets who knows where.

As service winds down, the woman unloads in front of Edna, using an antisemitic slur to describe the people she's been serving. Edna pops. She says, "There's nobody *here* but us [n-word]s and fairies!", as if to say, *Girl, you're in the wrong place.* As if to say that what animates Café Nicholson is the spirit of being marginal together. What gives it life is queer wonder: the magic of appropriating cheap or discarded things to conjure magnificence.

As the bones of Café Nicholson are being assembled, Johnny and Edna go searching together for pieces to furnish it. "We shopped on the Bowery, going into basement after basement" Edna would recall years later. "Before we opened we put sheets all over the walls and called them curtains."

Cultural anthropologist Esther Newton, describing how Broadway costume designer Miles White likewise, in 1948, covers the interior walls of his Fire Island beach cabin with sheets, uses the phrase "an alchemy beyond money." It's bohemian virtuosity, a transformation "by trained eyes and deft hands that could make something witty and appealing out of the most unlikely materials."

Edna's cooking reveals a similar alchemy. Consider what is arguably the most famous dish at Café Nicholson, individual chocolate soufflés baked in small ovenproof soup bowls.

What is a soufflé if not the transformation of unlikely materials? A dense, sticky base of flour-sugar-yolks improbably lifted through the magic of leavening?

In her first book, *The Edna Lewis Cookbook*, she describes feeling her way with them.

> *The first chocolate soufflé I made at Café Nicholson was so warmly accepted by the few customers who sampled it that I began to make them every day. . . . At that time I was unaware of all the supposed pitfalls of soufflé making . . .*

For Irma Rombauer in *The Joy of Cooking*, first published during the Great Depression, the soufflé could be a casserole with aspirations, a vehicle for stretching the chopped remains of past meals with a veneer of style.

In the 1950s, the soufflé reaches its quivering apogee. Authors of food stories in glossy US magazines go mad for the elegance of soufflés. A *New York Times* review of Myra Waldo's 1954 soufflé cookbook *Serve at Once* takes them as requisite for dinner parties, appropriate for every course—"only one to a meal, though, please." Authorities like Waldo tout how achievable the soufflé is, never mind how intimidating it may appear. This only reinforces how finicky and terrifying soufflés are, how you need to buy special dishes to get the rise right . . .

> *. . . I baked them in small soup bowls . . .*

. . . How you need a precisely heated oven with no fluctuations in temperature. How you need to minimize noise and movement in the kitchen—suppress unnecessary vibrations—or you'll find it collapsed into an eggy slump. Edna's soufflé finds its voice in its peculiarities of taste: its minimal sugar and sparing use of yolks to keep the focus on pure-chocolate flavor; its preservation of cacao's edges, its bitterness, acidity, and tannins . . .

*. . . I never measured ingredients, but each day shortly before the
dinner hour I made about a pint of roux and added a lot of grated
bitter chocolate. . . . I had no set time for cooking them . . .*

But primarily in how it's made: improvising, feeling its way, paying
attention and adjusting; using ordinary soup bowls because, presumably, real soufflé ramekins are too expensive; adjusting your timing
to an oven being constantly opened and shut because it also needs to
accommodate the roasting chickens . . .

*. . . Our waitress developed a fine sense of timing with experi-
ence, [was it Virginia Reed, or the restaurant's other server, Jean
Matlega?] and she would tell me when it was time to set the soufflés in the oven for each table.*

The soufflés' evanescence, fragility, conditional status; their forward
taste of barely sweetened Baker's Chocolate, the spirit of conviction
Edna suffuses them with: It all codes them as queer; marks them as the
inspired work of an outsider—somebody who, according to the standard literature of cookbooks, doesn't know any better, and yet by lis-
tening to her interior voice, creates something transcendent.

Say that the only true essential of queerness is the end point of that
magic, which is metamorphosis. Say that Edna cooked to match the
scale and ambition of Johnny's open sky.

BROTHER HA OF
PELL STREET

[1952]

IN HONG KONG, POSTWAR INFLATION AND THE TUR-
moil of civil war on the mainland that would end in Mao's ascension
ends Esther's filmmaking career there. Back in the US, she becomes the
lead for her father's movie distribution business, traveling the country
to promote Chinese-language films in Chinatowns and other enclaves.

In 1946, *Seattle Times* reporter Betty Cornelius describes Esther's
hair and clothes with typical amazement. "Her shiny blue-black hair
is cropped in a mannish bob," Cornelius writes, "and she wears power
blue slacks [Does Cornelius mean "powder blue"? Is this a Freudian
slip?] and a T-shirt under a tailored off-white jacket." She sports a pin-
kie ring she designed herself, and a wristwatch Cornelius calls "rather
masculine," with diamonds for numbers and a wide mesh band. Esther
is thirty-one. Cornelius says she looks seventeen, "a fact she has had to
fight against since her first picture."

Esther's not done directing pictures. *Blue Jade*, shot in Hollywood,
premieres in 1947. *Back Street* appears a year later, and in 1949, *Mad
Fire, Mad Love*, a full-length color feature filmed in Hawaii.

That same year, Esther shows up in New York City. She's managing
the family business, the distribution of Chinese-language movies to
Manhattan theaters like the Sun Sing, wedged under the Manhattan
Bridge in Chinatown. With its noise, its families chowing on picnic
lunches, its children running up and down the aisles with paper dragons, the Sun Sing preserves an echo of the distant Mandarin. Surely it

feels like home to Esther, this Chinatown nearly three thousand miles from home.

Something else must also feel familiar: An opera troupe, reluctant to return to China after Mao's proclamation of the People's Republic in late 1949, has left the actors stranded. Quickly, it seems, backed by investors with connections to opera, Esther launches a restaurant in Chinatown at 20 1/2 Pell Street. It's named Bo Bo, after one of the stranded performers. She sets it up for a family called Tan, according to Eng scholar S. Louisa Wei. It gives employment to idle actors. It's a hub for the opera community: "A kind of home or place to eat for the actors and actresses sojourning in New York," Wei says.

Esther stays in New York. She becomes a host and manager, one of the faces of Bo Bo. Does it conjure for her the collective energy of the old backstage world of the Mandarin and the ad hoc feel of a budget movie shoot? The creative spirit of queer family, bonded by grit and the daily rush of putting on a show?

Bo Bo eventually captures the buzzing neon plasma energy of Chinatown: packed Formica-topped tables under the dazzling light of canopy chandeliers, with mirrored walls reflecting the sidewalk's endless flow. Bright, Cantonese-style dishes have a depth and simplicity that seem to surprise those more familiar with the chop suey school of American Chinese.

Craig Claiborne, writing in 1958, calls the food both novel and "notably excellent": winter melon soup with chicken and a rich broth, peas, and "Chinese zucchini" (luffa perhaps); butterflied shrimp; duck with snow peas and cellophane noodles (he calls it "wooly lamb"—a whimsical transliteration?). A blogger who goes by Hungry Gerald recalls eating at Bo Bo. "It set a new standard for Chinese food in New York," he writes. Unlike in chop suey houses there was no menu—you asked for what you wanted. Hungry Gerald always ordered the lobster roll. He describes it as "a giant sized egg roll stuffed with big chunks of lobster. To die for, as the cliché has it."

And of course, there was Esther, slim and compact, in her mid-thirties, presenting in traditional male fashion: trousers, sport shirt, loafers, and the most amazing hair—short, with a side part, combed across. In photographs, Esther's hair is always like this, always perfectly, handsomely combed, beautifully short and shiny, polished with pomade. In photographs she shows the same smiling composure, the same poise. Obviously she knows the camera; seems to know what she wants it to capture, even through somebody else's lens.

There's gossip about Esther, but she's part of the neighborhood, the communal fabric. "People do remember Esther for her dress and life-style," Wei tells me, "but since her immediate community was mainly composed of cinema and theatre people and their families, I am convinced that she did not encounter major issues." Plus Esther came from a family of status and middle-class wealth, and she was respected for her pioneering film work. And she wasn't alone in pushing public gender expression, as historian Tze-lan D. Sang points out.

"Soong Mei-ling (Madame Chiang Kai-shek) had a niece who dressed up in man's suits in public all her adult life," she says. Born in Shanghai in 1919, Kung Ling-wei moved to Taiwan with the great exodus of 1949, and in the 1950s was general manager of the Grand Hotel in Taipei, a public role of some importance.

As Wei says, "Gay culture, like everything else, has a long history in China."

Once the Tans can run Bo Bo, Esther sells it to them. For another family, she opens MongKok (known in some records as Macao) next door at 19 Pell. There's a third restaurant, Hing Hing. And in the mid-1950s, she opens her own place, Eng's Little Corner, at 1 Mott Street.

In 1959, Esther makes her biggest restaurant move yet with the uptown launch of Esther Eng, a small, two-story restaurant on Second Avenue just above Fifty-Seventh Street. (A second branch of Esther Eng eventually opens on Pell Street.) It's got swanky touches befitting its location on the threshold to the Upper East Side: a few tables and a bar on the ground floor, and a dining room upstairs with "walls in contrasting colors and the effective use of dancing figures in shadow boxes," writes newspaper columnist Betty Ryan.

Reviewing Esther Eng the same year, Craig Claiborne marvels at "what may be an innovation at the restaurant," deep-fried sausage-shaped dumplings of ground shrimp and walnut. But he seems most taken with a dish he says, that "will be totally unfamiliar to diners who are not conversant with Chinese cuisine."

By 1965, Esther Eng in Chinatown features theatrical, Trader Vic's–style flexes: sliced "prime beef" with onion and pineapple ("a specialty of the house," says John H. Kuhn, a New Jersey restaurant critic), a list of steak dishes, and a "glamorous" dessert of various ice creams and fruits "set on illuminated chipped ice in a multicolored bowl." Surely Esther's reading the room, playing for the uptown and bridge-and-tunnel crowds. At the same time, she's still—uncompromisingly—Esther, offering an image to the public with no apparent fear.

In his Chinatown memoir *Tea That Burns*, the late Chinese American writer Bruce Edward Hall considers Esther through the eyes of his older uncles. "Esther is . . . unusual because she is an outspoken lesbian," Hall writes, "always seen wearing men's suits and 'mannish' haircuts. Her ex-girlfriends (of whom there are several) manage her other places uptown."

And, Wei says, for a while, Eng's Corner was a bar that was, as she puts it, "known to gay people." In his review of Esther Eng, Craig mentions Esther's physical presence—her "diminutive" five-foot height—as if it were inseparable from what it feels like to eat there.

FUTURE QUEER HISTORIAN Jonathan Ned Katz is maybe twelve. It's 1950, and for the small, buzzy circle of food writers and editors in New York City, there's excitement for Bo Bo. Jonathan's aunt is the food editor for the Associated Press, Cecily Brownstone. One day Cecily takes Jonathan and his parents to Chinatown.

They sit, and Esther, maybe because she knows or guesses that Cecily is someone important, takes their drink order herself. Jonathan's a precocious little gay kid. He's grown up in a progressive household in Greenwich Village that includes Cecily. Food people and queer people or both, in the case of James Beard, are in and out all the time. The mood is gossipy, sometimes campy—young Jonathan's heard a lot. He must have heard the word *dyke* batted around.

He's aware of the word *daiquiri*, too, though apparently has never heard it pronounced. The spelling makes it a treacherous word for English speakers.

Anyway, Esther's poised above the boy, waiting to take his order. I can just imagine the patient, gracious smile on Esther's face as she waits. And maybe Jonathan doesn't realize that a daiquiri is boozy, or maybe, being smart, he does, but the point is he wants one. So he looks up at Esther and asks for a *daiquiri* the way he thinks it's supposed to be pronounced.

It comes out of his mouth as *dikery*.

In relating this story decades later, Jonathan says how mortified his aunt was, zooming in fast to correct the boy. Maybe Esther doesn't think anything of it, or maybe she finds it funny. Maybe, in recollection, Jonathan's faux pas has grown bigger and more embarrassing than it was. But it points to an essential thing about the story of Esther Eng. In some ways her lifelong public-facing presentation as masc was the most salient thing about her, even eclipsing her film career, yet it wasn't supposed to be mentioned, not by strangers anyway, not in the open.

You were not to acknowledge the dykery in the room.

Esther's assertion of queerness was a little like a harelip, or a large facial birthmark. A defect in the eyes of some.

Despite everything she was, everything she was able to do, Esther was invisible. She lived a life of episodes erased almost immediately after they happened, like the lost prints of her films. She forced the world to acknowledge her queerness through the passive act of looking at her. The world responded by pretending she wasn't there. In the end, Esther became the story of her restaurants.

I keep coming back to one dish in particular, the one that seems to stick in the minds of non-Asian diners at Esther's restaurants. It's paper chicken, the fancy banquet dish I pictured was offered to visiting divas to the Mandarin Theatre in San Francisco. In his review of Esther Eng's,

Craig Claiborne names it cellophane chicken. "To prepare it, small bits of chicken are marinated in a mixture of hoisin sauce and peanut butter, wrapped in cellophane [actually glassine] and deep-fried." He describes hoisin as an "inscrutable mixture of spices and plums." Another critic in 1959, Betty Ryan, also finds this dish amazing. "In the preparation," she says, "the chicken loses any distinctive poultry flavor. The result is a tender, pinkish morsel, delicate and delectable."

Paper chicken is a dish that both masks and reveals, operatic in its dramatic manipulations, and with a fluid identity at its heart. It transforms base poultry into something pink and transcendentally perfumed.

You weren't permitted to be publicly queer in most places in the US in 1950. You weren't supposed to flaunt your partners or wear clothes not sanctioned for your perceived gender. Even in a queer bar in 1950s Greenwich Village, recalls Audre Lorde, you had to be wearing at least three pieces of clothing the police deemed acceptable for your gender or risk arrest in a sweep of the establishment. Esther lived to flout those taboos.

She seemed determined to live as if bigotry toward Asians, toward women, toward lesbians, didn't exist. It wasn't just her clothes or her hair. What Esther displayed was the attitude of the warrior.

Back in Hong Kong in the 1930s, the *Sing Tao Daily News* reporter, Lei Qun, who seemed both contemptuous of and fascinated by Esther, wrote this:

"In old China, there was a case of a masculinized woman called Mulan. . . . No one bats an eye at this. But in the case of Esther, there's something else that completely bewilders our sense of what's strange and bizarre with regard to humankind! It's not just work, address, manner, and dress. . . . It's her sensibility." Esther brought fearlessness to her restaurant life: fearlessness delivered as a rich and delicious form of sustenance. Café Nicholson delivered a coded flavor of queerness, and the Paper Doll still existed partly in the guise of a queer bar. Esther brought it outside of the protective cage queer food had always sheltered within.

When she dies from cancer in 1970, at age fifty-five, Esther's *New*

York Times obituary notes, as if in passing, that she'd broken ground making films in Hong Kong and Hollywood, as if her most notable accomplishments were as a restaurateur. The headline reads, "ESTHER ENG, OWNED RESTAURANTS HERE."

Maybe the thing she should be remembered for, above all, is her sensibility.

SATURDAY NIGHT
FUNCTION

[1956]

ON A FRIDAY NIGHT IN JANUARY, A PARTY OF SIX OR seven people forms in Paris. Eventually this night, and the weekend it launches, will solidify into a *thing.* And for me, it's a thing with an outsize significance: the diverging of two queer approaches to coming together around the table. Tonight, though, in the first weeks of '56, it's just some friends getting together in a large apartment on the Left Bank.

> *Call it a soirée, baby. Or let's say a messy ki-ki swirling around*
> *the themes of love and hunger and sensual need, which is a rather*
> *grandiose way of saying that everybody got absolutely stinking*
> *drunk on Scotch, listened to sides, and probably never—probably*
> *not even once—stopped talking.[1]*

It's a party that sprawls, despite its size. Here's who was there:

Jimmy Baldwin, thirty-one, in his eighth year of self-exile from the States (though he's drifted back and forth). He has one published novel, *Go Tell It on the Mountain.* He's had a book of essays published, *Notes*

....

1. Shall I explain these italics? That in the absence of a full accounting of this party and the ones to follow, we have to imagine a little of what was said, eaten, and done; to re-create the flavor of this particular moment in the life of queer food.

of a Native Son, and a play, *The Amen Corner*, which premiered at Howard University in Washington DC. His sure to be controversial second novel, *Giovanni's Room*, which one American publisher rejected and which has at its center a homosexual relationship, will appear later in the fall.

The artist **Beauford Delaney**, fifty-four, Jimmy's longtime mentor, his aesthetic and spiritual poppa, arrived from New York two and a half years ago. As a gay Black painter refusing to mask his sexuality he struggled to make much of a living in New York, but in artist circles Beauford is admired for his fusing of primitive and expressionist styles; for his brilliant portraiture that's a kind of thermography, revealing the radiance of his subjects' inner lives.

Richard Olney, twenty-eight, a painter of flowers and portraits from a nowhere speck on the Iowa map, in Paris on a year-long monthly stipend from his banker daddy. This is Plan B for Richard, after Uncle Sam killed his Plan A. He has a natural-born arrogance though, which protects him like armor—that and his stipend.

Bernard Hassell, twenty-five, Richard's boyfriend, and beautiful. Richard meets him one night at the gay bar La Reine Blanche with Jimmy; when they first touch, Richard would say, "there was something like an electrical explosion." Bernard arrived five years ago from Mount Vernon, New York, for a journalism apprenticeship arranged by Josephine Baker. Now he dances at the Folies-Bergère, the music hall in the Ninth Arrondissement known for skin, suggestiveness, and a sprinkling of exoticized Black performers, including Baker, once, and Senegalese gay icon François "Féral" Benga. Bernard's working tonight. He'll arrive after midnight, no longer technically even Friday.

Mary Painter, thirty-six, the party's host. She's an economist from Minneapolis working at the American Embassy to set up the European headquarters of the Marshall Plan. She has a salary, and one of those old formal, grand-windowed Left Bank apartments that Americans working for Uncle Sam (like Paul and Julia Child) were able to score in the scramble after Liberation. That, plus access to the American PX (the post exchange), where military personnel and some civilians can buy familiar goods for cheap, notably liquor and cigarettes. Mary's hetero but unconventional—she spent a couple of years in a sort of emotional throuple with Jimmy and Lucien Happersberger, physically if not sexually, and she still has a deep, deep bond with Jimmy. She "loans" him money. Soon after they meet in 1950 at the Montana Bar in Saint-Germain, she invites him and Lucien home for a meal. Dinner at Mary's becomes a regular feature of their lives. Surely this is the meaning in Mary's world—her passion for friends, food, and drinking. Though because her job at the embassy ties her to office hours, she limits her liquor consumption to weekends.

And the sixth, and possibly seventh: Is it **Lucien Happersberger**, twenty-three, Jimmy's Swiss-born best friend and one-time lover? Lucien's a struggling painter, tall and sort of forcefully sexy like Brando. His relationship with Jimmy is . . . complicated. At seventeen, when he and Jimmy met at a Paris gay bar, Lucien was earning his bread as a rent boy. Now he has a wife, Suzy, and a baby. (Jimmy's the godfather.) Lucien lives in Switzerland but he's often in Paris. Richard recalls him being at the Friday night party.

Baldwin biographer David Leeming, though, leaves the door open for Jimmy's current boyfriend in 1956, **Arnold**, being at the party, or maybe Lucien and Arnold both. What to say about Arnold? His surname and age have not been recorded in any account of Jimmy's life I'm aware of. He's younger than Jimmy. They meet in 1955, when Jimmy and Lucien are in New York. Arnold is Lucien's drinking buddy, and becomes Jimmy's lover. He's a twunky, light-skinned ex-GI with big shoulders (there's a picture of him from '56 with Jimmy in the sea in Ibiza); a jazz musician (vibes) who's had it rough: a troubled emotional life, mistreatment in the army, struggles with heroin and other addictions. Richard describes him as "a gentle, sweet boy who [drifts] easily with the tide."

In September of '55 Jimmy brings Arnold back to Paris. Arnold has some ambivalence being Jimmy's boyfriend, anyway an exclusive one. (He sleeps with women.) By the end of summer 1956, Jimmy, depressed in part by what feels like the end of the relationship, and after he and Arnold fight, swallows sleeping pills with the intention of killing himself. It's Mary he calls to say what he's done; Mary who rushes to Jimmy's apartment and makes him vomit before the doctor arrives—an averted tragedy that brings him and Arnold closer, at least for a while. In January though, the night of the party in question, summer must seem far off.

Back to the party.

Mary's apartment, the setting for this gathering, perches above a narrow street in the Fifth Arrondissement under the Panthéon's dome. Mary's ferocious Siamese cat, Caesar, prowls rooms stacked with paintings, records, and in the kitchen, Mary's small but growing batterie of pots and baking dishes from kitchen shop Dehillerin in the rue Coquillière.

Jimmy, holding the floor like always; reclining shoeless on the sofa, left heel braced on Arnold's (or Lucien's) thigh; slapping his glass down and slipping to the floor, head back on the sofa cushion.

Mary has the book spread open under a pot lid used as a weight. She's feeling nice from the booze, the cigaret she dangles from her lips, Jimmy's high laugh and Diz and Bird blowing "Mohawk" out in the salon. She's attempting Elizabeth David's Poulet au Riz Basquaise from French Country Cooking—she hasn't made it before (Mary reads cookbooks for entertainment), but she likes the little bit of Spain it conjures, Elizabeth's language—a memory of sun and espadrilles and the sound of the wind through pines, release from the relentless gray of Paris, the ubiquity of stale bread and potatoes.

Jimmy speaks with rhythm and a preacher's fire, audibly italicizing the crux of what he's saying like the italics rippling the printed voice of revelation in the King James Bible. It's a night of feeling good by feeling no shame, Jimmy declares. Going the way your blood beats.

> *But there are too many steps to keep fixed on her mind in its current state, even with Richard leaning in to help. The water boils away from under the chicken as it poaches, which scorches along with the sausage; the rice, cooked apart, has gone dry before it can swell and soften the way it should; and the tomato and sweet pepper ragôut is pink and mealy owing to the sad inevitability of November's fruit, and unbelievably hot since, unable to find the piment Basquais David calls for, Mary's substituted cayenne powder.*

The hours stack up like empty Johnnie Walkers crowding Mary's table.

> *They talk about art and the artist. About novels and pictures, Richard Wright, Norman Mailer, Henry James; Paris and Greenwich Village, Indochina, the Republican Front, Montgomery bus boycott, and the war in Algeria. About lust and the imperative of love.*

The booze makes edges recede and inhibitions drop like cigarettes on Mary's carpet, expanding its galaxy of burns.

> *Dinner at last comes together: a pilaf Richard's folded together from the various elements—the dry, hacked chicken and obstinate rice, stewed tomato and peppers. It's either a fucking disaster (Richard) or a radiant success (Jimmy). It has what Jimmy calls the force of life: raw, open. Because what matters isn't perfection, it's about sensuality, intimacy, connection. It's the intention behind it—who you cook for, the spirit in which you share it. The food itself—the material—is always just pork chops.*

The sun rises on Saturday morning. Even Caesar doesn't rouse.

Beauford, who's grown quieter, keeps the records spinning: Bessie, Billie, Charlie, Duke. To the cries of the other five he lifts the needle on a hot side soon as it ends and drops it again at the start: Bessie on "Kitchen Man," singing of food in the most profane way possible, as sex acts conflating nourishment and need, framing the dirty and the downlow not as aberrations but as part of the essential acts of being human, DRAGGING her man for lacking the groceries to fill her yawning need with anything more than a snack.

The party drifts across the divisions of the days. They burn through packs and packs of PX smokes. They lay down to rest, coupling and tripling up for warmth in the freezing dawn. They argue, fight, doze off, and wake up again, drunk, hungover. Revive with cups of coffee put right with Cognac. Revive with cigarettes.

Mary and Richard cook what's on hand: eggs, a little ham, apples. Maybe Lucien, or Arnold, runs out for bread.

Until suddenly it's dawn, on Monday, and Mary has to feel her way to the bath to get presentable for the office. Leaving Jimmy, Lucien, Beauford, Richard, and Bernard to emerge hungover, "their faces . . . gray and damp; [stinking] with weariness," Jimmy writes of similar people, likewise friends, bracing for the world beyond Mary's door.

It's agreed that Richard will do the cooking next time they're together.

Jimmy, Beauford, Richard, Bernard, Mary, Lucien, Arnold: They repeat the sprawling, days-long party in Mary's apartment on successive weekends: every weekend that they're all, or mostly all, in Paris or Clamart. It becomes a thing they look forward to.

A name for these camped-out weekend gatherings at Mary's sticks: Saturday Night Function. The name's from an old Duke Ellington / Barney Bigard ditty, a stomping spiritual immortalized on 78 by Duke and his Cotton Club Orchestra in 1929. I bet this particular side was in Beauford's collection of scratchy jazz and blues records in his studio back in New York, when part of his education of young Jimmy was playing the phonograph. You hear the orchestra's horns and Bigard's clarinet lurching around gin-drenched hooks. It sounds like staggering into church on Sunday morning still drunk from Saturday night, an act of rebelliousness executed with shitfaced panache, and a relic of a time in Harlem when desire was allowed to trust its appetites.

Lucien, since technically he lives in Switzerland, is unpredictable, but others become part of Function's cast. In June of 1956, Richard's younger brother John shows up in Paris post-college and becomes a regular. By then Function has picked up the predictability, intimacy, and intellectual openness of a salon, though not the longevity or the scale of the Neal Salon in New York. Saturday Night Function lasts only eleven months.

The last one unspools the weekend before Thanksgiving, 1956, just before Mary's job calls her back to Washington. (She returns in 1962 to work with the Organization for Economic Co-operation and Development. In 1969 she marries Parisian chef Georges Garin and takes on the role of patronne at his Michelin-starred restaurant in Paris, first, then in the South of France.) Tonight doubles as Mary's going-away party.

Jimmy and Arnold aren't there—they're in Corsica. Besides Richard and Mary there's Beauford, Bernard, John, and some of Mary's embassy co-workers. The meal Richard prepares is monumental in scale, operatic in volume and coloring.

First course: frogs' legs poached in white wine, served with poulette sauce, a velouté heightened with lemon juice. Second: a leg of venison larded with strips of pork fat and marinated in wine and olive oil, roasted pink and served with a buttery purée of chestnuts. Cheese follows, and for dessert, crêpes baked with an almond soufflé filling. The wines, including Chevalier-Montrachet and Nuits-Saint-Georges, are dazzling.

It's as if Richard finally, as Function ends, has mastered the Escoffier book of secrets he dreamed over as a boy in Iowa. But Richard's queered Escoffier: appropriated an esoteric language of cuisine to conjure in a place of fundamentally rewritten rules—social, sexual, racial—in a space like the one bell hooks describes as fundamentally queer, a place to "invent and create. . . . [A place] to speak and to thrive and to live."

Yet I can't help thinking that this meal, Function's grand coda, solidifies Jimmy and Richard's final divergence. It must feel somehow right that Jimmy's absent.

For Jimmy, I think of Saturday Night Function as a way of extending his imperative to embrace a frictionless, unquestioning love; to give an unqualified yes to the heart and its beating. Drinking and eating together is the physical practice not just of friendship but of a collective humanity that regards the act of doing those things *together* as our only true sustenance—an end to all the gnawing hungers.

Accepting a meal comes with so many possible manipulations. True kinship for Jimmy is a communion of shared need; a resistance to regimes of power that try to seduce and seek to manipulate us—with food, money, success. All of the bullshit trappings.

Hunger has a kind of nobility for Jimmy; the nobility of accepting our hungers together, as part of our humanity.

In Jimmy's 1962 novel *Another Country*—which he dedicates to Mary—Eric, an American actor vacationing in a rented house in the south of France, watches as his Yves, his boyish French lover, returns from the beach. Eric is leaving the next morning to return to New York. That evening, the house's prickly caretaker, Madame Belet, roasts a chicken for the couple before taking off for the night.

Yves and Eric let it sit on the table to get cold, though, and leave untouched the wine Madame Belet has opened for them. Because their real dinner, the only sustenance they need, is making love. The bed—"the only haven either of them had ever found," Jimmy says—becomes their table, the air scented with Yves's sweat that smells like garlic and pepper from having been in the kitchen with Madame Belet; with Yves *giving* himself to Eric, like Yves is this delicious sustaining thing; like queer lovemaking is the act of taking the most vulnerable things within you and offering them to another just as vulnerable, to nourish the starved places in both of you.

It's this moment in Jimmy's writing that happens sometimes, where time seems frozen, the air stills, and every noise becomes amplified, this safe space where queer love happens.

Where food becomes magical in Jimmy's world is when it's part of shared denial, a state in which love, if it exists, becomes nakedly obvious. In his later novel *Just Above My Head*, Arthur proposes to cook for his lover, Jimmy, so they don't have to go out—pork chops, cold red beans and rice he can heat up, a chicken wing. But satisfying physical hunger must wait for burning off pent-up desire. Arthur knows he's about to "grab Jimmy by those two dimples just above his ass, growl, and bite, into the nape of his neck . . . and grind Jimmy's behind against his own prick, playfully, while Jimmy protests—playfully—and lets the onions burn while he turns and takes Arthur in his arms: too late. The pork chops, too, may burn, unless Jimmy, as he often does, exhibits great presence of mind, and turns down the one flame, while both calming, and surrendering to the other."

Poised to fuck, as the pork chops send an ecstasy of airborne grease onto their queer bodies like a rain of stars. Food—the performance of cooking—is almost irrelevant to the broader human performance of connection.

I read Jimmy and find the blurred lines of sensuality, his merging of hunger, love, sex, and, need, incredibly moving. If Jimmy were ever to articulate anything as unlikely as a queer culture of food, it would begin with love. The material details, the edible particulars, would be subordinate to that. Many of us learned to express our sexuality as a kind of armor in the world, through protest and action. Can we find a deeper meaning in queerness by submitting to a shared silence, a communal vulnerability? Could this be the lesson of Saturday Night Function?

✳

FOR RICHARD, Function has been a kind of cooking residency: a testing of his skills. He finds shape and a voice for his gastronomic aesthetic: how to achieve a purity of effects, how to sequence a menu. I can't help thinking that Saturday Night Function has been a stage for Richard to practice the queer aesthetic that will find open expression for a wider audience in his books. The queer salon that Saturday Night Function represents seems the essential setting for lending space and community to work out these ideas.

In the semiprivate setting of the salon, a queer aesthetic could be forged: pieced together, tried on, tested for an audience both critical and supportive. What was deemed promising might then be floated in the wider world. It's a testing ground for a queer sensibility that could drift into the outside world, with all of its potential for danger regarding queer expression. The salon is a place where an aesthetic culture of queerness can find its footing before merging with the world beyond the street door. Tested at night and in liminal hours of the day, when we're rawest, and most real.

Café Nicholson is a kind of queer salon, too: a proving place, before (at least initially) a small, supportive community, for expressive ideas that will eventually spill into and transform the wider culture.

From my distance, I see Jimmy and Richard's divergence as a foreshadowing of what would be the two strains of queer identity building at the table: the egalitarian and communal, more interested in collectivity than purity of cuisine, versus the epicurean and hedonistic; the cliché of the politically and ethically grounded lesbian vegetarian potluck versus the cliché of the glittering gay dinner party.

Saturday Night Function is Jimmy's empathy circle, a place where everything's shared and absolute honesty rules.

For Richard, it's a stage for queer performance. And public performance, in the decades to come, would be a prime vector of the queer revolution.

UP THE GOAT PATH

[1961]

E VEN BEFORE THE FIRST SATURDAY NIGHT FUNCTION, Richard had moved from central Paris to Clamart, a suburb at the southwest edge of the city, to paint where rent's cheap. He took a second-story flat with a large garden to look on. Beauford Delaney moves downstairs; he tacks up white sheets to cover the walls and reflect light. Jimmy and Bernard and Mary and Arnold, the whole Function family, spend a lot of time there: sleeping over, bathing in the oldfangled tin tub in Richard's kitchen. They drink at a nearby bar called La Guinguette. They eat what Richard cooks.

Surely it's a relief from Paris: smells of turpentine and oil paints; coffee in the morning espresso pot on the burner. The scents of Richard's daily soup-making, sweet, sulfury leeks melting in butter before the potatoes go in; the everlasting stink of strong cigarettes. They have the garden to sit in, the wide-open sky between the houses. It isn't enough, though, especially with the tenuousness of Richard's existence in France following the end of his year's allowance from Norris.

Then, in the spring of 1961, Richard and his brother Byron rent a seaside house near Toulon. Friends take them for a walk in the hills above town, overlooking a valley and the Gapeau river. "Cherry orchards transformed the valley into a blanket of white blossom . . . ," Richard writes. "The poetry of Provence was in the air and tender tips of wild asparagus, invisible to the profane[,] were breaking the ground everywhere. I fell in love."

In the hills above the village of Solliès-Toucas they're shown an abandoned, half-destroyed old cottage with a cornerstone dated 1859. "The property was an enclave," Richard writes, "the only access from the road below, a precarious goat path bestowed with the oral tradition of a right of passage." Seven acres straight up a hill, terraced with dry stone walls, covered in neglected olive trees, to a small, long-abandoned limestone quarry.

With money from an Ingram Merrill Foundation arts grant, Richard puts down a deposit on the rotted house and its seven acres of unmanageable hillside. He wants to root here, at the other end of the world from Paris; from Saturday Night Function, also from Jimmy—they've drifted apart, though Richard's still close to Bernard and Mary. Still, a piece of Function will have a chance to naturalize in the generative soil up the goat path. Some queer spirit Richard had only ever known in in bars, apartments, and rented rooms can now grow wild.

Will it, though?

For a culture to take root, the circle has to expand beyond the physical table, into the realm of ideas. In a system determined to deny, prosecute, marginalize queer existence, who could leave a record of queer food? Who would have the freedom or the cunning, the courage or the audacity, to set down the meaning of food in queer lives?

Part Three

COOKING
IN
CODE

1946–1973

· ·
· ·

Our Cast of Unlikely Subversives
and Saboteurs

Genevieve Callahan

Louvica "Lou" Richardson

Craig Claiborne

Alice B. Toklas

Brion Gysin

Lou Rand / Lou Rand Hogan / Louis Randall

· · · · ·

Plus
Julia Child! M. F. K. Fisher!

· ·
· ·

GEN AND LOU

[1946]

CRACKED SPINE, OLD EVIDENCE OF BUTTERY HANDS, pages touched by so many fingers the paper feels like suede. Genevieve Callahan's *The California Cook Book*, released by Barrows in 1946 (four years after the same publisher trotted out *Stina* by Herman Smith), feels like a thing designed for use. It's from the era before *cook* and *book* were fused; a time when pink and jade-green Jell-O salads anchored a buffet without the burden of irony.

Genevieve—Gen—had been food editor for *Sunset*, the Western regional home magazine, based in SF then. In fact, she'd authored an earlier book for Sunset's imprint, the *Book of All-Western Foods* of 1936. In some of the headnotes and chapter intros Gen's voice thrills me with a certain sense of discovery that, I'll be honest, feels familiar. Take pizza, which she "discovers" at Tommaso's restaurant in North Beach ("The slap, slap, of Eddie's hands as he flattens the ball of sour dough into a very thin flat cake.") It's a thing so alien and exciting she has to tell her readers how to pronounce it: *peet-za*.

There's her crab cioppino, a set of guidelines rather than a fussy, teaspoon-specifying recipe—as if the process of cioppino should be loose and variable depending on the crabs, your kettle, how many people you're feeding—a performance: loading a few essentials into a big old kettle. Covering. Boiling.

And the performance continues at the table, as the cioppino's "heaped in soup plates," Gen writes, "with plenty of sauce," bibs and paper napkins essential. She suggests there's joy in intimate handwork, a project that results in faces stained with sticky broth, itchy fingers, forearms flecked with bits of meat and shell.

In the late forties, home economists rule the printed recipe in America. As a proud part of the profession, Gen shares her sisters' preoccupations: budgeting, efficiency, careful measuring. Yet at a time when a real woman is traveling the country as "Betty Crocker," i.e. a fake, Gen's naturalism breaks the fourth wall of cookbooks. Her persona is present and muscular; she ignores the conventional virtues of female daintiness and motherly nurture. She's not stressing over the price of hamburger or the planning of beanie-weenie parties for the kids. In fact she never mentions kids, only Lou Richardson, who, the context makes clear, is Gen's husband. Their surnames are different, but whatever.

The way Gen drops Lou's name with the comfortable closeness of couplehood, from the acknowledgment at the outset to the glimpses of a shared home life that flash intermittently across the pages—the married mojo rumbles deep in the *us*-ing and *our*-ing and *we*-ing. "The menus are for the sort of meals we like to serve our friends from the East and the South and the Northwest," Gen says up front, at the opening to the *Cook Book*, "when they visit us in our Russian Hill apartment in San Francisco, or in our little red cottage in Inverness [a coastal village north of SF], where we spend our weekends."

And Gen doesn't entirely ditch postwar homemaker conventions, the notion of eating right: meat protein balanced with milk protein, balanced with starch, sugar, and any vitamins that might be left standing in glazed carrots and canned peas. "Remember," Gen writes in that home-ec voice so familiar to readers of women's magazines in the 1940s, "you can always balance a rich, glamorous dish in both cost and digestibility by keeping the rest of the menu on the simple side."

Gen, however, takes it to a place no other food writer at the time was willing to go: the L place.

You can always balance that rich dish, remember she says, by keeping everything else simple. "Like Lou Richardson's dream of the 'perfect balanced menu'" she sets up the lesbian punchline like a pro: "sparkling Burgundy balanced with hamburgers."

First it tweaks me, because I know that in 1946, a woman cookbook author is not supposed to talk about a meal of wine and burgers in the same sentence as cost and digestibility.

Then, once I figure out that Lou Richardson is a woman, it absolutely smacks me.

I discover it years later, doing research about the early years of *Sunset*: that Lou was born *Louvica*, and was Gen's partner at home, and her collaborator in work, including at *Sunset*. They lived together beginning in the early 1920s, in Des Moines, as editors for the Meredith company, publisher of *Ladies' Home Journal* and *House Beautiful*. Their last shared home was in Fallbrook, near San Diego, where they died a few years apart in the early 1980s after six decades together.

They held on to all the tools of deniability: single gals bunking together to save their pennies, home-ec professionals too busy with war work and freelance careers to start families, talkity-talk, *things were different then*, blahty blahbbity blah blah blah.

Though it takes me years, I'm able to unscramble *The California Cook Book*, and find within it a diffuse memoir of queer joy.

PLEASURE EN FRANÇAIS

[1949]

CRAIG CLAIBORNE'S SAILING BACK TO NEW YORK from Cherbourg on the *Île de France,* a splurge he allows himself following his navy service in the war and its aftermath. He experiences the kind of food epiphany that parallels the founding mythologies of other American food writers: Julia's sole meunière in Normandy; teenage Anthony Bourdain's Brittany oysters on the half shell.

For Craig it's *turbotin,* a kind of flounder, in a white wine and fish fumet reduction bound with egg yolks, mounted with butter to yield a sauce with a smooth mouthfeel, no doubt plush; no doubt luxe. Years later he'll write about the "spiritual revelation" it delivers. "Never again has anything tasted so audaciously good," he says.

He writes in a cringey voice of passion. His turbotin is "the essence and extract of some sublime, supernal elixir that was all I'd ever hoped for without knowing what I'd hoped for." He gives it the weight of sexual rapture, a hedonist's initiation, the indelible intensity of a first orgasm. This is Craig at his most exuberantly queer. The way he leans into the sensuality: He does everything but come out. But every ounce of revelation—all the ecstasy—is securely embedded in the turbotin. Queerness lurks like a spell.

WHEN COOKBOOKS LIE

[1954]

I N HARPER & ROW'S 1984 REPRINT OF *THE ALICE B. Toklas Cook Book*, marking thirty years since the original edition, there's a publisher's note: Alice's editor, Simon Michael Bessie, describing the book's genesis.

Bessie's note features a cold open, a recalled conversation with Alice. Bessie's suggestion that she should write a memoir of her life with Gertrude Stein is implied. Alice's reply is the first line of Bessie's note:

" 'Oh,' said Alice, 'I couldn't do that.' "

He presses her; wants to know why she can't.

" 'Because,' said Alice in that cigarette-rough and sensuous voice, 'Gertrude did my autobiography and it's done.' "

"Since I could think of no response to that," Bessie writes, slipping into the editorial first-person plural, "I must have looked very sad; and since Alice had grown a bit fond of us in the years since Gertrude's death, she thought of something: 'What I could do,' she said as tentatively as she was able, which was not very, 'is a cook book.' And then, 'It would, of course, be full of memories.' "

But this origin story, appearing seventeen years after Alice's death, is a lie. Though in Bessie's defense, so much of Alice's own stories are lies; or if not lies, perhaps prevarications, a blizzard of half-truths. Or try untruths: fictions never intended to be taken as factual, because what lesbian could tell readers in 1954 the truth about her life?

Still, Bessie's story *is* a lie.

✳

ALICE WRITES TO A FRIEND IN 1947, the year following Gertrude's death, about how badly she wants a pass to the American PX in Paris, for all the lovely cheap food there. (She's sure that published American authors have freedom of access.) She writes, "Suddenly it came to me if I could get recipes printed in some magazine I'd be as eligible as Richard Wright—so why not gather my recipes—make the cook book . . . "

Here's evidence that even before she starts to write, she's thinking of a cookbook as a literary project, a work that would put her on the same footing as the expat novelist Wright. Even if she's half joking, it shows her state of mind. And that, as a literary effort, a cookbook should lean on all a writer's tools of persuasion: metaphor, allegory, narrative structure, voice. For almost forty years, Alice was Gertrude's sounding board, typist, ad hoc editor—her de facto collaborator.

When Alice finally writes her cookbook, she ends it with the famous kicker, *As if a cookbook had anything to do with writing*, tossed out like a challenge. *I dare you*, she seems to say, *to find the purpose in my words.*

✳

THERE WAS A PRACTICAL IMPERATIVE across mostly all of the twentieth century to scrub manifestly queer voices from cookbooks.

Say it was complicated, this imperative. Say the owners of those queer voices actively participated in it—an ongoing, unspoken act of collusion between queer authors and their editors and publishers. A tacit agreement with the cookbook-buying public to believe author biographies as stated: *the committed bachelor . . . a devoted companion.* To avoid questioning aloud. To swallow the plausible arrangement at face value—*the roommate*—no matter how unlikely.

Call it a system of acceptable lies, powered by agreed-on ignorance. A system to keep avowedly queer people out of view in the kitchen, even as a byline, an author photo on a cookbook jacket.

Say it was a system to scare queer people from avowal in the first place.

NOBODY EMBRACED THIS SYSTEM with quite as much public spunk and gusto as Julia Child did.

"I wish all the men in OUR profession in the USA were not *pedals!*" Julia writes to Simone Beck, her co-author for *Mastering the Art of French Cooking*, using a form of the vulgar French slur for faggot, *pédale*, a word rooted in *pédophile*, implying gays were psychopathological creeps with a taste for children. With friends, she fantasizes aloud about launching what she calls a "de-fagification" of food writing.

This de-fagifying would of course purge her good friend James Beard from the field of cookbook writing; also, over the years, Craig Claiborne, Richard Olney, Michael Field, James Villas, Maurice Moore-Betty—on and on. And this is where it gets complicated, because Julia's easy-sounding, exclamation point–inflected vitriol, while shocking, is universal in James's and Craig's and Julia's world, even among many politically and socially liberal people like the Childs.

"Homophobia was a socially acceptable form of bigotry in mid-century America," historian Laura Shapiro writes, "and Julia and [her husband] Paul participated without shame for many years."

I'm not saying Julia doesn't love her friend James. Not suggesting she isn't loyal to him, even using her influence and powers of persuasion after he dies to help found the foundation that bears his name, and secure James's Greenwich Village townhouse as a culinary center to preserve his legacy.

I'm saying she embodies the system of social enforcement of the closet and the open secret. That she seems to find it boorish and socially inconvenient for homosexuals to defy a system so efficient at making faggotry a private matter, silent and unseen. Seems to think it selfish of homosexuals to stir things up, if I can channel Julia's voice for a sec, when there's *no damn good reason* to!

What magnifies the cruelty of this for me is that I love Julia: the way she centered a particular experience of pleasure at the table; how she'd whisk into the dining room part of the set at the end of her early TV show—the set with the French provincial tall case clock and the framed botanicals and the paneling painted a grayish kind of artichoke-heart green and presented the dish she'd cooked and uncorked and tasted a wine. How she taped an entire show on serving wine with cheese for a party, as if *snatching* the corkscrew from the patriarchy, because in the world of 1970 men (waiters, sommeliers, so-called heads of households) are supposed to be the openers, the connoisseurs, the guzzlers of wine, but Julia shows she has . . . not even the balls, the *ovaries* to do it herself. Aficionados of the grape represent the seasoned appetite for pleasure. How could someone who freed herself from the gender bind cinch herself up so tightly in rah-rah homo hating?

Yet no amount of effort to squelch fagification could keep queer voices silent forever—some managed to slipped through the system. Queer subjectivities emerged in cookbooks from major publishers.

Cautiously. Cunningly, like coded letters passed through ghetto walls, cookbooks started making witness to the dishes that carried a record of queer lives.

EVIDENCE SUGGESTS THAT, years before she died, Gertrude conceived of a cookbook collab with Alice. On the inside cover of a James Fenimore Cooper novel, Gertrude's scrawl seems to plot out a cookbook of shared voices, with an outline of seven chapters, including "My Life with Cookbooks" and "Eating and Not Eating, an Occupation." Although Gertrude's been dead eight years when Alice's book at last appears, in 1954, you can feel her literary ghost pacing through it.

The longer you hold *The Alice B. Toklas Cook Book*, the slipperier it gets. It messes with two important cookbook conventions, challenging expectations of what a cookbook is, or could be.

First, Alice flips the central architecture of cookbooks. Instead of each recipe having an introductory headnote to anchor and contextualize it, Alice's recipe is often the introduction to the anecdote that inspired it. For instance, the spinach soufflé she makes for Picasso is actually only the setup for Picasso's mysterious remark on being presented with it, that the dish is a "cruel enigma."

Second, it has an unreliable narrator, "Alice." It masquerades as straight-up memoir, but there's nothing straight about it. "Alice" is not real, and the anecdotes she tells are enhanced reprises of episodes that "Alice," Gertrude's narrator in *The Autobiography of Alice B. Toklas,* related two decades earlier in that book. As scholar Anna Linzie says, Alice "hides in a carefully crafted textual persona, designed to veil the secrets of her intimate life with Stein."

Because of course neither Gertrude nor Alice could allow the public a peek under the veil. They resisted being essentialized, reviled as lesbians, or Jewish women, defined by perceptions they couldn't manage. Blurring was survival.

Here's Roland Duncan for UC Berkeley's Bancroft Library oral history project, recording a conversation with Alice in Paris in 1952. He's clearly trying to get Alice to cop to the late Gertrude's identity as queer and Jewish. Alice shuts him down.

Duncan: In the case of Gertrude Stein, do you think possibly that she felt that there was any cultural or religious minority which would have set her apart?

Toklas: No. Not the least.

Duncan: Perhaps made her strive towards certain social or cultural objectives? None at all?

Toklas: Never. We never had any feeling of any minority. We weren't a minority. We represented America.

Sooner or later, anyone who wants to write about Gertrude's work through the frame of sexuality feels Alice's fury. When she learns in 1947 that the writer Julian Sawyer took up Gertrude's lesbianism in a series of lectures in New York, Alice is livid. "You will understand I hope," she writes to him, "my objection to your repeated references to the subject of sexuality as an approach to the understanding of Gertrude's work. She would have emphatically denied it—she considered it the least characteristic of all expressions of character."

Denial is survival, and Alice is committed to keeping Gertrude's work and reputation out of the grubby hands of psychologists and overly clever critics.

In 1952, when she sits down with Duncan and his tape recorder, the American Psychiatric Association has just published a diagnostic manual classifying homosexuality under "sociopathic personality disturbance." It put queer desire in the same category as pedophilia, the rationale, for example, that fed Julia Child's homophobia. Also in '52, the so-called Lavender Scare, the persecution of gays and lesbians in US government service, was raging.

Yet despite Alice's fierce refusal to be seen—examined or psychoanalyzed—for what she and Gertrude were, she flashes signs in *The Alice B. Toklas Cook Book*. Onto the very screen that obscures the actual details of her life with Gertrude, Alice beams a coded celebration of lesbian sex.

FAREWELL TO FIRE ISLAND

[1957]

CRAIG IS OUT AT CHERRY GROVE WITH HENRY LEWIS Creel when the telegram arrives. Henry's at the cabin—he's the one who signs for it; he knows what it is. He doesn't wait for Craig to make his way back but jogs down the beach, the little envelope in his hand, to where Craig's laid out. Henry yells *Dobey!*, his private love name for Craig, if you can call it love, and maybe you can except to all the world it has to look like buddyhood since Henry's in the accounting division at Shell Oil—not the sort of job where you can be careless with public perception, and Fire Island on its own is risky enough. Anyway, Henry's yelling at Craig on the beach, waving the envelope as Craig stands up. *Dobey!* he says, Dobey it's the *Times!*

The editor of the women's page at the *New York Times* wants to meet with Craig to discuss the food editor job. Craig has had a short, disastrous run at the magazine called *Gourmet*, which might have been a sweet little place to roost except for the fact that the publisher is an absolute prick.

And this moment, this breaching of the gay enclave of Cherry Grove with a terse message with the iron gravity of the Gray Lady, as the *Times* was known, would become emblematic of Craig's dilemma for years—decades—to come. Was it reckless to even let the *Times* know he'd be on holiday in Cherry Grove and if they should wire him here? He's far from even having the food editor job and already he's running the risks in his head! But the fear Craig knew in Mississippi had never really left him, though there was a time it seemed he was free of it.

Chicago.

It was after the war ceased and his navy service ended, late '40s—
he took a kind of a nothing job as a PR flack for the local Windy City
ABC affiliate. And the reason he even went to Chicago was for a guy,
someone he'd met in the navy.

Lo and behold there's this entire gay world in Chicago, a crowd that
was just *wild.* Like all of the discretion anybody'd ever caged themselves
up in in the service was shattered: locks smashed, bars busted clean
through. Guys were still drifting into town, still coming back from the
war, leaving the navy or the army behind and with a frigate-load of stories. My God, the parties! The liquor! Craig learns how to go after the
guys he likes; learns how to take someone home from a party; learns
how to suck a cock, to give and take pleasure; to *imagine* that love is a
thing that he, the Indianola schoolboy with bruises and a scraped face, is
entitled to. The taste of freedom—a kind of euphoria none of these guys
experienced before the war. It was as if the bad old world cracked clean
open and scattered like rubble. Nobody was going to rebuild the cages.

Craig throws dinner parties, and successfully pitches a couple of
food stories to the *Chicago Tribune.* He even has the confidence to come
out to his boss at ABC. The boss shrugs.

And then Miss Kathleen sends Craig a souvenir of home: a school
composition notebook into which she has written some of her favorite
recipes in longhand. Great Grandmother Craig's Grated Potato Pudding . . . Sister's Sausage . . . Craig Wedding Punch, which is more
than two hundred years old. It reminds Craig who he "is": the scion of
a penurious but perpetually proud clan, with its rules and traditions;
its lines of succession.

It's like a squad of ghosts had come to refresh the old fear; to help Craig
build back the cage he probably always knew he'd have to crawl back into.

So that years later, when Henry comes running and hollering *Dobey!*
down the beach, waving a small envelope, Craig's ready. He knows
what to do.

✳

CRAIG BECOMES THE FIRST MAN to hold the job of food editor at the *New York Times.*

There is no coming out to one's boss at the *Times.* Under publisher Arthur Sulzberger Sr., fear stalks the halls and offices. This is true for almost every workplace in North America, but New York City, with its queer undergrounds and coalescing communities, heightens both the temptations and the hazards.

Craig cages his sexuality inside the unremarkable business suits and sober ties of a middling, mildly ambitious newspaperman, the workaholic bachelor too busy to take a wife. But Craig's published voice. . . . That's another story.

Some of Craig's earliest features for the *Times* have a preciousness that feels like dress-up, like he believes he has some divine gift of discernment. Take a look at Craig's recipe feature on asparagus from March 1958, six months into his tenure at the *Times*:

"The palate would be prosaic, indeed, that could deny that this tender product, now in profuse supply, was less than royal in flavor." The cadence, the thinking in clauses, the bombast—it's pure Blanche DuBois, the grand voice of theatrical pathos from *A Streetcar Named Desire*: "A cultivated woman, a woman of intelligence and breeding, can enrich a man's life—immeasurably!"

Craig again:

"And this, the first day of spring, seems a particularly suitable occasion for giving the vegetable—so closely associated with the season—its due."

And Blanche:

"Physical beauty is passing. A transitory possession. But beauty of the mind and richness of the spirit and tenderness of the heart . . . aren't taken away, but grow! Increase with the years!"

There's a flouncing rhythm to both voices, a quality of practiced artifice, the painted fan that flutters and snaps shut.

The story has a delicious photo to match, an arrangement of asparagus dishes styled in chic Dansk pans. Above them is an antique botanical print: a thick stalk of asparagus with a bullhead tip, lolling like a half-engorged penis.

When he started, Craig's job was marginal. Editor of food stories of the so-called women's pages of the *Times* was a grind with no glory, a job tossed to women, the lowest and most disposable workers in the male business of newspapering. But Craig applies gay magic; sprinkles so much preciousness around it makes it feel like what he's doing is work of sublime importance.

He has a hedonist's adoration of anything buttery and French; a devotion to the glorious high-calorie, low-nutrition foods of people who have probably never had and no doubt actively disdain small children. A really good early Claiborne feature reminds me of the lit candelabrum Liberace always kept on his piano for performances. A piece by Craig can open a mood that feels like a world view, a challenge to burn through layers of provincial habit and charm you into believing you deserve more elegance in your life. Maybe the fanciest thing you ever made was a cake from a Betty Crocker mix. Craig would like you to think of yourself as someone worthy of making and absolutely *flaunting* a Viennese chestnut torte.

Craig is haunted, though. He almost marries a woman but drops back in time. From the outside he's a success. By 1961, when he institutes starred reviews in the *Times*, he's the unacknowledged tastemaker of New York City and thus the nation. He has made a marginal job into a vertex of power in a city where restaurants respect only power, only status, only influence. Away from his byline—away from critic's meals, following dessert and the check and the goodbyes to the important people he invites to dine with him—he sinks back into a marginal life. The apartment on the gritty East Side he considers tawdry; the beer gardens and bars he haunts almost every night to drink himself numb before cruising the streets for daddies in uniform, including cops—cops out patrolling, not cruising for sex. As if the only thing he knows to do with being queer is live in the risk he would've known had he stayed in Indianola, trolling for flesh, terrified. His food writing is coded to bring recognition and maybe comfort to queer readers hungry for it, but Craig lives like a starving man.

STRANGLING THE DOVES

[1954]

LOOK TWICE AT "MURDER IN THE KITCHEN," A CHAPTER in *The Alice B. Toklas Cook Book.*

Alice begins by confessing her reluctance to kill: to wring the necks of chickens and other birds; bludgeon fish pulled flapping from a tank. She posits a parallel between cooking and murder mysteries; that the thing they have in common is that, for animal-based diets, both begin with a corpse, i.e. a carcass fresh from the abattoir. "Before any story of cooking begins," she says, "crime is inevitable." We are all dirty. We all transgress.

Meat is predicated on acts of slaughter most carnivores don't want to see; would prefer not to acknowledge the horror of. And it's the tension between this distaste for suffering and death and the pleasure that suffering and death transform into in the kitchen that serves as a sustained metaphor for the tension between sin and carnal pleasure. The real "crime" is acting on lesbian desire—a crime against the state, against religion, against conventional notions of decency. And yet queer sex is a source of concentrated pleasure, all the more intense for being forbidden.

Like an unsolved murder in the remote country mansion full of weekend guests in a detective novel, queer desire that can't be publicly acknowledged sows a fearful kind of disorder that must, somehow or other, find resolution.

Cookbooks are deeply conservative, upholding power and privilege as they validate assumptions of safety and order in the kitchen: the narrative steps in a recipe, the predictable timeline. Recipes talk to us with the reassuring authority of imperative commands: *Ask the butcher . . . Watch carefully . . . Do not allow to boil.* We sign an invisible contract with a recipe author for replicability—that the method will always be correct, always turn out just the same, unless we, the user, fuck things up somehow with substitutions, omissions, shortcuts— unless we bring our own failings.

But what happens when a kitchen is a place of vice and criminality? What if, just beneath the ordered surface of a recipe told in the com- forting voice of the narrator, a liar speaks to us? What if a recipe fools the unsuspecting reader into being complicit in queerness, which after all is a sickness; a threshold to criminal acts of perversion? What if a recipe were subversive?

For most of the twentieth century, queer sex can exist only as denial. Gertrude and Alice conspired to scrub certain obvious lesbian references from some of Gertrude's manuscripts. Others survived Alice's editorial pencil. "How are they all to say how do you do how glad we are all to see you," Gertrude writes in one of these rare cases, "and we are not at all pre- pared to see all of you." The only lesbians most people were prepared to see were terribly confused and desperately unhappy ones, like the tragic Karen and Martha, played by Audrey Hepburn and Shirley MacLaine in the 1961 movie adaptation of Lillian Hellman's *The Children's Hour.*

Maybe mystery is really the only way to represent queerness in the mainstream in 1954. Knowing that something exists but not being able to see it; to understand it. Describing the mystery stories that fascinated her as a young woman, Alice tells Roland Duncan that merely *suggesting* a crime, without ever having to show it, is the surest way to create tension. "The mystery was held back," she says. "In fact, the mystery was so great that you were enthralled with it, and it was never divulged. The mystery existed and that was sufficient."

✳

WESTERN TRADITION says cooking belongs to women. It says killing belongs to men.

In "Murder in the Kitchen," Alice describes, at various times in her life, watching men kill fish: the Puget Sound fisherman in Seattle; a Parisian fish monger. When Alice is forced to kill, because the market men are busy or distracted, she also frees from the gender binds that strangled her like that cerise corset on the train to Florence. She slits the throat of "poor Mr. Carp." Guts him, emptying "a great deal of what I did not care to look at"—a symbolic castration. She feminizes Mr. Carp: stuffs him with dressing, drenches him with white wine, flocks him with cracker crumbs and bakes until he slips from the oven wearing a crisp, buttery, ruffled chemise. It's an emasculation both grisly and elaborate, like dressing a twentieth-century corpse in the wig and brocades of a seventeenth-century courtier at Versailles. She suggests serving him laid out on a pallet of "very delicate" noodles. She gives the recipe.

In another episode, Gertrude and Alice travel to the country with their cook, Jeanne. At an open-air market, Jeanne purchases live doves and immediately begins to smother them. But a bunch of rough market women object. They yell at Jeanne that the proper way to kill a bird is by decapitation. Jeanne resists. She tells Alice that smothering the birds allows the carcasses to retain their blood—it keeps the flesh of the cooked squab plump and soft. Jeanne's sensitive fingers find the correct place on the necks, to coax the life out of the doves as if she's teasing a clitoris; coaxing it to find release; palping each little body until it reaches the literal state of *la petite mort*, the little death—a French expression for the orgasm that wipes you out; leaves you utterly, blissfully wrecked. Strangling the doves is foreplay: readying their bodies for the indulgence to come.

The worst kitchen murders are done in acts of testosteronic brutality. The best, the ones yielding the most pleasure, are slow, patient acts of domination.

In the book, back in Paris, Alice applies Jeanne's technique to six white doves someone sends as a gift from the country; learns how to feel with her fingers the precise point of asphyxiation on the necks, "poor innocent Dove's throat," she says. When she's finished, she lays out "the sweet young corpses."

The chapter's ending unfolds like allegory.

There's this love triangle: a live-in cook at 27 rue de Fleurus, the Austrian Frederich, and his innocent fiancée, Duscha, who's "pretty, dainty, and . . . elegant," Alice says. An "angel." The third point of the triangle is a woman with dark eyes Alice calls the Devil.

The Devil's determined to seduce Frederich, to steal him from Duscha, and if she can't, to kill him. It gets weirder. Frederich is from Adolf Hitler's hometown. Alice says he's strange like the Führer, but with an exquisitely feminine touch with Sacher tortes, Linzer tortes—all sorts of pastry. Even for allegory, this is warped.

It's less than ten years since the end of the Nuremberg trials, and Alice can intuit a connection between their cook and Hitler, who oversaw the relatively recent slaughter of six million Jews and tens of thousands of actual or suspected homosexuals. (See Janet Malcolm's brilliant *Two Lives* on the problematic opacity of Alice and Gertrude's politics; their internalized antisemitism and possible Vichy sympathies; the casually racist shade they toss at Nguyen and Trac, successive Vietnamese-born cooks in the Stein-Toklas household.)

Still, it's not the shadow of genocide that seems to matter here, only subversion: how lesbian erotics and masculine humiliation can be the correctives in a world where violence and duplicity rule. I think Alice wants us to *feel* how the sting of control and manipulation coils within hetero desire.

By the end of this episode, after the Devil essentially drags Frederich offstage by the balls, leaving Duscha to Gertrude and Alice, there's nothing for the women to do but share the final slices of the last tart Frederich will ever make for them, in a poignant scene that plays like a lesbian gustatory ménage à trois. Alice titles Frederich's final work of art "A Tender Tart" and declares it exquisite: buttery pastry top and bottom, and between, a filling of vanilla, sugar, and finely chopped hazelnuts.

The hazel tree, *Corylus avellana*, produces nuts in soft and hairy, frilly-edged leaves that sheath them tightly in an involucre that appears exploded, appearing frankly genital. I regret buying them shelled all my life, never knowing the pleasure of harvesting from the tree. Were there hazel trees growing alongside the fruit trees in Bilignin, in the country houses where she and Gertrude spent fourteen summers, huddling during war and occupation?

I've made A Tender Tart—the recipe Alice Waters reconfigured for *The Chez Panisse Menu Cookbook* of 1982. (Waters says she couldn't get the original Toklas recipe to work.) It's a fifty-fifty balance of taste and feel: buttery, friable pastry with delicate browning; oily-fleshed hazelnuts radiating their gorgeous birch-bark sweetness; sticky, pebbly filling in pastry that collapses under the tag-team pressure of teeth and tongue. Even to pronounce it—*a tender tart:* the way the lingual apex taps four purposeful beats on the hard palate; the way you tongue-flick a nipple or a clit.

The forbidden lesbian experiences—Alice's "crimes"—have a heavy tactile dimension. It's as if a defining feature of queerness is reclaiming the sense of touch numbed from the culture at large: an outlaw tenderness. The name of Alice's tart carries an echo of *Tender Buttons,* Gertrude's 1914 book of poetic explications of foods and objects. *That* book's title is unexplained in the text, though of course there are theories. Is a tender button a nipple? The spongy, sensitive clitoris?

Gertrude's queer friend and collaborator, the composer Virgil Thomson, thought she may have been making a bilingual pun, a play on *tendres boutons,* the first signs of budding in a tree, maybe the emerging bumps in *Corylus avellana.* "In that case," Thomson mused, "it would mean that the writings included were a new development like the eclosion of leaf, flower, or branch. And whatever erectile suggestiveness may go along with this would imply that we are in the presence of a natural force moving toward explosion."

Baked by a weak and feckless man, Alice's exquisite hazelnut tart carries the narrative excitement of an orgasm—it's literally the climax of "Murder in the Kitchen." The logical end to a chapter built on the wicked ministrations of fingers and tongues.

"The realization had never come to me that before that one saw with one's fingertips as well as one's eyes," Alice says in "Murder in the Kitchen." "There was no denying one could become accustomed to murdering."

Like the Alice that Gertrude describes, in a private amorous note, as always shining "full of love and dove." Like the Alice who ID's herself in a love note to Gertrude as "your dove."

You couldn't slip anything criminal (let's say lesbianism) into a cookbook in 1954, but you could hint at crime. You could introduce murder, albeit with bathos, in a droll way about killing animals, as a metaphor for the outlaw thing you can't say. Because that thing, queerness, is simply unthinkable in a cookbook. "Fulfillment as a woman had only one definition for American women after 1949," Betty Friedan writes in *The Feminine Mystique*, published in 1963: "the housewife-mother."

Granted, Alfred Kinsey's *Sexual Behavior in the Human Female* dropped a full year before Alice's *Cook Book*. As he did with gay behavior in his 1948 report on male sexuality, Kinsey and his team attempted to plot the incidence of lesbian desire. Based on interviews with almost six thousand women, Kinsey determined that 1 to 3 percent of US women were exclusively queer, compared with 4 percent of men. So lesbians were *thinkable*, at least in a clinical context, hypothetically. But an unambiguously out lesbian claiming visibility on the Betty Crocker, Fannie Farmer, or Better Homes & Gardens cookbook shelves—girl, no.

It's not until 1989 and the publication of *City Cuisine*, by Los Angeles chefs Susan Feniger and Mary Sue Milliken, that a cookbook from a major US publisher would feature the voice of an out lesbian (Feniger). And Feniger wasn't even expressly out in the book, or later, starting in 1993, on Food Network; she just let the optics of being a lesbian coexist with life as a chef. (In 1996, culture critic Camille Paglia would praise Feniger's visibility on food TV for doing more to liberalize what she calls the "quality and meaning" of life in America "than any of the doctrinaire leaders of the feminist or gay-activist establishment.")

There was a gap wider than a generation between Alice's book and Feniger's. Across the vast conservative terrain of cookbook publishing, silence filled that gap. And in the rare moments when queer or dissident voices managed to break through, a kind of panic took hold.

AN EDIBLE FOR SAINT TERESA

[1954]

"RECIPES FROM FRIENDS" IS A CHAPTER IN *THE ALICE B. Toklas Cook Book* made up of eighty-five dishes Alice solicited and never bothered to test. (She confided to a friend she needed the recipes to pad her manuscript; to make it add up to the 70,000 words she was obligated to send her publisher.)

The chapter's a mini queer cookbook all its own: Francis Rose's eggs in soy sauce, Virgil Thomson's shad-roe mousse, Georges Maratier's liver custard, Pierre Balmain's tarragon chicken, Natalie Barney's sweet stuffed eggplant, Carl Van Vechten's garlic ice cream (a frozen dressing for avocados), Cecil Beaton's iced apple pudding.

And queerest of all: Brion Gysin's hashish fudge.

A British-Canadian artist and writer born in 1916, Brion met Gertrude and Alice in the 1930s. Their brief acquaintance was casual. He was seated next to Gertrude at a dinner once; afterwards they sent letters back and forth. When Gertrude dies Brion takes up a friendship with Alice. She becomes a kind of mentor to him in letters, encouraging him to persevere in his art. In 1950 she nudges him to accept an offer by Paul Bowles, the American composer and novelist, to come to Tangier. Brion goes.

Tangier in the 1950s is a haven for British and American writers and artists, many gay, lured by fucking and getting high. Before Moroccan independence in 1956, Tangier was an international municipality governed by several European nations; "a utopia of dangerous, unknown pleasures," says historian Andrew Hussey. Orientalism was baked into its French colonial culture. There were cheap, plentiful drugs and abundant sex workers, and as long as you were *relatively* discreet and didn't violate certain cultural taboos, nobody got in your business.

Brion hooks up with an aspiring young painter named Mohamed Hamri, and it's Mohamed who acts as Brion's fixer, lover, helper around the house (Brion's moved out of Bowles's place)—including how to pack a pipe with kif, tobacco mixed with weed. Brion writes a stoned, rambling treatise on kif. And when Alice asks him for a recipe to help fill her book, he doesn't go far for inspiration.

By 1954, Americans had been persuaded to think of cannabis as pernicious and corrupting, on par with Commie infiltration and sex perversion. A psychologist in California who consulted vice cops laid out in 1950 all the slippery slang for marijuana that parents should listen for: "Miggles, mooters, reefers, greefa, griffo, Mary Warner, Mary Jane, hay, love weed, stick, giggle-smoke, bumbalacha, mohasky, moocah, grass, tea, gungeon!" They had the low-life ring of the streets, nighttime worlds unknown to decent people, folks who kept their nose clean, and whose backsides knew the righteous feel of a church pew.

The papers were becoming littered with stories of kids getting hooked. Congress passed the Boggs Act in 1951. It set mandatory sentences for drug convictions. A first offender could get ten years in a federal pen. Like queerness, weed was a deviation from the straight and narrow, a trip to a world of pleasure so intense that once you took even a single puff there was no coming back. Marijuana existed in a realm of freaks and oddball pleasures.

Take twenty-four-year-old Mary Louise Truly of Greenwich Village, described in the *Daily News* as "a willowy platinum blonde model." In 1954 her apartment was raided on a vice tip; she was found to be in felony possession of two packets of love weed she'd scented with lilac—"a feminine touch," the *News* noted.

Into this hazy half-world of dropouts, jazz players, and the lusty damned, crazy for giggle-smoke, walks a little old lady and her recipe for what her cookbook calls "Haschich Fudge." It becomes infamous—a minor scandal—before *The Alice B. Toklas Cook Book* even makes it to bookshops.

Brion's confection isn't fudge, and contains no hashish. It's an appropriated version of the Moroccan edible *majoun*. In Brion's formula, you pound a bunch of spices in a mortar and set them aside, then pound cannabis, the stickier the better, into an oily, resinous powder. Separately, chop dates, dried figs, almonds, and peanuts. Knead the spices and cannabis into the chopped mixture, along with a cup of sugar you've worked into a big lump of butter. Work everything together and roll into bite-size balls, or form it into a cake you nick pieces from when desired.

The lines *Time* ascribes to Alice are clearly Brion's—phrases that make you think of William S. Burroughs, Brion's future collaborator, mocking popular medical literature and the voice of women's magazines, deadpanned like a true smartass:

> This is the food of Paradise—of Baudelaire's Artificial Paradises. It might provide an entertaining refreshment for a Ladies' Bridge Club or chapter meeting of the D.A.R. [Daughters of the American Revolution, at the time an all-white "heritage" organization] . . . Euphoria and brilliant storms of laughter; ecstatic reveries and extensions of one's personality on several simultaneous planes are to be completely expected. Almost anything Saint Theresa [sic] did, you can do better if you can bear to be ravished by *"un évanouissement reveillé."*

"Artificial paradises" nods to queer poet Charles Baudelaire's 1860 book of essays *Les paradis artificiels*, about getting high to reach some meta state of consciousness. And that last phrase, *évanouissement reveillé*: the state of fainting while fully awake, or what it feels like to get fucking baked.

Of course, Saint Teresa of Avila is known for her chew-the-pillow night of divine revelation after hooking up with this angel, who thrusts and *keeps* thrusting his gold spear with a red, searing tip into her flesh. "The pain was so great, that it made me moan," Saint Teresa testifies. "And yet so surpassing was the sweetness of this excessive pain, that I could not wish to be rid of it."

Girl, *unf.*

What Brion's saying is that his fudge is an excellent edible for bottoming. It's sex food.

Compare that to Alice's carefully coded literary parable of lesbian desire.

Maybe Alice never really looked at the finished galleys for her book, or maybe she did but was just clueless about Brion's insinuations. It's clear from letters she has no clue what cannabis is. Besides, the whole "Recipes from Friends" feels like something Alice doesn't really want to own. It feels a little like an appendix accidentally inserted before the final chapter.

When Harper & Row, Alice's publisher, hears of the potential scandal they dash off a telegram to the office of US Attorney General Herbert Brownell Jr. Is it a crime to publish a recipe that specifies an illegal substance? What happens when making a recipe inevitably calls for the commission of a crime? Brownell's office informs Harper that it is wholly legal to *publish* the recipe, but Harper is skittish anyway—no doubt they've gamed scenarios where the papers report on the arrest of another willowy platinum blonde in Greenwich Village, busted while whipping up Brion's fudge, with Alice's book propped open on the table. The potential for PR nightmares is too real. They pull it from the American edition, though it appears in the UK. (It's included for American readers six years later, in the 1960 Anchor paperback.)

Alice tells a friend she only figured out the meaning of Brion's recipe after she read *Time*'s wickedly smug notice. *The late poetess Gertrude Stein . . . and her constant companion . . . Alice B. Toklas used to have gay old times together in the kitchen . . .* She signals that she's pissed.

Is she, though?

The *Cook Book* is a success. It goes into a fourth printing in only its third week. It would eventually become as beloved and ubiquitous as *The Autobiography of Alice B. Toklas*. How much did the controversy surrounding Brion's expurgated recipe contribute boost sales? Alice's good friend

Thornton Wilder considers the whole controversy a brilliant piece of marketing. "Thornton said that no one would believe in my innocence," Alice writes to a friend, "as I had pulled the best publicity stunt of the year." The edginess it confers on Alice makes her seem vibrant. Necessary.

Yet it's a rare moment when Alice can't control the narrative about the character Alice B. Toklas. A moment when the closet door pops slightly ajar, jammed open by a wadded-up piece of subversion placed by a queer provocateur from a newer, hungrier generation. Hashish fudge becomes the only memory of Alice's book that sticks.

THE QUEEREST ASPECT of Brion Gysin's hashish fudge might be that it's a recipe almost nobody will make; that almost nobody in 1950s North America and Britain *could* make. This makes it a purer distillation of Alice's book than even Alice is capable of: the most un-makeable recipe in a book of essentially un-makeable recipes.

It challenges the premise of a cookbook; questions the assumption that a recipe should deliver utility, standardization, replicability—all the bourgeois things. It challenges the purpose of a recipe as a formula for nourishment; bringing the family together; reinforcing its power structure, What is a recipe for? Is it only supposed to yield a dish that tastes good? That smells nice? What about the psycho-spiritual senses? What about the erotic possibilities of a recipe?

In the '50s, when queerness is criminal, a coded queer cookbook challenges straight power and straight values, even as it appears to support those values. Alice's book displays subtle powers of undermining straight power honed over decades as Gertrude's collaborator; Brion's contribution is bolder, less cautious in its subversion.

You sense in Brion, in his queer generation, more urgency to be out in everyday surroundings. Others were cautiously projecting queerness into public space. Dressing up subversion to look like something as familiar, as anodyne as a recipe—some queer voices would begin testing how far a cookbook could sashay into the realm of the outré.

CANNED CAMP

[1965]

I N NOVEMBER, LOS ANGELES-BASED SHERBOURNE
Press adds a real flamer to its catalog of novelty titles. *The Gay Cook-book* is a collection of recipes written in the voice of a queen, Chef Lou Rand Hogan, a.k.a. Lou Rand, a.k.a. Louis Randall. (Hogan is Chef Lou's maternal family name.) Lou's the author of a gay detective novel, *Rough Trade*. Like James Beard, he's a frustrated stage artiste. Around 1930 he becomes a steward and eventually a cook on luxury Pacific liners, including the *Lurline*, nicknamed the *Queerline*, since so many of the five hundred stewards working any given cruise are gay.

Sherbourne's cover line for Lou's *Cookbook* calls it "The complete compendium of campy cuisine and menus for men . . . or what have you." A tease of the chapter titles, styled in femme cursive, includes "That Old Tired Fish" . . . "Swish Steak" . . . "Oysters, Lobsters, Shrimps . . . And What to Do with Crabs."

The title font is in a girleena shade of rouge, with a caricature of a faggot drawn in the breezy ébauche lines of a department store lingerie ad. He poses before a tuffet-shaped barbecue grill, hip dropped like a model's, foot extended. His chef's toque's been pushed back from his blond fringe bangs. He sports an apron in a stylized floral, tied with a fashion bow; the word "hers" scrolls along the hem. In one hand he holds a barbecue fork, cocked like Audrey Hepburn's opera-length cigarette holder in *Breakfast at Tiffany's*. In the other he dangles a limp, red steak above the grill. The vibe is *heavily* Paul Lynde, the actor who brought his camp, *seriously* gay-coded character Uncle Arthur to national TV in 1965—same year Lou's book appears—on season two of the ABC sitcom *Bewitched*.

On the back cover a bearded, furry-chested girl with a blond bob in a marmalade-colored décolleté chats with a fellow in a turtleneck at a cocktail party.

On visuals alone, the book's a real scream, and Lou's copy shrieks just as loud. He reminds you, for instance, to tell your "butch" (girl, your butcher) how to "grind his meat."

It's a gag, a novelty to stash at the back of a kitchen drawer along with the naughty cocktail napkins. A book to pull out at a party after the second round of Gibsons hits.

There's a much stronger case for the subversive bending of steel-clad gender norms in the books of Marcel Boulestin, James Beard, Michael Field, Genevieve Callahan—authors working in the complicated open secret, who influenced how home cooks folded pleasure into their lives. You don't need a punch-line butch to grind his meat when James Beard's steakburgers are on the table, coded with the sort of transgressive desire that can leave a permanent stain, or when the rustle and clatter of Gen Callahan and Lou Richardson's queer domestic life sounds between the lines.

A lot of Chef Lou's recipes are long and kind of dreary: dull versions of American standards. Despite being peppered with sass, there's not much life in Lou's pages. The parenthetical asides that address you in an array of old-fashioned auntie names—"Not too much there, Gertrude!"; "I'm telling you, Myrtle!"—fade into formula.

It feels canned. For all its suggestiveness about living a mad and lecherous life, *The Gay Cookbook* feels like adapted recipes extracted from a culinary textbook: duck a l'orange, goulash, cheese sauce. I mean, sure: By the early '60s Lou had decades of experience cooking on cruise ships, but I've got a feeling the source for some of the recipes is *The Gold Cook Book* by Louis P. De Gouy, an author Lou adapts in one of his future "Gourmet Shoppe" columns for the *Bay Area Reporter*. Published in 1947, De Gouy's book is a thick bible of more than 2,400 recipes, dull as a Saturday night in Fresno, Agatha.

Judging by the ads it placed in large-circulation papers, Sherbourne Press is betting on straight buyers. An ad in the *San Francisco Examiner* calls Lou "the acknowledged dean of gay gastronomy"—a resonance that would hoist Lou into the same pantheon as Beard, the dean of American cookery. I don't know, though.

Halfway through the '60s, queers have seeped into the culture. In 1963 the *New York Times* drops a front-page exposé on how "sexual inverts colonized three areas of the city." *Life* Magazine goes next with a sprawling coast-to-coast report titled "Homosexuality in America," published in 1964—the year Susan Sontag's "Notes on 'Camp'" appears as an essay in the *Partisan Review*. Before long the *Washington Post* runs a five-part series on homosexuality, followed by a six-part series in the *Denver Post* and a four-part series in the *Chicago Daily News*.

There are reported pieces and moralizing essays in *Time, Look,* and *Playboy*. In their clothes and postures, some of the figures in David Costain's illustrations in *The Gay Cookbook* look plausibly like Bill Eppridge's street photos of young gays for *Life*: the boy in pegged pants and pointy-toe loafers loitering in LA's Pershing Square; the one in skinny jeans and a bulky sweater strolling through Washington Square . . . Costain's campy renderings suggest caricatures from the eye of an outsider looking in.

Most of these stories rehash the prewar trope of the gay fairy, the swish who's unmistakable in public, like the nelly figure on *The Gay Cookbook*. They also identify a more insidious threat: a new crop of homosexuals you can't identify at a glance; queers who dress, talk, and act like straight men. They display no less psychopathology than the fruity boys, but they're invisible, and as such, more menacing than pansies.

It's the *optics* of *The Gay Cookbook* and other popular depictions that both mock queers and seek to contain them; brand them as obvious faggots; bind them to a queeny stereotype in defiance of the normie new generation filling the ranks of the homophile and civil rights movements. I don't think it's accidental that ABC brings Paul Lynde onto one of most-watched programs in America the same year Sherbourne brings out *The Gay Cookbook*, and vice versa. Camp queens, modern rehabs of the swishy character actors of pre-Code Hollywood, are the culture's new-old swirl. I wonder if the old-school queen (and remember, Lynde's Uncle Arthur is nominally straight!) is a comfort to the guardians of the mainstream, a yearning for innocence amid the brooding menace of the strident new masc gays.

Lou's book gets picked up by an imprint of Crown Publishers; they sell an estimated 10,000 to 12,000 copies. *The Gay Cookbook* is a moderate success—a surprise for a book so seemingly ultra-niche.

"Homosexuality shears across the spectrum of American life. It always has," Paul Welch wrote in *Life*'s epochal 1964 report on queer life in the US. "But today, especially in big cities, homosexuals are discarding their furtive ways and openly admitting, even flaunting, their deviation." Forced to accept a degree of visibility, straight power can at least try to sway public perceptions of queers.

That's the frame around Lou's cookbook, the cover, the illustrations. I wonder if the book's editor encouraged Lou to add a little extra swish for the tourists, as it were, the straight audience in the market for gags—same as the literal tourists who packed Finocchio's nightclub in San Francisco to chortle at the comedy drag queens delivering risqué one-liners about blow jobs. Because if you read Lou's food column in *The Advocate* magazine, or his short-lived *B.A.R.* column, "The Gourmet Shoppe," the camp voice softens almost to a whisper.

Lou's columns were for an exclusive readership of gays, i.e. *family*. But in the *Cookbook*, Lou plays it camp for the straights, working it so even homophobes in the cheap seats get a look. Turns out that instead of being coded gay, Lou's cookbook is coded straight.

LOOK, I GET THAT Lou Rand is writing for a niche audience, and if I sound harsh maybe it's because the possibilities for out queer food writers in the 1960s mainstream were exactly, uh . . . zero.

This is what brings me, again and again, to James Beard.

In 1965, when *The Gay Cookbook* arrives, James has just ascended to national fame in the US as the Dean of American Cookery, an epithet published in the *New York Times* a decade before, but by the mid-'60s it finally seems true. His sprawling *The James Beard Cookbook* (with his ghostwriter Isabel Callvert, though acknowledged here), dropped in 1959, first in a cheap Pocket paperback edition that put James's roomy face, beaming above a platter of pork and sauerkraut, in drugstore racks and in newspaper stands across the country.

His image, his friendly hedonist vibe, his brand, as we say in a more media-saturated time, of New York City bachelor with gastronomic passions—they become stamped on the collective psyche. To a nation where the massive, tube-lit, piped-music supermarket with its trophy freezer cases was a triumph, not just for agriculture, manufacturing, and distribution, but for Western capitalism, the American work ethic, and the nuclear patriarchal family structure. Yet there was James, large and smiling, urging us on to cook and eat better. He's the dissonant note that, paradoxically, seems to support the imposed harmony of the dominant system.

But within that dissonance that James is allowed to represent— allowed by magazine editors and book publishers—is a campaign of dissent, a whole arsenal of queer-coded speech, language, and image that James seems on the verge of using to tear through the normative fabric of his time.

And behind that fabric was a big old queen, who lived a private, often joyous life among a close, mostly queer circle of friends.

In his books, his articles for popular magazines like *House & Garden*, James was the subtle yet persistent voice of queer subversion. Though his first books in the early 1940s covered acceptably masculine subjects in American cooking, barbecue, game animals, and cocktails, a decade later James was defying the unspoken prime directive of cookbooks, which is that women, exclusively, were bound to the domestic realm, the three squares a day of home life. And once he was in Americans' home kitchens, James was an advocate for pleasure, not moderation. He snuck in quiche and cassoulet, steak au poivre and French omelets, pan cubano and rolled chocolate gateaus.

Even if James's identity wasn't overtly queer, like Lou Rand, his food, which Americans everywhere cooked, was fucking *queer.*

LES CHEF BROS

[1965]

"MOST OF THE TIME HE WAS THE COMPOSED AND courtly gentleman, perfectly dressed and groomed, almost prim in manner," Claiborne biographer Thomas McNamee writes. "Then suddenly he'd be grabbing some poor dinner guest by the balls and cackling like a maniac."

McNamee wonders, "Did these lurches in behavior correspond to some sudden interior shifts in identity?" Or is it a question of how many vodka gimlets Craig puts away? Because the effort of keeping a tight hold on his non-secret secret takes epic strength, and when the vodka loosens those particular muscles, things can get messy. Balls might be grabbed.

Craig has learned to hide behind Pierre Franey, the French-born former chef of Le Pavillon, New York's temple of French cuisine. Craig is the journalist, his IBM Selectric planted at the corner of his kitchen worktable at East Hampton, watching Pierre cook, deferring to Pierre, recording Pierre's measurements, he movements. He treats Pierre like a ghost contributor, co-opts his recipes and mines his thoughts and his palate for restaurant reviews. (A byline for Pierre won't come till 1976, some fifteen years after their collaboration begins for real.) Pierre gives Craig cover. Hitching himself to a straight male chef is a way for Craig to partially resolve the problem of being a male food writer when a strict gender binary rules food in North America.

His envy is complicated. Surely it's Craig's desire to be French like

Pierre, to have a chef's training like Pierre. To have all the privileges of being straight like Pierre.

On weekends Craig entertains lavishly in East Hampton, where he's had a house built from an architect's prefab kit, on a four-acre plot he bought with royalties from sales of *The New York Times Cook Book*. He orchestrates an elaborate Lucullan clambake on a private island in Gardiners Bay, called a "pique-nique," with the French chefs he's surrounded himself with: Pierre, Roger Fessaguet, Jean Vergnes, even White House chef René Verdon, Jackie Kennedy's favorite—a masc Franco-fantasy, performed in front of a photographer for *Life* magazine. *Pigeons crapaudine* smoking on a vast grill lent by Abercrombie & Fitch . . . Dom Perignon in Baccarat crystal . . . a sinewy, super-hot Jacques Pépin in tiny beach-boy shorts, carving watermelons to fill with a macédoine of fruit . . .

It's like some replay of Craig's Chicago days, only with Beaujolais and stuffed lobster instead of beer and bratwurst; and with straight men instead of gay ex-servicemen: safer, I guess, in Craig's mind. The coding is gay, but it plays out manlier, more pro-grade, less domestic than in his first years at the *Times*. The aspiration Craig communicates is learning to cook like a trained chef, not like an amateur. The home cook attempting to conjure buttery magic gives way to meaty hetero man-chefs trained under the brutal kitchen brigade system. Like Pierre and Jacques, they came from rough country villages, places more like towns in the Mississippi Delta than Paris.

In *The United States of Arugula*, Betty Franey, Pierre's wife, reveals to author David Kamp how Craig, when they first met him, confessed he had a "problem"—his euphemism for liking men. That wasn't a betrayal of the system of queer silence, since the rules of the closet allowed a reasonably passing gay man to make his open secret explicit, as long as he never brought it up again. So when it came to Craig's relationship with his French chef bros, Kamp says, it was understood that his sexuality would have to stay contained within an indestructible crust of don't ask, don't tell.

In one of the most telling photos of Craig I've seen, captured by

Mark Kaufman, he's on a beach, surely on Gardiners Bay—and probably he doesn't even realize he's being shot—where he's standing on a vast drained tideland of sea rocks under a scouring sun, absolutely small, shrunken in the landscape. Completely alone.

Yet there's the warmth of his journalism, like he's figured out how to capture the radiance of his subjects, as he struggles to contain his own. No positive affirmation of queerness seems possible in Craig's world. Instead he stands drunk in the periphery, a shadow watching, recording with his typewriter the work of his French men. He floats alone on a raft in the stone-lined pool he never swims in, sipping a margarita through a straw. He arrives at the Franey holiday party late, already blitzed, swooping in with too-lavish gifts for his goddaughter—a puppy in a red-bowed Champagne bucket—drinking too much, laughing too loud, before being the first to depart, squinting through the windshield to make out the road on his swerving drive home.

THE UNSHOWN BED

[1973]

A LONELY JUNIOR HIGH KID IN A CALIFORNIA SUBURB, I keep a special word locked in my gay little heart.

That word is brioche.

If nobody's home I might slip my mom's copy of *The New York Times Cook Book* from the shelf in the hutch and flip through it. I always stop on page 473 and study the black-and-white picture: a small round table in front of window scrimmed off with sheer drapes filtering a too-harsh daylight. The table's set for two, there's only one chair visible: one solitary, empty chair. *Golden brioche*—the caption—*can be a festive addition to a leisurely weekend breakfast. Here brioche is shown with marmalade and butter, and glasses of orange juice encased in ice.*

"HERE BRIOCHE IS SHOWN." The elegant, ambiguous perfection of the passive voice.

Whose leisurely breakfast? Whose hands will tear at the fluted, shiny-skinned brioche crowned with plumped-out nipples of dough? Or slip these elegant juice glasses out of their crushed-ice sheaths?

The person-less table, the invisible chair, presumably pushed back out of view to allow the photographer in: There is a subjective ambiguity that saps agency from the viewer, casts them as a lonely adolescent voyeur—which I was. A sexual mute living with the secret of my gayness as if it were a second, separate me. Maybe that's why I felt I had this extra palette of senses I could use to disambiguate truth from situations presented without face and in the passive voice: Here brioche is *shown*.

From this one shot I swear I could catch a whiff of bodies just beyond the frame: guys with Sunday-morning shadowbeards waking together in a thrashed bed, about to brace for the cold shock of juice.

I figured out much later that the vignette in my mom's 1961 edition, the image I scoured for its every detail, was staged.

Those brioche weren't photographed in anyone's Manhattan apartment. They were shot in the New York Times studio on West Forty-Third Street near Times Square: a dummy apartment, fake window casting spotlight radiance on a table with borrowed prop plates and glasses. The original story, by Craig Claiborne, appeared in the paper on June 18, 1959, with the headline "Brioche Add Elegance to Week-End Breakfast, Brunch."

Also appearing in the *Times* that day was a story about a jury in London awarding Liberace a libel settlement of £8,000 against the *Daily Mirror* tabloid. A columnist had described him as "The pinnacle of masculine, feminine, and neuter. Everything that he, she, and it can ever want. . . . A deadly, winking, sniggering, snuggling, chromium-plated, scent-impregnated, luminous, quivering, giggling, fruit-flavored, mincing, ice-covered heap of mother love." Which, to me, explains almost everything about Craig's brioche. Explains the mood of fear they exist in; explains the intricate coding applied to them—a cryptography so effective that even a dumb virgin kid, fourteen years and a couple thousand miles away from where that photo was staged, could crack it.

All you needed to be was queer.

Also: It was almost ten years to the day before the Stonewall rebellion when the dual stories of brioche and Liberace arrived to readers in the New York metropolitan area. That Liberace won his case suggests things were starting, slowly, to change. There were situations and places where you needed to be *slightly* less batshit crazy when verbally fag-bashing someone.

Cookbooks from mainstream publishers, though—they were going to hold on to their homophobic ways for as long as they could.

That 1984 edition of *The Alice B. Toklas Cook Book* from Harper &

Row, the one with the untrue anecdote by Simon Michael Bessie about the book's genesis, has a foreword by M. F. K. Fisher that has to be one of the strangest ever to frame a cookbook.

When she's not talking about Janet Flanner's gluttony for Parisian patisserie and M. F. K.'s own regret at not meeting Alice when she had the chance, she talks a lot about how hideous Alice was—"probably one of the ugliest people anyone had ever seen," she writes. About Alice's mustache, "not the kind that old women often grow, but the sturdy kind"; about her "clunky" sandals over thick woolen socks, "almost offensive."

Is it homophobic? She registers extreme dislike for Alice's objectified queer body and the way she dresses it—a body M. F. K. never, she admits, has come face to face with. And yet, she's a grotesque old lesbian in unforgivable footwear. What in the hell was anyone associated with this edition thinking?

To me it's clear. This is part of a broader cultural cliché of queer people, the straight world's distancing of us. Part of a hetero gaze that vilifies, exoticizes, and ridicules queer people for how we dress, style ourselves, move, sound; a gaze that objectifies us as categories, butch, flamboyant, normie, femme. By 1984, the year I began my search for queer voices in cookbooks, the dominant culture was able to rip open Alice's queer coding and press its scattered pieces into a hideous caricature of us as the other.

And then you open the book to find the original scribbly Francis Rose frontispiece, where Alice looks monumental in the classical mode—a Minoan lady in profile, a goddess from the palace at Knossos; serenely peeling pears with enormous hands in the drawing room at Bilignin, in the house in Belley she and Gertrude rented in summer; the sandals that so offended M. F. K.'s eye, with straps crisscrossed above her ankles, disappearing under her caftan. It's a representation of a woman who dwells in mythic space, a kind of bookend to the photo of Alice with Harriet Levy in Fiesole, from that summer in 1907, when Alice and Gertrude wedded one another.

I look at Rose's illustration and think of Monique Truong: "GertrudeStein [as Truong styles her name] thinks it is unfathomably erotic that the food she is about to eat has been washed, pared, kneaded, touched by the hands of her lover." This is the voice of Binh, Gertrude and Alice's semi-fictional live-in cook, gay and from Vietnam, the narrator of Truong's 2003 novel, *The Book of Salt.* "She is overwhelmed by desire when she finds the faint impressions of Miss Toklas's fingerprints decorating the crimped edges of a pie crust."

In 1984, queerness could exist only as the story buried in a dish: a cake, a pot of stew, a salad, or a quiche. Food was a site for concealing the care we couldn't show under the open sky in daylight; for displaying the bruises of our dislocation; for airing the silence we were forced to keep through times of loss, and the joy of finding love and connection. Food was the empty page onto which we wrote our stories, signed with our true names, in letters the haters could not or would almost never make out.

Part Four

THE RICH, AUDACIOUS TANG OF LIBERATION

1973–1986

Our Cast of Rebels, Quiche Eaters, Assholes, Reclaimers, and Counterrevolutionaries

Richard Olney

Lou Rand / Toto LeGrand

The Members of Sha'ar Zahav Synagogue

Truman Capote

Bruce Feirstein

Craig Claiborne

Ernest Matthew Mickler

Plus
Andy Warhol! Simone Beck! Sandor Katz! Iliana Regan! Dorothy Allison! The B-52s! Vito Russo! Lily Tomlin! Thom Gunn!

RICHARD'S DIRTY SALAD

[1973]

THE LUNCH TABLE SITS IN THE HALF-SHADE OF AN arbor, where filtered sunshine glances over glasses half-filled with pale, green-gold wine. Richard Olney is standing, spooning soufflé puddings onto plates. Seated next to him is Simone "Simca" Beck, Julia Child's collaborator on *Mastering the Art of French Cooking*. She's a wiry, genial, upper-middle-class Frenchwoman of about seventy, peering over her sunglasses, her blond hair set in loose curls, a string of pearls above a light sweater, a second sweater slung around her shoulders like a cape.

Richard has a ruddy tan and a light veneer of hair on his chest and forearms. He's in a short-sleeved shirt of some peach-nectar shade of oxidized pink, hiked up and tied at his belly button. Below that, a pair of white bikini briefs. A fat bulge of scrotum, soft penile shadow—they're a foot from Simca's face. She has her head down as if to focus her eyes on the pudding. Her gaze appears riveted to Richard's crotch, though, with an expression more curious than freaked.

This isn't some special show for Simca—this is how Richard receives his guests in warm weather, in cheap underpants and almost nothing else. For first-timers (especially straight ones) he might throw on a shirt, tied at the waist, as here, to crop it high; or unbuttoned, which is how he wears it when Alice Waters makes her first walk up the goat path. She notes the kitchen towels at his waist (she calls it a "skimpy bathing suit") and a worn pair of espadrilles.

He appears like some ancient lustful nature spirit, a silenus concealing his goat's horns and tail, welcoming the unsuspecting under the dappled arbor, around the table with the linens and the silver and the correct little bubble-shaped glasses for the Riesling.

This is who Richard is, how he blurs the line between gay performance and culinary performance; a baring, as it were, of a new domestic identity that also feels ancient. It's the forward edge of queer food in the heady years after Stonewall and the liberation consciousness—the public openness—that has churned and swirled in its wake.

Granted, at least part of Richard's audience (we don't see who else is at the table) is at ease with the quirks and peccadilloes of artists, queers, and the unorthodox. Unlike Julia, Simca seems perfectly chill around men who step outside the straight world's rules for life in the gay open secret. (Simca's longtime assistant Michael James, a young gay American chef who dies in 1993 from AIDS complications, lives transparent in his sexuality.)

How can we look on those puddings as anything other than part of the performance? I'm sure they're Richard's *soufflés à la suissesse*, delicate savory custards flavored with Parmesan, baked in one large savarin mold or individual ramekins as in this picture, so rich and fragile they've flopped half over on the plates. You cook them twice, first poached in molds in a bain-marie, then teased out and baked with cream till they swell up and gratinée, a technique for achieving intensity through delay and resurrection, a kind of culinary edging. To serve, you spoon some rich sauce around them: a cream-enriched bechamel flavored with mushrooms, or sorrel, or both. There is no hedging, no pulling back. No sauce on the side.

This is cooking as a process of stoking desire, cooking as a disciplined gesture of patient teasing until the critical moment of release. He explores menus as pleasure narratives, exercises in keeping the palate "fresh, teased, surprised, excited," he writes. "The moment there is danger of fatigue, it must be astonished, or soothed into greater anticipation, until the sublime moment of release . . . "

Richard affirms the nature of cooking as sensuality, an articulation of pleasure. He forms this language using the traditional culinary vocabulary of France. He rescues French cooking from the sad and compromised internationalized thing it had become by 1973; rescues it from the deeply held idea in the English-speaking world that you can master the art of French cooking out of a shopping cart of industrial foodstuffs sourced in suburban supermarkets. Richard roots his cuisine to the garden: the herbs and mushrooms he's foraged on the hillside high above the arbored terrace, the cream and butter produced in the region where he is; the sorrel, salad greens, and artichokes from the cultivated rows in his garden.

He roots it in the bikini bulge on display for his guests, a whole relief map of desire in the bumps and curves and shadows. It's an assertion of Richard's absolute faith in the sensuality James Baldwin talks about in *The Fire Next Time*, where he says to be sensual "is to respect and rejoice in the force of life, of life itself, and to be *present* in all that one does, from the effort of loving to the breaking of bread." Surely this is *the* lesson from Saturday Night Function; surely it's become part of Richard, or was always part of him and now has now found its explicit form. On that terrace, he is *present* in his semi-nakedness in a way that might make even Jimmy momentarily speechless, peeping over his sunglasses like Simca. Richard is out there, baby, breaking that bread.

He's reclaiming French cooking for his generation; making it new, paradoxically, by reviving ancient ways; embracing sensuality with such commitment that to modern orthodox sensibilities can only seem dangerously, transgressively queer.

In his study of French gastronomy, Richard wallows in the forbidden.

He beguiles an elderly aristocratic French lady to eat the *pieds et paquets*, earthy specialty of Marseille, lamb's trotters braised with stuffed mutton tripe. The lady adores this dish, but considers it "dirty," low-class—she would never serve it at her own table, but conspires with Richard to eat it at his, and presumably offer small details as she recalls it, in Solliés, castigated as "backward" and "inbred" by inhabitants of surrounding towns. Richard's status is marginal—queer in every respect—but he uses it to build his storehouse of pleasure.

Much of what he knows about the rustic cooking of France—

women's cooking, *le vraie cuisine de bonne femme*—he's charmed from
men who make their living with skill and muscle. "Masons, carpenters,
truck drivers, plumbers, blacksmiths," he says, "with whom I have been
in contact over the years as I consolidate one corner of the house or
another." He learns from a couple of *Ardèchois* if the tripe and potato
pots-au-four they recall from mothers and grandmothers contained
green olives or black; a calf's foot or pig's trotters. He seduces them for
details of past succulence.

The intimate knowledge can flow the other way: Workmen catch a
whiff from Richard's pots, and it sparks a memory of something in their
past, a rabbit civet or snails *a la suçarelle.* They ask him to jot down recipes they take to their wives, who no longer cook the old dishes in the
old ways, in the hope that Richard's formulas might spark a renewal
in them. (Would they cook Richard's recipes, though, these wives?
Wouldn't they be pissed? Indignant about their husbands praising the
food of this *célibataire Américain,* usurping their kitchen primacy and
bewitching their men?)

Richard's cooking becomes an engine of yearning in a dynamic of
triangulated desire, an audacious appropriation of something older
even than nineteenth-century *cuisine de bonne femme.*

On this ancient goat-worn hillside, Richard has morphed before our
eyes into some pure queer spirit.

Skim American cookbooks from the middle-'70s and you imagine salads as static plates of embalmed produce, or dank hippie health
bowls of sprouts, raisins, carrot shreds wet with miso and tamari.

Here's a paperback randomly pulled from a stack of seventies cookbooks on my shelf, *Craig Claiborne's Favorites from the New York Times,
Volume 3,* from 1977. On page 42 you find "Tomato and Heart of Palm
Salad," with Craig's call for "6 to 8 red, ripe, firm tomatoes, about
3 pounds," and "2 14-ounce cans heart of palm." He has you make a
dressing from red wine vinegar and olive oil, mustard powder, sugar,
garlic, water (as if vegetables from cans weren't already watery) and
spoon this over. What are you likely to get? A soppy platter of fanned-
out slices sure to strike you as weirdly plastic, suffering from a kind

of disassociation: tough-skinned fruit from thousands of miles away, probably, and metallic palm slices from thousands further. (Craig suggests it as a side for feijoada, recipe given.) Craig's salad must be one of the unsexiest things ever attributed to Brazil.

Now look at Richard Olney's salad manifesto, from his 1974 book, *Simple French Food.*

IMPROMPTU COMPOSED SALAD
(Salade Canaille) . . .

. . . One need not . . . respect any of the endless and precisely defined classical recipes for composed salads (Niçoise, Waldorf . . . and so forth interminably) to be struck with the puerility of such a pastime and to realize how much more valuable and exciting is the imaginative and playful, self-renewing invention of a giant composed salad, never once repeated, its composition dictated by the materials at hand . . .

Richard's five-page "recipe" is a detailed hypothetical for early in summer, probably: yellow potatoes cooked and cooled under white wine; sweet peppers grilled on the coals, if you can; artichokes pared to the heart and boiled until just done. You slice garlic into a salad bowl, pound it with a pestle, add vinegar, olive oil, and the juices you collected from the roasted peppers. Add sweet, tender leaves of lettuce, plus purslane or arugula, plus basil leaves and flowers. Drop in small, tender green beans you've blanched but not shocked (do *not* dull their sweetness with unnecessary water!); cubes or a julienne of cold leftover pot-au-feu meat trimmed of fat; wedges of tomatoes, sharp-tasting hyssop leaves, peppery nasturtium flowers you've collected (with a few buds and leaves), quartered eggs, hard-cooked but with the yolks still a moist yellow-orange.

You toss this at table, first arranging it with an exacting look of carelessness: greens mounded atop the crossed salad fork and spoon, suspended above the vinaigrette, with the meat and the flowers and the bright or pale vegetal things scattered as if the breeze had blown them there, and presenting it like this for your guests to see. Then, still at the table, you toss by holding fork and spoon with firm authority, but with a definite slackness to keep the tender or fragile things from being crushed, and to keep the pile of leaves and petals light and airy. If you can't manage that, Richard says, you must use your hands, working gently but purposefully "to arrive at a loose but intimate intermingling of elements."

But as the three pages of description that precede this template make clear, Richard's "impromptu" salad of meticulous thought and planning—a composition in the most rigorous sense—is a cosmology, a dive into the nature of salad itself. Of salad as *essence*; as *practice*, not a thing or a promise of health or a squeaky-clean colon: of salad as a ritual for discovering and holding your place in the universe.

> . . . Given the fanciful but far from frivolous presence of flowers and a sufficient variety of green things, presented in a vast, wide ceramic or earthenware vessel (you need the space for easy tossing and the large surface for decorative effect), nothing in the entire repertory of food possesses the same startling, vibrant visual immediacy—the same fresh and casual beauty . . .

A kinetic performance of pleasure. Finding ecstasy where the possibility of it exists, no matter how small or how camouflaged the way in.

> . . . It is a concentrated, pulsating landscape of garden essences and must absolutely be tossed at table, for, no matter how delicious, the visual explosion of joy, mixing intricately and lastingly with your guests' memories of mingled flavors, adds a dimension . . .

A staging of deviance; riding the queer vibes that pulse and ripple through the universe.

> . . . This salad, in the seasonal round of my own life, symbolizes the happiest time of the year—that which is lived

almost entirely out of doors with the table set daily on the
terrace in the shade of a grape arbor, the sparkling play of
light heightening the effect of the table display of variegated
greens and bright-colored punctuations . . .

A gesture of rebellion; of archness, perversity. The art of flaunting.

To baptize this kind of salad canaille, underlining the French
affection for the delinquent and the demi-monde, is to suggest a quality of refreshing vitality allied to insolence—a
certain flaunting refusal to respect accepted formulas.

The word *canaille*, meaning "rascally," is kind of toothless and jejune in
modern French, but its roots are savage. It's from the Italian *canaglia*,
indicating a disreputable gang, a bunch of goons. That was from the Latin
canalia, a literal pack of dogs. But, like an aging hound, *canalia* eventually
lost its bite. And when it showed up in France as *canaille*, it still carried
"dishonest" or "immoral," but had mellowed out considerably to end up
"raffish." In context, Richard's choice of the word seems to taint canaille
with a sleazier cast than the sticky-sweet faux-innocence of "naughty."
His description for Salade Canaille that embraces "delinquent"; that adds
"insolence," and nods to the "demi-monde," mapping this dish definitively on the fringes of decency—Richard is signaling a meaning closer
to canaille's unsavory, pejorative past: dirty—a salad at the opposite pole
from Craig's source-blind tomatoes and sexless palm hearts.

Can we conceive of a salad with the musty tang of Genet? One that
roots us, with its restless and unstable elements, to a specific landscape? Can we see queer food as a performance of reclaiming space?

AT THE SAME TIME that Richard is reclaiming physical and cultural
landscapes radically unlike the ones he knew as a boy in Iowa, others
are reclaiming closer worlds.

The back-to-the-land movement is sweeping up seasoned hippies and fresh-eyed kids by the VW vanload, restless seekers itching to leave New York and San Francisco and feel the salt of honest sweat on their skin. A parallel move after Stonewall sends dykes and fags onto collective farms and into lone-wolf homesteads, living arrangements where a feminist, anti-capitalist ethos takes root. The romance for a countryside imagined as a place where homophobia had not taken root; the perennial non-Indigenous romance in North America for a new world built on righteous principles, even queer ones based on radical forms of love and equality—these work their way into food.

Inside homesteader tents and cabins, in shared kitchens fed by cooperative gardens and fields, a new kind of domestic culture rises. There's a sense that *nature* is queer, standing outside the patriarchy and its institutions. The capitalist system is a savaging of Goddess Earth: caging Her children and snatching Her gifts, selling them off for the greed of shareholders in that desert called America.

On a continent where Indigenous two-spirits and third-genders find shamanic power in culture-keeping; where Walt Whitman sang of his love for Union soldier boys as ecstatic connection, a tribe of faggots and faeries rediscovers a long-lost forest world of cosmic queer power and possibility.

"I built my little house alone," a contributor with the simple byline Olaf writes in country queer magazine *RFD* at about the same time half-naked Richard is serving his souffléd pudding to Simca on the terrace. "I walked alone in the woods, and fell asleep each night to the sound of whippoorwills. I awakened to the sounds of birds and chipmunks. I danced naked in hot summer rainstorms and awoke with frost on my beard in November. . . . The birds began to fly to me, the deer weren't bothered by me when I watched them browse. . . . I lacked only peacocks and a pale, white unicorn."

Country dykes and faggots munch wood-stove millet and lentil loaves that get their husky tang from wild-soured milk, sipping wild-foraged ginseng brew; eating according to the infinite calibrations in the movement of the stars and the seasons—under the same canopy where faeries stir, pale white unicorns graze, the elements of *salade canaille* grow, and queer love rises. They have reclaimed their status as spiritual intermediaries between nature and personkind, uniquely blessed to heal the world, with food and desire as balm and medicine.

This culture of faeries and queer communards mentors Sandor Katz, author, teacher, and self-described fermentation revivalist. In 1993, Sandor moves from New York City to a Radical Faerie commune in rural Tennessee. In *Fermentation as Metaphor*, Sandor celebrates the queerness of ambient microorganisms, which operate in ways contrary to the so-called purity of reductive, human-imposed systems—the kind of unnatural divisions that result in concepts like the gender binary. Feminist food and science scholar Stephanie Maroney talks of Sandor's passion for "the shape-shifting queerness of microorganisms through fermentation."

What liberation means—what's possible in the immediate aftermath of Stonewall, when lesbians and gays are re-examining almost every aspect of life through a queer lens—is that food, in the right context, can be imagined as queer.

In their memoir *Burn the Place*, queer chef Iliana Regan, in the midst of battling a string of self-destructive impulses that include rages and addiction, finds peace by returning to the scarred and dusty northern Indiana landscape where their grandfather farmed, a place of no bullshit and little commercial value. But the frogs Iliana forages—gigs, in Midwest vernacular—for their restaurant in Chicago represent wisdom outside of time: lingering spores in the ground, airborne bacteria invisibly drifting—the old forces that free Iliana to embrace who they are, or own the identity they were born with, along with the ground their family still owned but had abandoned. Iliana learns to cook according to the personal narrative they read in the dirt. They find their voice.

Richard finds his in a sensuality attuned to the laws of the universe; a sensuality that serves us a purified taste of humanity.

"The formalization of gastro-sensory pleasure," he says in *Simple French Food*, "must be an essential aspect of the whole life, in which the sensuous-sensual-spiritual elements are so intimately interwoven that the incomplete exploitation of any one can only result in the imperfect opening of a great flower, symbol of the ultimate perfection which is understanding, when all things fall into place."

And that great flower in full bloom—why, it's a big old salad: roots, leaves, flowers, all, in Richard's narrative, having the force of urgency. A "concentrated, pulsating landscape of garden essences," he says in *Simple French Food*. Salad is a work of fingers, softly, simultaneously drumming against multiple receptors: optical, lingual, tactile. It's a work of truth-telling; of dressing only to become naked of everything but the essential.

THE WELCOME TABLE

[1973]

JESSICA B. HARRIS IS A TWENTY-FIVE-YEAR-OLD PROFESSOR of French at Queens College in New York, traveling in Provence with her boyfriend, Sam Floyd. Sam is a friend of James Baldwin.

At Jimmy's house in Saint-Paul-de-Vence, above Nice, Harris sits at the outdoor table sheltering under cedars and the rough slats of an arbor. Jimmy appears, walking from his secluded writing studio at the rear of the tall old structure under a roof of sun-bleached tile. Bernard Hassell, still beautiful, is Jimmy's literal gatekeeper. He lives in the caretaker's cottage at the entrance to the property and greets visitors, of which there are many: Miles Davis and Cicely Tyson, Josephine Baker, Nina Simone, Harry and Julie Belafonte, and a constant stream of young writers eager to meet their idol.

Jimmy's cook is a local woman, Valerie Sordello, "la mama." She does the marketing, then rides to Jimmy's house on her scooter, wearing sunglasses that were a gift from Miles.

Today she's prepared one of her specialties: *soupe au pistou*, with its mosaic of vegetables and a spoonful of pistou, eastern Provence's cousin to Genoese pesto, stirred through the broth, triggering a fragrance bomb of garlic and basil.

Underneath the rough slats of cedar is what Jimmy calls the Welcome Table. The queerness of this setting is inescapable. From his state of necessary exile—now a quarter of a century old, despite a rambling life that's brought him back to the States for stretches—Jimmy shares meals around a table where the borders of gender, race, and sexuality fade into irrelevance. He disidentifies with "gay." He eases instead, at Saint-Paul-de-Vence, into a site of queerness some locals calls "the house of sin." Jimmy celebrates a state of androgyny he views as universal. His table sits outside the American idea of masculinity.

The constantly changing chosen family Jimmy shares his table with are the blood kin of a different sort than genetic: the blood of communion; of a common language beyond what Jimmy called the "useless vocabulary" of the dominant world.

Valerie's rich, fragrant soup is part of that common language. It nurtures the ongoing queer project of fashioning identity, a stitch in the cloth of intentional kinship. Jimmy's Welcome Table is a coalescence. What began in the realm of the profane, the years of Saturday Night Function, has found a site of sanctification under the arbor. Where Richard learned the art of queer performance at Function, Jimmy learned to erase lines of difference.

The soup is fucking delicious. Every spoonful.

LEARNING TO COOK FROM MOTHER

[1974]

LOU RAND KICKS OFF HIS NEW COLUMN IN THE SAN Francisco *Bay Area Reporter,* "The Golden Age of Queens," under a pen name: Toto Le Grand. He's sixty-four.

Young queers are flocking to the city. A 1976 estimate puts the number of LGBT residents in San Francisco at 150,000, nearly one in three adults. And most, as Toto Le Grand might put it, don't know shit: have no inkling of queer history, don't want to listen to their gay aunties and daddies talk about the before times.

Mother, as Toto refers to herself, has been around—was born near Bakersfield in 1910, and spent their teens and early twenties toggling between SF and LA, as a runner boy for gin bootleggers; having lots of sex for money, fun, or both.

Mother is weary now.

She means to use "The Golden Age of Queens" to make all these young dumb studs at the disco learn something, and has no time to waste. Her debut begins with a scorching, archly punctuated *read:*

> To hell with your modern "gay" bars (which aren't . . .); the mad, modern cruising (but where . . .); the "anything goes" Baths (where there are no REAL men, and who wants cat meat . . . ?) . . . Yes, 'twas better back then, when there were MEN! Men who treated a "girl" like a lady. And paid for it. Brought their own booze, and appreciated the service. A "trick" was for a whole weekend, or 48 hours, or lon-

ger. Many even lasted out the year, possibly the next, too. And, you stayed at home, and cooked and drank a little, and loved, and lived! Nowadays, it's to the Baths for 6 quick "ki-ki" numbers with other fags . . .

She's saying that cooking should be central to any queer life, the way it used to be. She's saying that the project of constructing gay domestic life is the work of generations, and that what these dizzy, dick-hungry post-Stonewall boys lack is the wisdom of elders. Remembered stories, shared tastes, rituals of connection—these are things the movement needs, in 1974, to build a culture.

In this kickoff and the columns that follow, Lou describes in detail how to master three dishes for a quiet little dinner party: green salad, fried chicken, risotto Milanese. It's a practical plea to younger gays to define themselves on their own terms; to build a queer new world of the home that's also a reclaiming of something old. He's reminding the Stonewall kids that even revolutionaries need to eat. Even radicals need to throw a dinner party now and then.

He doesn't have much time to spread the message. He dies in 1976. Until then, Mother does what she can. But you know what children are these days.

FRESS, DARLING

[1977]

A BUNCH OF LESBIANS AND GAYS IN THEIR TWENTIES and thirties form a queer synagogue in San Francisco. They name it Sha'ar Zahav, Hebrew for "Golden Gate," and dedicate it to a liberated, progressive practice of Judaism. A drafting committee produces a Friday night prayer book and Passover Haggadah wiped of sexist, militaristic language. They de-gender the Torah, scrub it as best they can of patriarchal, heterosexist framing. They riff for laughs: "Bless you, She, our almighty but nonaggressive Concept, who creates the crust of the quiche."

Months later, in a borrowed church basement during the High Holy Days, Sha'ar Zahav's members flip the gender roles that had always been unflippable. At the Rosh Hashanah seder, the women sound the shofar and say the blessings, while the men, who've done all the cooking, spread a feast of straight-up Ashkenazi holiday dishes: brisket, kugel, challah, apples with honey—re-created recipes from Jewish cookbooks every bubbe has on her shelf, or zealously guards on the stained index cards she keeps tucked away. Even Harvey Milk, fiercely secular, shows up to nosh and schmooze, weeks before his death at the gun of an ex-colleague on the Board of Supervisors.

It tastes just about like Rosh Hashanah always has. I imagine that's bittersweet for some, nostalgic flashes of home and blood family, the mothers and bubbes who cooked them first—but also reminders of banishment from those things for being queer and out; all the complicated feelings of exile: relief, pain, sadness, joy; and all the customary flavors of the holiday. But these briskets simmered with prunes and Lipton onion soup mix, these poppyseed kugels and marble cakes: They're queer versions of their prior selves, thanks to an alchemy of intention and circumstance.

The inversion of *men* handing round the gefilte fish; a *male* voice noodging a table to finish the carrot-raisin tzimmes because we are not doing leftovers, darling—there's the thrill of subversion, the joy of a new culture being born to replace one from an expired, intolerant past. Surely the presence of gay city supervisor Harvey Milk, only weeks before his assassination, helps to make it feel audacious, the snatching back of a promised heirloom unjustly locked away.

It makes it taste like liberation.

TRUMAN SERVES LUNCH

[1978]

T RUMAN CAPOTE LIFTS IT FOR ANDY WARHOL'S CAM-
era, a real beauty of a quiche: three inches high, with a fluted crust
and a pale surface roughly set with something darker, maybe spinach.
Truman holds it on a china pedestal stand for the camera, actually *bears*
it like one of the magi with a coffer he's hauled across the desert only
it's a quiche he probably carried from La Côte Basque on his lap in a
taxi. He presents it to Andy's lens like it's a gift. Or maybe a cypher to
decode. A message baked in a crust.

Truman poses with it in his apartment high above the East River.
He has on a floppy-collar shirt and cinch-waist jumpsuit; his head's
bare, spread with strands of hair as fine and rare as a baby's. He looks
the way Truman never does in the open—no huge tinted glasses, no
scarf or white fedora like at Studio 54; no mask of peevishness like he
puts on for Dick Cavett. Here in the apartment it's just Truman.

Armed with nothing but the quiche.

In another shot we see the quiche alone, sans Truman. It casts a sad
shadow on the dining table's paisley cloth, in an apartment that feels
stuffy and irrelevant: a toleware tray painted with fussy flowers, the
shadow of a scalloped window shade devouring a wall, tissue-paper
poppies drooping from a tarnished metal vase.

In other shots on Warhol's contact sheet, Truman looks sapped
and weary—over it. He's about to turn fifty-four in September 1978
(he would die a month short of sixty). The late '70s are difficult for
Truman. Perhaps he'd been drinking when Andy shows up, or feeling

the effects of the tranquilizers or the anti-alcoholism drug Antabuse, which causes agonizing nausea if you slip and take a drink. Maybe he hasn't had enough sleep.

He hasn't written anything the critics liked since 1965's *In Cold Blood*—hasn't published *anything* substantial, actually. He lost his closest friends when they felt he'd savaged them in an excerpt, published three years earlier in *Esquire*, of his long-delayed novel, *Answered Prayers.*

But in this one second, this pause before Truman takes the quiche to the kitchen and cut it with a sloppy knife into curdled-looking pieces for lunch with Andy, and probably *Interview* editor Bob Colacello, Truman looks radiant. There's something perfect about the quiche at the start of the narrative—a quiche that can make even Truman Capote smile in the most genuine and unaffected way. Something that signals joy and connection, even if only for a flash, about being queer and alive.

Because quiche is the thing: our food of queer reclaiming.

IT BEGINS LIFE AS THIS NON-QUEER THING: a savory French tart, not particularly elegant in France but suffused with this American cultural veneration of Paris in particular. But as the decades fall, quiche becomes a matrix for queer identity, fracturing into all these specific expressions. By around 1980, quiche is super-gay.

> *Our code and our power, in a solitary syllable en Français: quiche. The word in the mouth, a sharpness up front, smoothing into a frictionless vowel, with a landing in velour, an easing in: keeeessshhhhh.*

Meanwhile, in the straight world of power, quiche has become a vector of anxiety.

> *In his book published in the fifth century CE, Apicius gives a recipe for tyropatina, honey-sweetened custard. Did the ancient*

Romans evolve the process of thickening milk with eggs over fire that would become the heart of quiche, or was the knowledge a spoil of some culture with more fluidity, a society more matriarchal than Rome's? After all, coaxing fluid into a semi-solid thing is a work of magic, a celebration of liminality, harnessing heat and time to make liquid resemble curd cheese or soft flesh. It subverts a material duality assumed to be fixed—a queer sort of alchemy.

Richard Olney, writing in 1979 for the journal *Petits Propos Culi-naires* under essentially a drag nom de plume, Tante Ursule (Aunt Ursula), runs his finger around it: "In the past a quiche was rolled out bread dough garnished usually with lightly fried pieces of green bacon [unsmoked belly meat], smeared with cream or a cream and egg mix and baked, much the same concept as that of a pizza."

It sucks up all the joys and anxieties of queer life and serves them back: class struggle in the LGBT community, racism, ghettoization.

It's a francophone rendering of the German *Kuchen*, meaning cake, but also the name of a flan-like custard. Below quiche's simple surface there's a complex historical layering, the vicissitudes of its homeland, Lorraine. Within it lurk the ambitions of those who would control the region's wealth and occupy its strategic location at the crossroads of temporal power—given to France in full by 1648; in 1737 transferred to ex-King of Poland Stanislaus Lesczinska, then repossessed by France in 1766 when Lesczinska dies. After 1871 Lorraine becomes a duchy with an independent existence in Germany, and after that, well—it's at the heart of twentieth-century European conflict, *twice*: a witness to shelling, invasion, displacement, murder, starvation.

Straight power stuffs toaster waffles and Egg McMuffins in your face and you think it's what you deserve. In quiche we queers find an accessory to our identities, our realized selves, cloaked in the collective we. Quiche is Paris, Milan. Miss Diana Ross as Tracy

Chambers in Mahogany, hitting a runway pose in plum-colored
silk charmeuse. Quiche is Champagne brunch: a mouthful of
Moët, a forkful of quiche, and a sip of Chandon: rinse and repeat.

Kuchen-quiche would have stayed relatively the same over time, fixed to the land by tradition. The modern form was unknown in Lorraine in the 1500s. It included no cheese or applewood-smoked bacon; it was likely to contain cream, onions, and white poppy seeds. It was definitely not contained in pâte brisée casing.

Each of us has navigated a difficult pathway to brunch—to
quiche. Each of us gets here, though. Though we eat a thousand
different quiches in a thousand separate dining rooms, we eat
together. No matter what they say about us—what they do to
us—here we quiche.

Its communal nature was set from the start. Every quiche was a collective project involving a baker and his oven, a cheese maker with her thick sweet cream. And the eating of it was a shared undertaking too, part of a celebration. Think of those sixteenth-century paintings of peasant weddings by Pieter Breughel: feast-day food, hauled in on a board from the baker's by thick village boys. Revelers get wasted on strong beer. Players blow their shepherd pipes. Couples dance. Men pop unembarrassed boners that strain their codpieces. But kuchen-quiche was noble food for *jours maigres*, meatless days dictated by the Christian calendar; still, a food of celebration, however sober it was supposed to be, a shared taste of pleasure, fuel for thrashing in barn or bed.

Quiche is custard, and custard is collectivism in action.

Its collective production and communal dimensions survive the centuries, at least in rural places. British food writer Elizabeth David, driving through the hawthorn-scented spring countryside southwest of Strasbourg in about 1970, comes across a beauty measuring fifteen inches across, made by three women who run a *pension*. But by then, even away from cities, quiche has become delicate, lighter, more refined: "the filling risen like a soufflé," David writes, "supported only by the thinnest layer of pastry."

> *Quiche is an offering, a key to a new identity, handed to us in a silk-lined box. Straight people devour a cruller from a bag and slurp coffee from a paper cup on the subway, no thought to the ride. We lift forkfuls of quiche from restaurant china to a Sunday soundtrack of Sylvester slow grinds.*

Formerly humble quiche picks up a luxury aura that eventually lands it on gay and lesbian buffets: a charisma known as *eleganza*, the power to give life.

UNLESS YOU SPENT SOME TIME in France before World War II or read French cookbooks, chances are the word "quiche" would have thrown up a blank. But in 1948, newspaper readers in dozens of US cities would have found a nearly identical recipe for quiche Lorraine in their local dailies.

It happens by design.

At Manhattan's Waldorf-Astoria, during a national convention, the imperious banquet manager, Claudius Philippe, walks through the hotel's vast basement kitchens more than a hundred food editors, all women. "Avenues of heavy-duty ranges polished to a satiny finish stood ready for service," reports a clearly awestruck Harriet Cooke of the *Buffalo News*.

After the tour, Philippe leads them to a buffet of Champagne, ladyfingers, and something called "quiche," open tarts "without a top crust," notes Wilma Phillips Stewart in the *Des Moines Register*, with three different fillings, one with bacon and Swiss cheese (i.e., Lorraine). Baked in pie plates and cut in small wedges, they were "something that most men would enjoy," Stewart says.

Philippe passes out recipes scaled for home cooks, and in coming weeks the Waldorf's formula for quiche appears on women's pages across the nation. At a time when New York City hopes to lure back tourists after the disruptions of war, it's a public relations win, a reminder of the magnificence right there for the gawking at the Waldorf and other gilded sites in Manhattan.

From far away, say a farmhouse in a clapboard village like the one that formed Richard Olney, magic ripples through the unpronounceable *quiche*.

THE WORD "HOMOSEXUAL" arrives in the US at almost exactly the same moment the neologism "brunch" does. Though the latter was probably squeezed together by university students in England, "brunch" officially appears for the first time in 1895, in the British periodical *Hunter's Weekly*. Meanwhile, according to historian Jonathan Ned Katz, the first print sighting of "homosexual" in the US is in a Chicago medical journal of 1892.

An early mention of quiche in the *New York Times* comes via reporting from an organized wine tasting in London in 1931. Author Charles A. Selden characterizes the quiche served with a Riesling as "incelibate," by which I think he means sexy; offering a mouthfeel creamy and slippery enough to feel transgressive.

In the decades after World War II, Sunday brunch becomes queer church.

A 1941 story in the *New York Times* on how to throw a party suggests the queer takeover of brunch was already under way even before the war. Author Susan Sheridan refuses to use the word ("This column hopes that word 'brunch' will pass into oblivion soon . . . "), but offers plenty of subtext even without it. Sheridan writes, "An older lady we know, who lives alone, started having these [Saturday or Sunday late] breakfasts last winter. . . . She soon found herself playing to a full house, with everyone bringing someone 'who lived alone.'"

Those inverted commas say what Sheridan can't. Brunch is queer to its bones, boozy comfort for all those poor, lonely bachelors and single women shackled to their jobs.

By the late 1960s more and more Americans are doing brunch, but it *belongs* to the gays. It has cheap booze, hollandaise, quiche. It stretches the cruising hour well into Sunday morning and blesses—formalizes—the Sunday afternoon hookup, or aspirations for one.

It challenges rules of straightness's devising, heterosexuality's "economically useful and politically conservative" system of coupling and child-rearing, Foucault says; capitalism's imperative that workers lead strictly regulated lives so they'll show up at offices and factories sober, non-hungover, and on time; to obey capitalism's imperative to maximize production.

But the bottomless Bellini brunch?

Brunch is a feeder of Foucault's "fruitless pleasures," an enabler of queerdom's "genitally centered sexuality" unsanctified by procreation. Cruising over crab cakes Benedict becomes an identity—"a way of living time outside the linear progress of history," as writer Kevin Brazil puts it, "and the organic continuity of biological reproduction." With the incelibate creaminess of quiche fresh on our tongues, we are fortified for the long Sunday ahead. We are ready to fuck up the linear progress of history and maybe, while we're at it, to fuck up capitalism, too.

In San Francisco, the rise and fall of quiche corresponds to the post-Stonewall project of creating the gay citadel—a safe, almost self-contained village of queer-owned businesses: the gay ghetto.

A FRACTURED TIMELINE
OF QUICHE

This is the part in the story where queer food becomes a character, like Herman, Alice, or Jimmy. The part where a critical mass of societal deviants raises a totem. Confident enough to let it lurch off into the straight world to charm, annoy, or strike fear in the hearts of our oppressors. It's taken us long enough to get here, the part where food becomes embodied, a queer presence moving through the world, free of camouflage.

[1971]

Jackson's, a piano bar, converts to a brunch restaurant on Sundays, placing ads in queer weeklies promising the city's finest quiche Lorraine.

[1972]

A 1972 report on the Butch Brunch party notes the tastiness of the quiche Lorraine served before the start of a trio of contests: leather, cowboy, and hot pants. Quiche becomes a draw for daytime fundraisers, fortification for spectacles devoted to harnesses, boots, and butts.

[1979 . . .]

The Duo restaurant opens near the corner of Eighteenth Street and Castro, physical and spiritual heart of SF's gayborhood. It's got bistro looks, a new style for the Castro, posh and shiny, but with the same old quiche served at leather bashes in the faux-garage and bunkhouse bars. "Lorraine" has been decoupled from quiche; it's going extinct. Maybe it rings too femme for the Castro's growing monoculture of masc men in Levis and Freddie Mercury daddy-staches. Up the street from the Cafe, 6 a.m. Saturdays and Sundays at the Balcony, a bar packed with boys still coked up, bennied, and poppered, spins the new track from Gloria Gaynor, "I Will Survive," which might as well double as an anthem for quiche.

[. . .]

Twentysomething lesbian Joni Gold self-publishes a hand-lettered illustrated recipe booklet, *Their Friends Were Young and Gay: A Fairy Tale in Food*. It's about life at the table with her partner, Barbara King, through a series of cheap SF apartments, including one that looks down onto the corner of Castro and Seventeenth. This is the inspiration for Joni's "Castro Corner Quiche," featuring a veg-oil crust and a custard baked with sliced onions and "any handy vegetables," Joni says. It's a recipe about permissiveness: making it your own, using what you have, accepting it the way it turns out—a recipe for a generation that had to fight myriad obstacles to come out. Quiche has become a canvas for self-expression and improvisation, a dish of variable flavors, a range of affinities, and elastic dimensions.

[. . .]

Near Polk Street, the city's older, more patina'd sexual deviance zone, Our Kitchen opens with a $3.85 weekend quiche and Champagne brunch. The empowerment vibes are heavy—the *our* in Our Kitchen is emphatic, but also exclusive. The logo features a dude in a chef's hat that looks just enough like feathered-shag pornstar Sky Dawson—an avatar both bland and studiously hot, like precision-manicured pubes or the name "Sky." One calculated to invite specific membership, a warning to straight men and *all* women, cis and trans, that they might feel more comfortable at the diner up the street. Black and Asian gays? Latinos judged too dark, too "ethnic," to sip Champagne in *Our Kitchen*? Quiche as the emblem of a cis white gay bougie power class: the flaky-edged, bacon-studded snack of the post–Harvey Milk capitalist takeover of homo mecca.

[*1981*]

Twenty-six-year-old Rick Leed authors a queer cookbook for Gay Sunshine Press, *Dinner for Two*. "My original idea was to write a 'how-to' cookbook for gay men who never learned to cook," Leed says in the introduction. He includes a recipe for quiche with bacon and chopped frozen spinach. Like the other recipes in the book, the quiche is bland, unchallenging, profoundly normie. This is a cookbook for the gayborhood and its white, straight-presenting power class. Even the title, *Dinner for Two*, signals exclusion, keeping gayness a private, privileged affair where street gays, along with flavor, are kept at bay.

[*1985*]

Black drag queen and comic Billi Gordon publishes a cookbook: *You've Had Worse Things in Your Mouth*. Billi's the face of campy drag greeting cards sold at bookshops and gift boutiques in gay enclaves and beyond. She does Mammy drag: Hattie MacDaniel from *Gone with the Wind*, bandanna head wrap and apron, wielding a rolling pin, an ugly cluster of tropes that sparks a protest. Maybe Billi feels she deserves to make a dollar feeding gays the Black stereotypes they can't resist; maybe she feels it's her right to offend. *You've Had Worse Things in Your Mouth* is likewise raucous, shiny, and just too much. It has redeeming edges, though, including the recipe for Quiche Lawanda, a straight-ahead Lorraine plus shallots and mushrooms: quiche with an earthy floor. "They say that real men don't eat quiche," Billi's headnote reads, "but honey please. Real men eat anything, and that's why they're real men." I believe she means *anything*.

[*1980 . . .*]

The album *Wild Planet* by the five-member B-52s, four of whom identify as queer, includes the song "Quiche Lorraine." It's a midtempo
bop with the band's signature sound: slashes of spooky Farfisa organ
lines woven into guitarist Ricky Wilson's angular surf licks. The lyrics
are about a miniature poodle named Quiche, a cute, sassy little thing.
Quiche abandons her owner for a Great Dane, and the song's a scorched
lament for the joy Quiche's absence has killed. Singer Fred Schneider
yowls about joy turning suddenly to pain, a line with bitter prescience.
Five years later Wilson falls to complications brought on by AIDS.
Pain turns real. In 1980, quiche seems capable only of rising on clouds
of queer exuberance, an expressiveness that allows for both vegetarian
earnestness and New Wave camp. But the epidemic to come will sink
everything. Quiche included.

[*. . .*]

San Francisco's International Gay Freedom Day Parade, i.e. Pride,
includes Gays Against Brunch, a small group of anti-capitalist sati-
rists. They march with a sign that reads "Cut the Quiche!".

[*1982*]

In February, as he stumps in the primary for one of California's US
Senate seats, patrician gay gadfly Gore Vidal blasts First Lady Nancy
Reagan by casting her as a brunch-loving Marie Antoinette. To the
poor seeking food stamps and other assistance, he says, Nancy's attitude is, "Let them eat quiche!"

[*. . .*]

In May, Pocket Books publishes *Real Men Don't Eat Quiche: A Guidebook
to All That Is Truly Masculine.*

It's a slim paperback, parts of which have appeared in *Playboy,* by a twenty-six-year-old little-known screenwriter named Bruce Feirstein. The book blows up overnight to become a cultural and political phenomenon. Two years into Ronald Reagan's first term, America rushes to elevate a satirical reader—a joke book for the shitter—that pushes back on the New Left, the sexual revolution, environmentalism, feminism, and fags. Especially fags. Soon it's on the *New York Times* bestseller list.

In interviews, Feirstein denies being homophobic, says some of his friends are gay, but it's like . . . shut up. "Real men don't eat quiche, don't catch rays, don't get *behind* (~rolls eyes~) anything." "Real men don't disco. Real men don't eat brunch." Real men don't live in San Francisco.

Feirstein's list of things "you won't find in a real man's stomach" include quail, pâté, tofu and bean curd (listed separately, as if distinct), and "arugola salad." The missing item, the one thing Fierstein doesn't *need* to spell out of course, is cum.

That this dumbass little book should become a phenomenon feels like an echo of Disco Demolition Night at Comiskey Park in Chicago in 1979, when, under banners proclaiming Disco Sucks, a mob in the thousands riots. A local rock station explodes and burns a pile of dance records, blowing an actual crater in the outfield—a symbolic erasing of the collective soundtrack to gay and Black selfhood. An unleashing of white patriarchy's pent-up fury. Feirstein's dumbass little book gives columnists in dailies across the nation cover for writing homophobic pieces milking reactions from male hair stylists and mocking what they say. Quiche-eating gays are less than: less than fully male, not quite worthy of empathy or respect.

Five months after *Real Men Don't Eat Quiche* appears, Reagan press secretary Larry Speakes fields a question about AIDS in the White House Briefing Room. The questioner, talk radio host Lester Kinsolving, notes the CDC's recent classification of AIDS as an epidemic, with officially more than six hundred cases in the United States. "Over a third of them have died—it's known as the gay plague," Kinsolving says, as reporters in the Briefing Room laugh.

"I don't have it," Speakes says to more laughter. "Do you?" The laughs grow louder.

Kinsolving wants to know if the White House looks at AIDS as a big joke: a redundant question.

Not long after, hard-right antifeminist Phyllis Schlafly sends a quiche to each of the fifty-three US Senators (all but one, Nancy Kassebaum, are men) who have sponsored reintroducing the Equal Rights Amendment six months after it dies. As if to shame them with quiche, perhaps reminding the male senators of their masculinity, and marking all as traitors to Christian patriarchy and the idea that the gender binary must remain firm and unequivocal. (Schlafly's especially worried about women being drafted into military service if the ERA were to pass.) In a statement following the quiche drop, Schlafly refers to the senators as "wimps."

There are two male classes in America: *real* men, who come home to a wife and kids and expect meat for dinner; and quiche eaters, who move to disco, eat jizz, and die in a plague they bring upon themselves.

[. . .]

In a satirical spoof on the Gay Freedom Day Parade, writer Dennis McMillan imagines Gays Against Brunch burning a huge cardboard effigy of a fat quiche slice on a plate.

[*1983* . . .]

B.A.R. reader Bob Hart writes to the paper's editor with a theory about AIDS, a response to something published in a previous issue. Reader Jim Boeger's letter called the CDC's growing evidence that the virus is transmitted sexually or through exposure to blood "a BIG lie," and pushed a conspiracy theory that the government is introducing AIDS into gay populations as genocide. In his sarcastic response, Hart offers an alternate theory, an idea sparked, he says, by the 1982 murders outside Chicago from cyanide-laced Tylenol planted on store shelves. He wonders, "Could that innocent-looking little lady who runs the cafe where we love to brunch be poisoning our quiche?" It's a grim joke that reveals how quiche and brunch have become essential to gay identity. If you're not brunching on quiche you better check yourself, queen. You might not be gay.

[. . .]

Activist and film historian Vito Russo produces a video bit around quiche for his WNYC-TV series about the LGBT community, *Our Time*. The bit is a spoof: Vito reports, evening-news style, outside a gay bar in Cleveland, Ohio, as comedian Lily Tomlin steps from a taxi, in character as the tightly clenched Midwestern housewife and mother, Mrs. Judith Beasley. She's bearing a dish she calls the Quiche of Peace—a gift from the straight world to show support for the queer community. The comedy hangs on Judith's naïve assumption that queers and straights can come together, but she freaks out in the bar, gaping at what people *actually* do in queer spaces. The Quiche of Peace becomes the ironic symbol of an unbridgeable gap. Straight power cannot stomach even the tamest manifestations of queer lust.

Until straight people can accept that fucking is the heart of queerness, allyship is a lie.

In the middle of her passive-aggressive performance of Calumet City nice, Mrs. Judith Beasley realizes that quiche is an emblem of queer difference, which is to say a sign of queer power. In a year when HIV/AIDS is exploding, the implications are deep. Moralizing critics, both gay and straight, have been quick to blame gay promiscuity for the epidemic, instead of a toxic mix of government inaction, systemic racism, corporate greed, antifeminism, and deeply rooted homophobia. With the failed Quiche of Peace, Vito and Lily hint at sex as the true emblem of queer difference, the source of queer power—especially when public opinion has cast gay sex as an evil source of contagion.

Quiche and sex are who we are, though. They are identities we flex.

✳

HOMOPHOBES AND OTHER CRITICS blame AIDS on promiscuity; they say gay men brought AIDS on themselves, and not a dime of government funding should be spent on the problem. Prominent gay moralists, especially those of Randy Shilts and Larry Kramer, tell us the gay party's over. That monogamy and other acts of queer renunciation are the only things that can save us from excruciating illness, not condoms in bathhouses; not a reinvention of sex, or remaking our sites of sexual liberation as places of collective care. Shilts and Kramer would have us believe that the cruising sites themselves are dehumanizing and shameful; that a culture of sensuality is a culture of death. That we don't need some café owner to poison our quiche because we're poisoning ourselves.

"Our promiscuity taught us many things," writes critic and activist Douglas Crimp in 1987, in response to the moralists. "Not only about the pleasures of sex, but about the great multiplicity of those pleasures." The voices of James Baldwin and Richard Olney echo around that line—Jimmy rejoicing in the force of life; Richard describing the great flower of understanding that opens in thrall to pleasure. Hedonism can pull us deeper into our own humanity, and quiche—food of queer resilience and queer power—is fuel for the journey.

"Having learned to support and grieve for our lovers and friends," Crimp writes as a kicker, describing a queer response to AIDS built around safe sex and community education after the epidemic's initial years of panic and paralysis. "Having joined the fight against fear, hatred, repression, and inaction; having adjusted our sex lives so as to protect ourselves and one another—we are now reclaiming our subjectivities, our communities, our culture . . . and our promiscuous love of sex."

This is the heart of the great project that began with the Stonewall uprising: seizing the narrative about queerness, taking it back from psychologists, judges, and clerics; from political hucksters. Trusting in revealed identity and the measure of our hearts. Protecting the families we've made. Living our dignity without ever having to justify it.

I'd like to think that's what Truman Capote shows Andy Warhol's camera the day Andy pops in for lunch—that a ferocious queer subjectivity twists and thrashes in the incelibate body of a quiche.

A CULINARY
EXTRAVAGANZA

[1982]

P AUL PRUDHOMME BRINGS A PAIR OF STOVES FROM
New Orleans for blackening redfish and heating vats of jambalaya
and red beans and rice; he hustles them up to Long Island in a spe-
cially tricked-out mobile home. Alice Waters flies in crates of red and
yellow peppers from California. Maida Heatter spends weeks at home
in Miami baking and freezing walnut tortes and cookies before loading
up the car and hitting the I-95.

In the heat of August, a culinary extravaganza oozes in and around
a yellow-striped party tent on the East Hampton property of America's
premier food writer, Craig Claiborne. It's planned as a triple jubilee:
Craig's sixty-second birthday, the twenty-five-year anniversary of his
becoming food editor at the *New York Times*, and the publication of his
memoir, *A Feast Made for Laughter*.

It's a gourmet jamboree: three dozen chefs and cookbook authors
dispensing tastes of food they haul in or cook on site, either in Craig's
kitchen or in the kitchen of one of his indulgent neighbors. Two hundred
people are invited; more than twice that many show up, gate crashers
like the lady in a bright pink dress, carrying a shopping bag, who gets
word of the bash and walks right through the gate on Kings Point
Road, past the trucks, local news vans, and a sea of cars.

Artist Larry Rivers leads numbers from his swing band, as Jacques
Pépin spoons tastes of ceviche from a carved watermelon. Roger Fessaguet, chef of Manhattan's haute-French temple La Caravelle, dishes

out roast veal, while Marcella Hazan pries spinach cannelloni from a stack of baking dishes.

There's Marion Cunningham, slinging wedges of apple pizza, a recipe in her forthcoming *Fannie Farmer Baking Book*. From Poilâne, the Parisian temple of wood-fired, naturally fermented breads, come enormous rounds of levain with Craig's name baked into the crust. *New York* magazine restaurant critic Gael Greene, sporting a sassy oversized newsboy cap, serves the mousse-filled chocolate pie she once described as an aphrodisiac. "The more intense the taste of chocolate," she said, "the more erotic the spell." Indeed, a very peculiar kind of spell hangs over Craig's four acres in East Hampton.

Diana Kennedy flew in from Mexico. "Have you tasted my turkey mole?" she asks *Chicago Tribune* reporter Paula Camp. "The cooking event of the century," declares cookbook author Ken Hom, as he serves tastes of his Chinese ratatouille. "A bit of conspicuous consumption," says Kurt Vonnegut, sounding jaded, as Betty Friedan, author of *The Feminine Mystique*, sips Champagne.

Craig looks hammered and a little lost: grinning, seated solo at a table covered with cakes, wearing a summer-stripe shirt with a couple of buttons undone, a mic clipped to the opening. (CBS is shooting a mini-doc.) Adoring chefs and famous insiders in restaurants and media, the glamorous and the influential, stand three-deep behind him for the cameras. Craig is the center of an international foodie culture elite—a culture Craig has largely spawned and fed.

The no-shows, including Truman Capote and Lauren Bacall, are conspicuously absent. And many of the celebrities here have something to sell, some product or personal branding to flash at the lenses. "Certainly," observes the *San Francisco Chronicle*'s Jeannette Ferrary, "there was an element of enlightened self-interest."

"As soon as the food tables were decimated," Camp writes, "the guests drifted away from the party as quickly as they had come." The TV crews turn off the mics, reporters close their notebooks. The mystery crasher in the pink dress stuffs the last of Maida Heatter's cookies into her bag.

And even though Doubleday, publisher of *A Feast Made for Laughter*, is footing the bill for this event of the century, Craig's memoir seems the last thing guests seem inclined to talk about while the cameras are running. Because even before it goes on display in bookstore windows coast to coast, Craig's book has already left an awkward stain.

✳

It's on page 20 where Craig publicly comes out. Remember how the Depression-ravaged Claibornes take in boarders in Indianola? Remember how, amid the scarcity of beds and the decision his parents have made to sleep apart, young Craig shares a bed with this father, Lewis?

"That happened," Craig explains in his memoir, "at the time when I had just achieved seminal flow."

He says it like a first wet dream is some kind of merit badge.

"I slept next to him, spoon-fashion, my slender upper arm securely holding him around the chest."

Definitely creepy. Definitely not okay.

"It was my father's custom to retire shortly after supper each evening, pausing first to take a hot tub bath before entering the bed."

Blanche DuBois still haunts Craig's voice. Also: WHAT?

"In the beginning, my going to bed with him was a casual, unplanned affair. Until one winter evening when I put my arm around him and onto his left arm . . ."

No . . .

"I followed that arm . . ."

. . . Nuh nuh nuh nuh nuh nuh . . .

" . . . onto the hand and discovered his fingers . . . "

. . . NO HAND! NO FINGERS!! NO DISCOVERY!!! . . .

" . . . enfolded around the throttle of his lust, the object that best reflects the strength and status of a man's desire."

OH CHRIST NO! . . . Just . . . aw, fuck it. Just ugh.

"In the years that followed I was to relive—in my cultivated daydreams—the enormity of that experience in my mind and I tried many times to describe the ecstasy of it . . . "

Seriously? He's doubling down on "ecstasy"?

It's as if the fear that never left Craig keeps him ducked behind Southern Gothic tropes: incest, madness, the death of a noble blood line blahblah *yech*—all of Craig's alcoholic self-deceptions curdled into a cliche of forbidden lust.

The revelation feels somehow like a drilling deeper into the closet. His daddy-fondling reads like bad fiction, a clunky homosexual pastiche of Faulkner: a lie. Craig pretends he's revealing all in his memoir, but much of his life remains obscure. His heart, his vulnerabilities, how he feels about Henry Lewis Creel, a constant friend—Craig's book illuminates little that's important, except maybe his deep, deep ambivalence.

This extends to food. The coded magic that suffused his writing in an earlier era, that gave it life and a certain insistent energy is gone, replaced by a numb sort of deflection.

Coming out like this seems a shield of self-delusion for Craig, an act of self-directed homophobia that maybe, possibly, somehow has the power to protect the small, scared boy within. The boy eating Aunt Catherine's clabber out behind the Sunflower house, gazing at walnut trees, feeling the comforting cold of the soured milk and the sandy grit of sugar against his teeth.

When queer food couldn't speak in its own voice, queer food needed Craig. Now that it can speak, Craig's become voiceless.

In July 1997, nearly twenty years after readers of the food pages of the *New York Times* could count on Craig's queer Southern rhythms and gilded evocations, the *Times Sunday Magazine* publishes a recipe for Salade Gourmande, by Craig Claiborne with Pierre Franey. It's a mix of blanched asparagus, green beans, and sliced avocado, heaped on plates and laden with an obnoxious cap of black truffles and hunks of foie gras from the can. It rests uneasily on lettuce leaves, drizzled with a vinaigrette containing Dijon or Düsseldorf mustard. "Do not use the hot dog variety," Craig warns the reader, because, sure, this is *fancy*.

Craig's text reads as bored as the salad it describes: stiff and clunky, sneering, flaunting a joyless kind of luxury—a voice seemingly unconnected to the material, emotionally flat, sealed against any possible incursion of queer magic.

IN THE OCTOBER 14 ISSUE of San Francisco's *Bay Area Reporter*, porn critic John Karr reviews the latest crop of gay skin mags, including *Three for All* and *Bullmeat* (which, to Karr's professional eye, shows some hellaciously fine photo work).

Karr has an interview a few pages on, though not with a subject you'd expect—not the dopey blond centerfold of *Sweat* or the freakishly hung star of *Huge*. Instead, Karr goes one-on-one with Craig Claiborne.

Credit chance and Karr's instincts. In the lead-up to Craig's book-tour stop in SF, someone in Doubleday's PR department sends Karr *A Feast Made for Laughter.* Maybe they think he's a conventional critic, maybe they don't care, he's just media. This is not a book Karr's remotely interested in (he's no foodie) until someone, a buddy, tells him to look on page 20, at Lewis Claiborne's throttle of lust. And just like that, a writer who opines on the jerk-off value of mags and VCR cassettes gets a sit-down with the undisputed king of American food.

It doesn't go well for Craig, though I'm not sure he realizes it. The spooning scene with daddy? He presents himself to Karr as some kind of gay hero.

> "I know this will sound altruistic," he says, "but there was one reason I was serious about wanting to write this book. It was a chance to state my homosexuality. The lack of awareness in this country is incredible and there are so many women across the country who respect my work. I felt that if I could increase their awareness that being gay is not a bad thing, doesn't make you an evil person and that they don't have to be ashamed if their child is gay, or if I could give comfort to one kid because of my coming out and declaring my homosexuality, the book would have been worth having been written."

Craig's delusional. He talks like he's the second coming of Harvey Milk but declines to witness the truth of his sexuality in any affirming way. He doesn't describe the resilience and joy of queer communities like the one he knew in Chicago after the war; doesn't site his own fear in a wider context of homophobia and queer oppression.

Karr sees it. You can tell he's like, *This queen may know Brie from Camembert, but she's fucking confused.* Karr writes that Craig's "general sophistication" may have "clouded his vision." Which is a generous take, since Craig's entire career has been about projecting sophistication to shield an inconvenient identity.

Craig tells Karr something important, though, something he kept from his memoir. That in the early '70s Dr. Howard Brown, New York City's Health Services Administrator, privately urged Craig to come out—to use his fame, his prestige, to lean into the post-Stonewall fight against stigma, fear, the closet. Because Craig had left his position at the *New York Times* (he returned a couple of years later), there was no risk he'd lose his job. Brown himself came out in 1973, and helped establish the civil rights nonprofit now known as the National LGBTQ Task Force. Craig could not.

He tells Karr, "I'm afraid I was a coward about it, and I've felt guilty ever since." But if he did feel remorse, you'd never know it from *A Feast Made for Laughter.*

It was Craig's opportunity to acknowledge the courage of others who came out.

He declined.

ERNIE AND THE
RAINBOW CAKE

[1986]

I N KEY WEST, FRIENDS OF ERNEST MATTHEW MICKLER throw a book release party.

Ernie's *White Trash Cooking* flouts every convention of respectable cookbooks: the serious, sepia-washed, rigorously tested ones published by Knopf, for instance, edited by the great Judith Jones. Ernie's book is spiral-bound, 160 pages of Mock Cooter Stew and Goldie's Yo-Yo Puddin, a whole bunch of garish, disreputable things.

With *The Taste of Country Cooking* and *In Pursuit of Flavor*, Jones positions Edna Lewis as the oracle of a *cuisine* of the American South: a tradition almost as serious, buttery, and canonical, in Jones's framing of Edna, as cuisine bourgeoise. In fact, Edna's often tagged "the Julia Child of Southern cooking," an epithet both patronizing and inaccurate.

Ernie will never seriously be known as the Julia Child of anything.

White Trash Cooking celebrates the make-do recipes of folks living in rural poverty. A jokey, puckish spirit pervades the book, but Ernie seems to laugh with, not at, the people he collects recipes from: Bonnie Jean Butt of the Banana Puddin; Freda of the Five-Can Casserole; Clara Jane Vickar of the Creamed Tuna Lunch.

It's also, though not specifically queer, gay as hell.

✳

ERNIE WAS BORN IN 1940 in Palm Valley, a scrubby fishing town on the northeast coast of Florida. He makes it to San Francisco, where, across the bay at Mills College in Oakland, he receives his MFA, walking across the stage during a 1972 graduation ceremony fitted with psychedelic butterfly wings and a hiked graduation gown cinched at the waist to look like an A-line frock.

He writes the *White Trash* manuscript at the urging of friends, mostly in rural Northern California, mostly stoned. He shops it around to every publisher he can think of in New York and Boston. Most like at least *something* about it; all turn him down. The publisher David Godine sends his admiration, but finds the title and subject matter too risky for a distinguished house such as his.

And then, thanks to one of Ernie's persistent friends, the manuscript finds its way to The Jargon Society.

The Jargon Society is an indie press founded in San Francisco in 1951 as Jargon Books by David Ruff and queer poet Jonathan Williams. Williams, who grew up in North Carolina, became associated with the Black Mountain Poets, many of whom Jargon published. Williams was into found language, the spoken culture of Appalachia. Guy Davenport, writing of Williams and his literary mission, quotes William Carlos Williams's line, "The poet's business is to let the world speak for itself." And it's that quality of letting the cooks Ernie's rounded up speak in their own voices that makes *White Trash* more than a jokey insult to the poor ways of the South. Ernie's photographs of country kitchens and roadside market stands express his love for the culture of the marginalized.

The book is a roundup of humble recipes from real cooks across the hardscrabble South: mayonnaise-tomato sandwiches and icebox cakes, potato pones and cooter pie. Ernie's reverence for these cooks shines, all these poor women cooking in teensy kitchens in shacks and even teensier galleys in trailer homes.

Before we go on, I want to say something about the toxicity of "white trash," the poorest of poor whites in the South. In *Where We Stand*, bell hooks describes their place in the traditional race hierarchy as just above Black people of any economic circumstance and just below lower-middle-class whites. "White trash were different because they flaunted their poverty, reveled in it, and were not ashamed," hooks says. "White trash were folks who, as our neighbors were fond of saying, 'did not give a good goddamn.'" Unable to sink any lower in the racialized caste system of the South, white trash had nothing to lose and were therefore dangerous. Can we read Ernie's book as an attempt to show poor whites that they did indeed have something to lose? A rich legacy of food and language? Perhaps by ennobling this heritage, suggesting it has every right to take its place in American culture, Ernie is tempering dangerousness by persuading folks to give a good goddamn.

AGAINST ALL ODDS, *White Trash Cooking* takes off. Within months the charming, chatty, salt-and-pepper-goateed Ernie appears on David Letterman, and drips his languid North Florida drawl all over NPR. Public radio correspondent Vertamae Smart-Grosvenor, author of *Vibration Cooking*, declares, "I *do* like the flavor of this book." Bryan Miller, the *New York Times* food critic infamous for prickly judgments, calls *White Trash* "the most intriguing book of the 1986 spring cookbook season." Ernie's book does the impossible: finds praise across cultural barricades.

In 1988, after Ten Speed Press acquires the rights to *White Trash* from The Jargon Society, they lean on Ernie to produce a follow-up. Within the year, they rush out *Sinkin Spells, Hot Flashes, Fits and Cravins.* Less than six months later, Ernie disappears: dead from complications due to AIDS.

Sinkin Spells, Hot Flashes, Fits and Cravins: The text, the vignettes, short stories, sketches—grounded in queerness. Aliens, outsiders, social miscues, lust, longing outside the bounds of what's acceptable in the cloistered White Trash world. There's a sweet, sensitive quality to the sketches. Subversion of norms, blood family, parental and community expectations.

Ernie navigates between what Susan Sontag identified in 1964 as "naïve camp" and "deliberate camp": a road where Ernie, a queer exile from corrosive blood family in the conservative coastal Florida towns where he grew up, finds acceptance, or at least forgiveness: a kind of benediction, a form of solace. In the end, it offers Ernie a way back home.

✳

IN STEPHAN ELLIOT'S 1994 ROAD MOVIE *The Adventures of Priscilla, Queen of the Desert*, drag queen Felicia, played by Guy Pearce (all three of the film's protagonist queens carry the scars of family trauma), poses in an enormous throne-like spangly silver stiletto anchored to the roof of the girls' tour bus as it cruises the Australian outback, a long train of silver mylar whipping across the vast blue sky: gay wings slapping heaven. All the while, Felicia lip-syncs to Aussie diva Joan Carden's aria from Verdi's *La Traviata*, "Sempre Libera," *Always Free.*

Camp is a force for liberation and for protection, with the power to spin deflector shields of pure glam.

"To be camp," writes Mark Booth, "is to present oneself as being committed to the marginal with a commitment greater than the marginal merits." Is returning to a Walmart town with the cruisy highway rest stop or the subdivision with its Denny's and its donut shop and its high school drama teacher in the closet really such a powerful act of reclamation? I mean, homophobia and alienation from family are only two reasons we flee. Mostly, these places don't offer much to return to, apart from the act of return itself.

I read *White Trash Cooking* as queer reclamation not so much of place as of populist culture. A correction for the bourgeois foodie-ism that had turned food magazines into lusty, patriarchal adorations of male chefs, their Cuisinart recipes; their pasta primavera and balsamic glaze and red pepper coulis; their "decadent" flourless cake. Ernie's camp, his commitment to the marginal, declares his humanity and actually stretches the meaning of camp. Having grown up like all queers in a psychic exclusion zone, Ernie doesn't point at the marginal and laugh at it. He slides in to soak up the artistry there.

Instead of othering the trailer park women who make okra omelets and potato chip sandwiches, Ernie levels up the camp equation; binds himself to the marginal with devotion equal to the marginal.

It's the queerest message: that the things elites and cultural influencers throw away has a value equal to what they tout as precious. Maybe that's the regional, pastoral, hard-scratch country foods of Marcella Hazan or Diana Kennedy; *cucina povera*, food of the least, the worst; "peasant food" in restaurants for the privileged; panzanella and ribollita, dishes wringing every last calorie from the crusts and hard heels of precious bread loaves; chilaquiles for salvaging and transforming yesterday's tortillas. The trash foodways appropriated by chefs ignorant of poverty, they defined '80s chic in a whole class of restaurants in LA and the Bay Area.

Authors of gay-themed cookbooks sought a homo language of food and failed—Lou Rand, the Kitchen Fairy: they copied the language of mainstream cookbooks, maybe in some cases copied recipes from mainstream sources, but queered the voice. Lesbian books were better at bending recipes into a new language of cookbooks; of forging a collective language of the potluck.

I think that's why *White Trash Cooking* resonates such a distance. Deep in the cultural revisions of Reagan and Thatcher, and a year before Oliver Stone's *Wall Street* trains a cinematic eye on the craven consumption of '80s capitalism, Ernie puts an invisible frame around trailer-park cooking: the queer food that can save the soul of a culture.

Where he might easily mock, Ernie's gentle. In a recipe for White Gravy, he says, "Always keep reminding yourself that it takes years of practice to make a good flour gravy. Nobody's perfect right at the very first."

In her short story "A Lesbian Appetite," published in 1988, *Bastard Out of Carolina* author Dorothy Allison, who grew up poor and Southern, offers a more nuanced taste. For Dorothy, trash food is a source of pride and embarrassment, food that provokes pissed-off reactions; banishment from the lesbian potluck table; food that's leverage for shaming among the middle-class feminists she fucks or dates or hangs out with in New York City.

"Poor white trash I am for sure," the narrator of "A Lesbian Appetite" declares. "I eat shit food and I am not worthy. Five of my cousins bled to death before thirty-five, their stomachs finally surrendering to sugar and whisky and fat and salt. . . . But my dreams will always be flooded with salt and grease."

Ernie finds his way back through camp, Dorothy through self-revelation: a coming out that never ends, publicly owning her queerness in view before her extended family, before the world of straight power at large, and before the lesbian feminists who've judged her for getting off on dom/sub sex; for not eating "healthy," vegan, in moderation, otherwise "right." It's connection, the collective queerness—fucked as it is; judgmental as it is—that gets Dorothy through.

Nobody's perfect right at the very first.

"The way we see ourselves," she says in "A Question of Class," "As parts of both our birth families and the extended family of friends and lovers we invariably create within the lesbian community. For me, the bottom line has simply become the need to resist that omnipresent fear, that urge to hide and disappear, to disguise my life, my desires, and the truth about how little any of us understand—even as we try to make the world a more just and human place."

For me, the recipe in *White Trash Cooking* that expresses all that; that resists any false, easy resolution about queer acceptance in the places where a part of us will always reside is this: Reba's Rainbow Ice-Box Cake. It's cold and bright; an intricate piece of layer-work you can adapt to your mood, or the dish you have; to the amount of ingredients on your counter, or your situation.

It's a process of assembly: layering a moussey whip of margarine, egg yolks, pineapple slush from the can, and pecans over graham crackers. On this you spread straight-up cherry Jell-O (made with the reserved pineapple juice), and once that's set you cover it with lime Jell-O, first frothed with an eggbeater to attain volume and exuberance; a contrast to the smooth purity of the red Jell-O below and, I guess, an echo of the pebbly texture of the pineapple-pecan layer. Whipped cream blankets everything, and you can dot that with cherries from the jar.

The way you can adapt it, according to Reba, is by adding extra layers of grahams, but the basic recipe already makes fifteen servings, so this is by nature a party. A rainbow without literal Pride stripes but with something like their optimism; the yellow-red-green of hope, passion, and new beginnings: an emblem of everything good in the margins. Ernie would have us taste compassion in every layer.

MONDAY NIGHTS AT ZUNI

[1983–1994]

I T CAME TO ME AS A RUMBLE, THE BACK-PAGE STORY that flicked my attention before drifting away.

When I read that the government had come up with a name for the gay cancer, or gay plague, or whatever the papers and the evening news had been calling it, I was pissed. Acquired Immune Deficiency Syndrome, AIDS for short. What a fucking stupid abbreviation, I remember telling my boyfriend. I am never calling it that.

Three years later, AIDS had recalibrated almost everything in my life. Me, every gay guy I knew: we felt a constant mix of panic, rage, and surrender. A schizophrenic mix of scared urgency and paralysis.

In the early years of HIV/AIDS, the months and years before testing, before effective treatment, before ACT-UP, sex seemed to want to wrench back everything it only recently gave us. In the liberation era unleashed at Stonewall, sex taught us how to love. But now, every visit to a bathhouse or glory-hole club (before many cities forced them into lockdown), every hookup, every act of making love with the boyfriend I was in an open relationship with—every formerly liberating gesture dragged a heavy chain of risk.

I wish I could tell you that I flouted danger as defiance, acts of political resistance. That in the face of annihilation I affirmed my queerness. It would be a lie.

Many of us scattered into our separate cells of denial and grief. We stayed home with our VCRs, our phone sex. We clung to weird-ass justifications for why the virus wouldn't find us, desperately trying to weave hope from strands of lies and magical thinking. Death was only part of the epidemic's cruelty. AIDS also tried to sap the narrative arc of our stories, the universal story where we come out, move to a city, and find love at last.

"What has it been about male/male love that has made me desire it so?" asked Lou Sullivan in his diary. Sullivan was a trans male activist who settled in San Francisco in the mid-'70s, and who would die at age thirty-nine in 1991 as a result of AIDS. As a gay man, Sullivan had to fight to obtain gender-affirming care from a homophobic system. His diaries ring with affirmations of gay desire.

"The fact that [male/male love] didn't *happen*—that the two people involved really *wanted* to be with each other, and that the other person chose to love him. . . . Not so much that it was two male bodies (not to minimize that aspect, though), but that despite all forces against them, they clung to each other with desire."

This is the great story of modern homosexuality: the power of love and desire to *sometimes*, because of determination and fortitude, speak through an imposed silence. The food that becomes part of this story, in acts of nurturing our own, or standing up around a potluck table, or decoding a recipe's message of resistance—that food gives us, to echo poet Judy Grahn, distinction and dignity. That food gives culture.

One of the many cruelties of AIDS is that it muted queer stories that had barely begun to be told. The cost of surviving—of being one of those left behind, purely because of stupid luck—was the responsibility of picking up narrative strands the dead were forced to drop.

For those of us burdened with the guilt and sorrow of carrying on, food and all its pleasures demanded that we survive; to taste joy in whatever time stretched before us.

Food took on a new role in queer culture as a brace for eulogy; something to sustain us as we remembered the lost. At memorials, food became part of mourning: a reminder of pleasures the dead would never know again; a witness of stilled desires.

Zuni Café, the restaurant Billy West founded in San Francisco in 1979, was dark on Monday nights. And as the wave of deaths crashed on the city, Monday nights at Zuni became space for memorials for customers, for workers—Zuni lost twenty-four employees to AIDS, Vince Calcagno, the restaurant's former co-owner, told me.

In 1987, the year Judy Rodgers became Zuni's chef, Billy organized a Monday night memorial for Todd Van Bortel. Todd's boyfriend was the gallery owner Jeffrey Fraenkel, one of Billy's friends. After Todd got sick, and struggled in his office job, Billy hired him as one of the hosts at Zuni. And when Todd got too sick to come in, Billy didn't fire him. He kept him on the payroll.

"After Todd died, it wasn't even a discussion that the memorial would be at Zuni on a closed Monday," Fraenkel says. It was typical of a Monday event: some fifty people standing to hear about Todd's life, and to say a few words, drinking Champagne or margaritas. Pick-up foods to keep everybody going; booze and food to both soften and sharpen feelings of loss.

In 1994, when Billy died as a result of AIDS, of course the memorial was at Zuni.

If you've ever spent time in a closed restaurant, a room without the hustle of the servers or people angling at the host stand, tinkling phrases from a piano, or the ambient drone of the hot-line's hood, you notice unexpected ghost fragrances: the acrid reek of the bar's rubber floor mats; the sweetness of pink hand soap from the kitchen; the lingering smells of rendered fats, browned chicken skin, vinaigrette. It's like a record of expired pleasures, a sensory memento that seeks to sharpen the will of survivors to cling ferociously to joy.

OPEN HOUSE

[1986]

IT'S FEBRUARY ALREADY: I TELL MY BOYFRIEND STEVE that we need to have a party. We need to have it soon.

Through the window of our dining porch in a reclaimed landing, the bare sticks and branches on the huge plum are already showing out. The porch is at the rear of the flat. In a few weeks there'll be this insane cloud of white and pink-washed blossoms through the glass, and it'll all end in a kind of anarchy that's become predictable, we've lived here so long (three years that's felt like forever): masses of flowers in a haphazard swirl. For days the yard will be a snow globe of petals twirling down and drifting onto the cracked patio two floors down, piling up like slush.

The party: an afternoon open house on a Sunday, marking the release of blossoms; a pagan-type witness for dead flowers freed according to the spring surge; the rising of the sap.

Of course the food will have to be gay. It has to be.

Because if you're not expressing queerness in your everyday, or defending the basic freedom to be out and vocal; to live your life out and not deserving the shame of AIDS—of dying—then there's something seriously wrong with you. You have seriously lost your queer humanity.

I feel I've found my place in a city with enough lesbians and gays to form a defensive herd: protection from popular contempt and discrimination, from queer-hating cops (basically every cop), from violent queer-baiting on the streets, the everyday assaults and common mur-

ders. A lot of us carry little metal whistles to sound for reinforcements
during bashings—we cannot rely on the police, especially now that
AIDS is "evidence" of our toxicity; epidemiological justification for our
pariah status.

The only way I can deal with everything terrible is finding valida-
tion in my growing stretch of funky cookbooks I keep on the splintery
shelf rough-nailed to the wall in the dining porch. The only thing I can
do is cook—cook with the same urgency as the plum tree coming into
bud. "Sap-swollen tendrils," to quote the poet Jim Powell, who (spoiler
alert) will be at our open house, "leafing to embrace the same infatuate
exuberance this year as last."

Because it's already February, and nobody gay can know what this
year's bringing. Nobody gay can count on being around next spring to
see the flowers twirl same as last.

The psychic, the moral cost of failing to do something—to fight
back somehow—is huge, especially since the next person I know to fall
to the virus could be my boyfriend; it could be me. There's no saying
how long anyone has.

I tell Steve we need to have a party: a Sunday open house to catch
the coming chaos of petals.

QUICHE, RIGHT? It has to be quiche, the Sunday icon—a cliché, but
I'll make it not. A word too tainted to show up on any menu with
ambitions. Quiche is "savory tarts" in the kitchen language I've been
taught. They say that Deborah Madison, the opening chef at Greens,
first restaurant I cooked at, banned *quiche* from the language of menus.
We served savory tarts, but they were still quiche: with Sonoma goat
cheese and a shitload of herbs harvested from the restaurant's farm up
in Marin County; with stewed leeks and Niçoise olives; with smoked
mozzarella and tomatoes in a marbled range of green-gold-red; with
asparagus and stringlike bits of red onion.

In so-called serious restaurants, quiche is too Castro; a pale, flabby-crusted thing under plastic wrap, pulled from a cafe fridge and nuked.

I'll queer the equation. Instead of making quiche and calling it savory tarts, I'll make savory tarts and call them quiche—a reclaiming, I guess.

✳

STEVE, WHEN HE ISN'T WAITING TABLES, is a poet. He asks his poet friends to come by: Jim Powell, Aaron Shurin, Kenny Fries, almost everybody queer. There's a buzz when Thom Gunn arrives, clomping up the stairs from the street door, looking tall even in the high cavern of the hallway. Dressed in denim, a belt with a chunky brass buckle, biker boots—he glances at me after my boyfriend's intro, then looks past me to the kitchen where everyone's clustered. The kitchen where I'm soon shuffling tart pans around our uneven-browning oven:

- Elizabeth David's Tarte Aveyronnaise, fancy quiche with a Roquefort filling and a yeasted crust, a stiff-ish brioche you roll out thin to line the pans. It bakes up with crisp edges and a light, buttery body. Quiche and brioche, basically a double gay flex.
- The goat cheese tart with herbs: fresh dill, parsley, and thyme, smelling like the dampest hillside in a Northern California spring.
- A quiche with saffron custard with Swiss chard and pine nuts on top. Saffron because its source is flowers, and this whole day is about making witness before a blossom-covered plum tree.

I spend the afternoon cooking, pulling tarts from our ancient white enameled range with the leaky oven door as the party drifts and swirls around me. People clear the way for my dash with a hot ring pan in my towel-covered hands to the porch table; to an upside-down old stainless restaurant soup insert, a rigged pedestal for coaxing the pans' sides from the crusts.

It's true I'm always happiest working, manifesting the eternal queer quest for refuge with food and drink. To enable all of us, if I might rephrase Jimmy Baldwin, to gather in the place where our blood beats. To fortify that blood for as long as fate allows it to surge through our hearts.

✳

THOM GUNN GAVE AN INTERVIEW IN 1992, after the publication of his book *The Man with Night Sweats.* That book includes a section of poems that deal with AIDS, the feelings of loss, and terror, guilt, and regret an epidemic unleashes. In the interview Thom talks about the so-called gay community, and how he never felt a part of it until AIDS changed everything. " 'The gay community' was a phrase I always thought was bullshit," he tells the interviewer, "until the thing was vanishing."

Irish writer and critic Kevin Brazil talks about how queer communities see themselves—how artists like photographer Catherine Opie, for instance, have made it possible for trans viewers to see in Opie's work their collective identity represented in the world. Brazil writes that Opie's portraits of trans models "are more than representations of a particular community in time and space. They are also about the process by which any community comes into being— perhaps only comes into being—by acquiring a collective representation of itself."

It's that way with food. Any dish that has sustained queer connection; that has nourished, comforted, or charmed us; has supported the old ongoing battle to define ourselves—those foods have been part of a process of collective recognition. We look up and see each other eating, and in that shared act we claim knowledge of ourselves.

Remember what Judy Grahn said? That what gives any group of people distinction and dignity is its culture. Our food is our culture, but our food is not a connected web of dishes and foodways; it's not a cuisine. It's our determination to cook and eat together; to sustain ourselves and those we love; to keep strong enough to fuel hope. We are adaptable. Any food is queered when we taste it together; when it sounds a shared story on our tongues.

Epilogue

THE
QUEEREST
FOOD

THE LANGUAGE OF CAKE, PART TWO

N OT LONG BEFORE I BEGAN TO PITCH THIS BOOK, I came across the story of David Warren, a trans man from Chico, California, who in the 1940s married Thelma Jane Walter in San Francisco.

David spent his toddler years being told he was a girl. But the age of five, he had the definitive realization that he was not.

In 1940, David—a woman in the eyes of civil bureaucracies—was assigned a shared room in a female dormitory at UC Berkeley. His roommate was Thelma. They fell in love, and in 1947 were *legally* married at Trinity Church in San Francisco. Legally, because, since David presented as a man, and since a clerk in Sonoma County, where they applied for a marriage license, apparently didn't bother to check David's birth certificate, they were granted the license. (Of course, an alternative theory—the one I'd like to believe—is that the understanding clerk *did* notice David's official, state-decreed gender and issued the license anyway.)

Later that year, as Thelma Jane shopped for groceries to cook Thanksgiving dinner, the FBI showed up at their chinchilla farm in the hills above Sonoma to investigate David's failure to register for the draft. Following a suspicion, an agent frisked David and declared him to be a girl. The couple were arrested and charged with three felonies.

"We couldn't figure out any other way to live," David told the *San Francisco Examiner* from his cell in a Santa Rosa jail. "Under our code, to be honest with each other, we decided the marriage was the only course. We considered living together without being married very improper."

The charges were eventually dropped based on a legal technicality. That, and because David and Thelma Jane appeared penitent—at the advice of their lawyers—both agreed to see psychologists to treat their so-called mental illnesses. Thelma Jane, previously a respected teacher at Sonoma Valley High School, quit her position.

What ate at me is how some of the contemporary press reports (and there were *a lot* of stories about David and Thelma Jane, almost all referring to them both as "girls") read as if the disruption of their Thanksgiving was the point. Papers reported with apparent glee that the couple had wanted to spend their first Thanksgiving together as husband and wife, but instead were eating the holiday meal in separate cells—not turkey, nothing traditional for Thanksgiving, but beef and whatever sad starch and canned veg the jail could dump onto trays.

It seems to me the glee in their disrupted dinner was the point—like eating the cultural foods you crave, the things you love or that have meaning for you, is a privilege of the straight power class; a privilege of conforming to some system, whether or not you feel you can. A generation after Herman Smith fled Portland in a panic, public outrage hadn't shifted very much. The policing of queer lives was still vigorous.

It struck me that queer food is the seizing of privilege from the straight power intent on policing and controlling queer lives; in defining queerness in social, scientific, and political terms. That the food itself doesn't matter as much as the ability to share it in the context of the lives we make for ourselves, and in the power we have to keep the stories of those meals alive. The queerest food is that which sustains a refusal to accept.

In "Sweet Southern Dreams," a 2012 story in *Saveur* magazine about mastering the American layer cake, author Ben Mims writes about turning his deep sorrow over queer dislocation into glorious, pastel-yellow slices of lemon cake. Mims described his coming out to his mother, Judy, preserver of Mississippi's rigid Baptist architecture.

"Prior to October 7, 2010," Mims wrote, "my mother and I were the best of friends. A consummate Southern lady, Judy Mims is a fantastic cook, gossiper, and mom—and in her relationship with me she had always drawn on all those talents. But on that October day, I flew from New York City to my childhood home in Kosciusko, Mississippi, to come out, at 25 years old, as a gay man to my parents. As anyone who grew up in the Bible Belt can imagine, the outcome was heartbreaking. My mother and I used to talk at least weekly; now months go by without a call. I miss her. And I can't help feeling like I've lost touch with not only my mother, but also my lifeline to the world I grew up in."

Ben teaches himself to bake the sort of layer cakes that belong to his mother and grandmother's historical tradition. His baking both numbs the pain of family separation and keeps the wound hurting; the scab perennially tender.

Ben's grandmother's coconut layer cake recipe, a painstaking formula that involves cracking and prying out the fresh meat, is an act of nostalgia that seeks to recast the trauma of rejection. Ben conjures his Mississippi past in an adult milieu of freely expressed queerness in New York City. He appropriates the past to heal, and to stay connected to his hurt: a reminder of who he is in the present.

"Whenever I get nostalgic for the South," Ben writes, "I break out my cake pans, butter, and sugar, and whip up a lemon cake like the one we shared; it buoys my hope for a future in which my mother and I are as close as we once were. The result—bittersweet and beautiful—reminds me of that afternoon, four years before our lives changed, when we sat together in that cafe without a care in the world and just talked about cake."

But here's another way to think about Ben's story.

Judy is only a middling baker. Ben relates the embarrassment of her red velvet cake one Christmas, when the whipped cream icing she took a chance on ended up dry and chalky—a moment of humiliation around the holiday family table. Clearly, Ben is the better baker, capable of wielding whisk and rubber spatula in ways that honor the Southern cake tradition. But as a straight Christian woman, Judy has the power to deny her queer son the rights to an heirloom it's obvious should be his.

And so Ben is forced to bake in exile, redacted from the family narrative of cakes. At the same time that Ben's story shows the limits of Southern culture, his nostalgia cedes all power to Judy. Writing as if he believed his imagination to be afflicted, Ben reinforces the hetero power structure he's spent his adult life escaping.

The irony is that Ben, as a writer, cookbook author, and pastry chef, has all the power. Judy can only assert her control using the worn-out artifacts of a past that wield only as much force as Ben decides they do.

Reinventing himself in queer-friendly city enclaves, Ben finds balm for trauma, but his loss of family goes on hurting.

My heart aches for Ben—for all of us queer and trans people who've lost mothers, children, friends. My only brother, who decades ago got sucked into this Borg world of extreme Christianity, can only think of me as a sinner in need of prayer; pity me as someone whose soul will blister in the never-ending fire, jabbed by devils in the forever time after dying. My father, as he lay on the hospital mattress that would be the last his body touched, in his final hours, took my brother's hand and asked him, as a final request, to accept me. My brother could not.

I know the decades of justification and denial, the rage and sorrow that pumps through this air of exile I breathe. And I know that there's a way to reclaim these lost places, spaces physical and emotional, and even the psychic, even the spiritual places we've been banished from. Our places of exile can feel like the margins of lives we once imagined for ourselves. But enough—no more gay trauma, no more queer pain. Not another tear to streak the buttercream.

We have learned to cook and eat together in the margins; to love in the margins—we *own* the motherfucking margins. It's where we discover our strength and realize our courage; where we find or make our families. We are the people who built our homes on the margins and made it feel like the center of the world: a place where cakes rise like hopes and even lemons taste sweet.

ACKNOWLEDGMENTS

MANY PEOPLE, IN WAYS LARGE AND SMALL, POINTED ME
to resources, offered ideas, or were generous with their knowledge.
Special thanks to:

Bailey Barash

Andrew Coe

Susanna Cuyler

Phyllis Eckhaus

Zach Fechheimer

Kadal Jesuthasan

Catherine Johnson

Kian Lam Kho

Celena E. Kusch

Judith Olney

Richard Orton

James Peterson

Carolyn Phillips

Tze-lan D. Sang

Amy Sueyoshi

Nancy Ng Tam

I can't express the gratitude I feel for my editor, Melanie Tortoroli,
and my agents, Steve Troha and Dado Derviskadic of Folio Literary
Management. Nor could I have written this book without the advice,
research wizardry, patience, support, and love of my husband, Perry
Lucina. It's all just pork chops, baby.

NOTES

A Word About Research

Digging for stories from the queer past sometimes feels like impossible work. Our ancestors were very good at hiding their private lives from the scrutiny of their contemporaries and those of us who consider ourselves their heirs. What can we make of the blank pieces they left us? My task for this book has been the diligent work of restoration: taking the fragments left to us and trying to see where the edges might fit. Where they don't, I've sometimes resorted to speculative reconstruction. I've pointed out where I have: Where the meaning I and others are so eager to find must be subject to restoration. I believe this is a way to honor the stories of those in the past who lacked the freedom to tell them. My wish is to give our queer predecessors the dignity of rich, fully assembled public lives, to match the private ones we sometimes can only guess at.

PROLOGUE: THE ROAD TO HUDSON

3   **"upstate's favorite downtown":** Home page, VisitHudsonNY.com, accessed May 18, 2024.

5   **Two founders:** Elazar Sontag, "The School of Lil' Deb's Oasis," *Eater*, June 2, 2021.

5   **gay tiki bar:** Von Diaz, "Queer Joy Is the Main Course at Lil' Deb's Oasis in Upstate New York," *Washington Post*, June 3, 2022.

6   **I told *Sentinel* readers:** John Birdsall and Steve Silberman, "Invitation to Autumn: Three Fall Fruit Pies," *San Francisco Sentinel*, October 17, 1987.

7   **Near the close of the nineteenth century:** John D'Emilio, *Sexual Politics, Sexual Communities: The Making of a Homosexual Minority in the United States, 1940–1970* (Chicago: University of Chicago Press, 1983), 15–17.

8   **a more nuanced view:** Ari Adut, "A Theory of Scandal: Victorians, Homosexuality, and the Fall of Oscar Wilde," *American Journal of Sociology* 111, no. 1 (2005): 213–48.

8   **French Penal and Napoleonic Codes:** "A History of LGBT Criminalisation,"
      Human Dignity Trust, accessed July 26, 2024.

8   **From the earliest years:** "Criminalization of Homosexuality in American His-
      tory," Death Penalty Information Center, accessed July 24, 2024.

9   **"We are apt to forget":** Charles Berg, *Homosexuality: A Subjective and Objective
      Investigation* (London: Allen & Unwin, 1958).

10   **"If happiness is of any value":** Charles Berg and Clifford Allen, *The Problem of
      Homosexuality* (New York: Citadel Press, 1958), quoted in Lillian Faderman, *Odd
      Girls and Twilight Lovers* (New York: Penguin, 1992), 131–32.

10   **Patricia A. Posten:** "Arrested 'Girl' Jailed as Man," *Oakland Tribune*, December
      29, 1962, Newspapers.com.

10   **a deadnamed story:** Dean St. Dennis, "Boy Who Doesn't Want to Be One," *San
      Francisco Chronicle*, December 31, 1962.

10   *Jet* **picked it up:** "Calif. Boy 'Passed' as Woman," *Jet*, February 7, 1963, 46–48,
      Google Books.

10   **"intimidated into speechlessness":** Faderman, *Odd Girls*, 99.

11   **McCarthy's Cold War purges:** Judith Adkins, " 'These People Are Frightened to
      Death': Congressional Investigations and the Lavender Scare," *Prologue* 48, no. 2
      (Summer 2016), National Archives.

11   **"You weren't only afraid":** Sasha Gregory Lewis, *Sunday's Women: A Report on
      Lesbian Life Today* (Boston: Beacon Press, 1979), 58.

11   **They gathered:** Lewis, *Sunday's Women*, 58.

11   **Tallulah Bankhead's variety program:** *The Big Show with Tallulah Bankhead*,
      Ep. 2, November 12, 1950, YouTube video, 1:21:52.

12   **"one of the nicest people around":** Lewis, *Sunday's Women*, 59.

13   **"Many things in the world":** Susan Sontag, *Notes on "Camp"* (New York: Picador,
      2019), Google Play.

THE LANGUAGE OF CAKE, PART ONE

17   **Clara Butters:** Mary Hart, "Mystery Cake: Secret 'Ingredient X' Revealed for
      Baking Mammoth 'Chiffon,' " *Star Tribune* (Minneapolis, MN), February 15, 1948,
      Newspapers.com.

17   **foreman at the local Standard Oil plant:** "Mrs. Frank Butters Passed Away
      While Being Conveyed to City Hospital," *Allen County Republican-Gazette* (Lima,
      OH), July 1, 1910, Newspapers.com.

18   **He tells his mother:** Hart, "Mystery Cake."

18   **lemon-scented Sunshine Cake and delicate Queen:** Two recipes from Fannie
      Merritt Farmer's popular *The Boston Cooking-School Cook Book* (Boston: Little,
      Brown, 1896), Michigan State Libraries Digital Collections.

MADDALENA'S PIGEONS

19   **praline ices as good as San Francisco's:** Alice B. Toklas, *What Is Remembered*
      (New York: Holt, Rinehart and Winston, 1963), 24–25.

19   **Casa Ricci:** Toklas, *Remembered,* 48.

19   **"Large and heavy with delicate small hands":** Toklas, *Remembered,* 23.

19   **amid clutter and smells of dog:** Linda Simon, *The Biography of Alice B. Toklas* (Garden City, NY: Doubleday & Company, 1977), 57.

20   **Alice's weakness:** Simon, *Biography,* 58.

20   **batik dresses:** Simon, *Biography,* 81.

21   **Alice took up the burden:** Alice B. Toklas, *The Alice B. Toklas Cook Book* (New York: Harper & Brothers, 1954), 97.

21   **Even the wood:** Simon, *Biography,* 18.

21   **Brownstone Front . . . Ribbons of Sarah Bernhardt:** Alice B. Toklas, *Aromas and Flavors of Past and Present* (New York: Harper & Brothers, 1958), 137, 139.

21   **"like a nun":** Simon, *Biography,* 21

21   **The train is stifling:** Toklas, *Remembered,* 48.

21   **"What a strange coincidence":** Toklas, *Remembered,* 48.

22   **"a hundred gradations of distance":** Henry James, *Italian Hours* (A Project Gutenberg ebook, August 2004), "Florentine Notes."

22   **In the novelette:** Gertrude Stein, "Didn't Nelly and Lilly Love You" in *As Fine As Melanctha (1914–1930)* (Freeport, NY: Books for Libraries Press, 1969), 219–54. Internet Archive.

23   **Alice is still crying:** Simon, *Biography,* 70.

23   *Our future,* **Gertrude writes:** Stein, "Nelly and Lilly," 224–25.

23   **pilgrimage walks . . . her camisole and bloomers:** Toklas, *Remembered,* 50–51.

24   **a photograph from that summer:** "Alice B. Toklas and Harriet Levy, Fiesole, 1909," Annette Rosenshine Papers, The Bancroft Library, BANC PIC 1964.049— ALB p.13, b. The date of this photo, 1909, appears to be incorrect, since Alice and Harriet did not return to Fiesole that year.

24   **"any and every kind of bird":** Elizabeth David, *Italian Food* (New York: Alfred A. Knopf, 1958), 226.

24   **"giant luscious birds":** Toklas, *Aromas,* 60.

25   **First she browns them:** Toklas, *Aromas,* 59–60. The recipe in *Aromas* calls for curry powder, but the editor of that book, Poppy Cannon, was infamous for "modernizing" Toklas's recipes to appeal to American cooks in 1958, as Cannon saw it, without showing Toklas the final edits. (Cannon says, for instance, that frozen rock Cornish game hens would be a fine substitute for fresh pigeons.) It's my firm belief that curry powder is Cannon's addition; that a Tuscan domestic cook of this era would not have used it, much less known about it. Read about Poppy Cannon's bastardizing of Toklas in Justin Spring, *The Gourmands' Way: Six Americans in Paris and the Birth of a New Gastronomy* (New York: Farrar, Straus and Giroux, 2017), 157–60, Google Play.

25   **no doubt fired by charcoal:** Technically it's speculation to suggest that Maddalena cooked over live fire, but it's almost certain that a cook in a semi-rustic part of Tuscany in 1908 would have. Here's Elizabeth David writing in *Italian Food,* 38, in the early 1950s: "Where the cooking stove is concerned it should be remembered than an enormous number of Italian households, particularly in country districts, still use a charcoal stove and grill . . ."

26   *I see you and you see me:* Stein, "Nelly and Lilly," 236.

26   *I love my love:* Stein, "Nelly and Lilly," 244.

26   *Not very many are well pleased:* Gertrude Stein, *The Making of Americans* (Strel-
      bytskyy Multimedia Publishing, 2024), 872, Google Play.

26   *the salads composed:* Toklas, *Remembered*, 69.

26   **"As a lesbian":** Julie Abraham, *Are Girls Necessary? Lesbian Writing and Modern
      Histories* (Minneapolis: University of Minnesota Press, 2008), 91, Scribd.

27   *Don't you understand:* H.D. [Hilda Doolittle], "I Said.," H.D. Papers, Yale Collec-
      tion of American Literature, Beinecke Rare Book and Manuscript Library.

27   **Before leaving Florence:** Simon, *Biography*, 72.

27   *Give us also the right:* Radclyffe Hall, *The Well of Loneliness* (A Project Gutenberg
      of Australia ebook, 2015).

VILE FUGITIVE

29   **Hermann Schmidt:** George Painter, *The Vice Clique: Portland's Great Sex Scandal*
      (Portland, OR: Espresso Book Machine at Powell's, 2013), 211. Painter writes, "His
      name is given as Schmidt in Portland directories and newspaper accounts of the
      Vice Clique Scandal. However, he put 'Smith' on his voter registration card in Port-
      land and is so listed in census records, his indictment record, trial transcripts, and
      autobiographical information."

29   **he volunteers some information:** Peter Boag, *Same-Sex Affairs: Constructing and
      Controlling Homosexuality in the Pacific Northwest* (Berkeley: University of California
      Press, 2003), 1.

29   **homosexual underground:** Boag, *Same-Sex Affairs*, 89–91.

30   **Lownsdale Park:** Painter, *Vice Clique*, 140.

30   **eleven men:** Painter, *Vice Clique*, 49.

30   **A local paper calls it what many believe it to be:** Headline in the *Portland News*,
      quoted in Painter, *Vice Clique*, 47.

30   **hobos . . . with their "punks":** Boag, *Same-Sex Affairs*, 26.

30   **Chinese, Asian Indian, Greek:** Boag, *Same-Sex Affairs*, 18–19.

30   **Among them is Herman Smith:** Painter, *Vice Clique*, 56.

31   **"an act . . . which grossly injured":** Painter, *Vice Clique*, 64.

31   **a homosexual house party:** Painter, *Vice Clique*, 108.

31   **he has seduced and corrupted:** Painter, *Vice Clique*, 145.

31   **prosecutors . . . begin dismissing indictments:** Painter, *Vice Clique*, 166.

32   **"boy . . . referred to a young man":** Boag, *Same-Sex Affairs*, 108.

32   **In the wake of the arrests:** Boag, *Same-Sex Affairs*, 203–4.

32   **she was close to two of the implicated men:** James Beard Foundation, *The James
      Beard Celebration Cookbook: Memories and Recipes from His Friends*, ed. Barbara
      Kafka (New York: William Morrow, 1990), 24.

33   **SS *Tenyo Maru*, sailing from San Francisco:** "Japanese Liner Sails for Orient,"
      San Francisco Call and Post, December 14, 1912, Newspapers.com.

33   **Hermann Georg Ludwig Schmidt:** US Census Bureau, "1900 United States Fed-
      eral Census for Herman Schmidt," Portage Township, Indiana, Ancestry.com.

33   **Friedrich and Anna Schmidt:** Craig Jacobs, "Did a Cook Called 'Stina' Really
      Exist in Niles Back in the 1870s?," *Niles Daily Star* (Niles, MI), October 17,
      2008.

34 **"The gay life which went on about us"**: Herman Smith, *Kitchens Near and Far* (New York: M. Barrows & Company, 1946), 68.

34 **boards a westbound train**: Jacobs, "Did a Cook?"

34 **The Chinese-born cook**: Smith, *Kitchens*, 85–87.

34 **"These wiry handsome bronzed men"**: Smith, *Kitchens*, 82.

34 **"bronzed . . . by the sun"**: Smith, *Kitchens*, 97.

35 **he registers as a Democrat**: Painter, *Vice Clique*, 211.

35 **Herman received money**: Smith, *Kitchens*, 120.

35 **"strange hunger of the heart and soul"**: Smith, *Kitchens*, 242.

35 **"gayest city in the Orient"**: Smith, *Kitchens*, 153–55.

36 **sometime in or after 1918**: According to his draft registration card, before September 1918 he's working for the US Ordnance Department. "U.S. World War I Draft Registration Cards, 1917–1918," for Herman Maurice K. Smith, Ancestry.com.

36 **a single yellow flower**: Smith, *Kitchens*, 270.

37 **he boasts to *This Week***: Grace Turner, "Crack Christmas Recipes," *This Week*, in *St. Louis Globe-Democrat*, December 24, 1939, Newspapers.com.

37 **Herman's job disappears**: Jacobs, "Did a Cook?"

REDEMPTION FUDGE

39 **Harry's wedding to Mary Fitzwater**: Wedding notice for Miss Mary Fitzwater and Mr. Harry M. Baker, *Cincinnati Enquirer*, June 23, 1912, Newspapers.com.

39 **baked bean and cake parties**: Mary Hart, "Mystery Cake."

39 **Harry sells insurance**: Mary Hart, "Mystery Cake."

39 **a couple of kids**: Joseph Hart, "When Harry Met Betty." *The Rake*, January 29, 2007.

39 **To relax**: Mary Hart, "Mystery Cake."

40 **Harry's been picked up**: Joseph Hart, "When Harry."

40 **Samuel Steward**: Samuel M. Steward, *Chapters from an Autobiography* (San Francisco: Grey Fox Press, 1981), 10–13.

40 **"such things must [therefore] be nonexistent"**: Steward, *Chapters*, 15.

41 **away from Mary's kitchen**: Mary Hart, "Mystery Cake."

41 **He moves to Los Angeles**: Mary Hart, "Mystery Cake."

41 **"Eden of the imagination"**: Robert Gottlieb, *The Next Los Angeles: The Struggle for a Livable City* (Berkeley: University of California Press, 2005), 18.

42 **"The number of faggots cruising"**: Hart Crane, quoted in William J. Mann, *Behind the Screen: How Gays and Lesbians Shaped Hollywood 1910–1969* (New York: Viking, 2001), 87.

42 **he lays her to rest**: Joseph Hart, "When Harry."

42 **Wilshire Community Kitchen**: Mary Hart, "Mystery Cake."

42 **April 14, 1927**: Mary Hart, "Mystery Cake."

NIGHTS AT THE MANDARIN

43 **Mudan Su**: Nancy Yunhwa Rao, *Chinatown Opera Theater in North America* (Chicago: University of Illinois Press, 2017), 236–37. Internet Archive.

44   **"A chattering kind of freedom filled the space"**: Wayson Choy, "Paper Shadows," in *The Penguin Book of Canadian Short Stories*, ed. by Jane Urquhart (Toronto: Penguin Canada, 2007), 450.

44   **dumplings and sweet egg tarts**: Choy, "Paper Shadows," 450.

44   **"pliant notes"**: Choy, "Paper Shadows," 446.

44   **"Cantonese opera at night bestowed upon me"**: Choy, "Paper Shadows," 451.

44   **a part-time job in the box office**: Frank Bren, "Blind Spot: Looking for Esther Eng," *Metro* (Australian Teachers of Media) 145 (2005).

44   **San Francisco's new Chinatown**: Rao, *Chinatown Opera*, 222.

45   **successful dry goods business**: Christianne A. Gadd, "The History of Esther Eng," OutHistory.org.

45   **"one of the world's great centers"**: Bren, "Blind Spot."

45   **the Mandarin stages a pop-up series**: "Chinese Theater Is Jazzed Up," *Los Angeles Times*, May 31, 1925, Newspapers.com.

45   **"drew from its aesthetics and expression"**: Nancy [Yunhwa] Rao, quoted in Wendy Maloney, "Inquiring Minds: Chinese Opera in North America," *Timeless: Stories from the Library of Congress*, August 1, 2017.

45   **"the emancipation of Chinese women"**: Robert Commanday, "A Western Pear Garden," *San Francisco Chronicle*, August 28, 1983.

46   **"a theater of actresses"**: Rao, *Chinatown Opera*, 236.

46   **As in Shakespeare's time**: Chou Hui-ling. "Striking Their Own Poses: The History of Cross-Dressing on the Chinese Stage." *TDR* (Cambridge, MA), vol. 41, no. 2 (summer 1997): 130+. Gale Literature Resource Center.

46   **"He would take out his cosmetics"**: "Guide to the Jade Shoots of the Dingyou Year," quoted in Wu Cuncun and Mark Stevenson. "Speaking of Flowers: Theatre, Public Culture, and Homoerotic Writing in Nineteenth-Century Beijing," *Asian Theatre Journal* 27, no. 1 (2010): 109–10, JSTOR.

47   **"hella queer"**: Amy Sueyoshi, email to author, January 5, 2024.

47   **Mu is a great star**: Rao, *Chinatown Opera*, 236.

47   **"To underscore the intimacy"**: Rao, *Chinatown Opera*, 238.

47   **"The collapse of the distinction"**: Siu Leung Li, *Cross-Dressing in Chinese Opera* (Hong Kong: Hong Kong University Press, 2003), 163.

48   **in her natural voice**: Rao, *Chinatown Opera*, 237.

BAKED IN THE BEDROOM

49   **non-hat-shaped second location**: Joseph Hart, "When Harry."

49   **Harry's cake is the first**: The Brown Derby Service Organization, *The Brown Derby Cookbook* (Garden City, NY: Doubleday & Company, 1952), 6.

50   **swells and browns**: Mary Hart, "Mystery Cake."

50   **"more beautiful than *Whistler's Mother*"**: Mary Hart, "Mystery Cake."

50   **Albert Ross McCarney**: US Census Bureau, "1930 United States Federal Census for Harry M. Baker," Los Angeles, Ancestry.com.

50   **Harry and Mac's relationship**: Joseph Hart, "When Harry."

50   **the fame of Harry's cake**: Mary Hart, "Mystery Cake."

50   **Marie Dressler . . . Dolores del Río**: Mann, *Behind the Screen*, 56, 80.

50   **a mark of status for the stars:** Mann, *Behind the Screen*, 48–53.

50   **First Lady Eleanor Roosevelt:** Joseph Hart, "When Harry."

50   **a registered Republican:** Los Angeles County Voter Registration, 1942, "United States Voter Registrations, 1900–1968 for Harry M. Baker," Ancestry.com.

50   **Cary Grant and Randolph Scott:** Mann, *Behind the Screen*, 159–60.

50   **flavored with grapefruit:** Joseph Hart, "When Harry."

51   **Kirmser's bar:** Ricardo J. Brown, *The Evening Crowd at Kirmser's: A Gay Life in the 1940s* (Minneapolis: University of Minnesota Press, 2001), 3–4.

51   **Washburn Crosby:** Jessamyn Neuhaus, *Manly Meals and Mom's Home Cooking: Cookbooks and Gender in Modern America,* (Baltimore, MD: The Johns Hopkins University Press, 2003), 169.

51   **the girls who ran the test kitchen:** Tori Avey, "Who Was Betty Crocker?", *PBS Food*, February 15, 2013, PBS.org.

52   **comic strip *Betty*:** "Betty by C. A. Voight," Barnacle Press-Comics 1.0.

52   **the first official face of Betty Crocker:** Betty Crocker Kitchens, "The Betty Crocker Portraits," BettyCrocker.com.

52   **"an ageless thirty-two":** Jean Libman Block, "The Secret Life of Betty Crocker," *Women's Home Journal*, December 1954.

52   **"Miss Betty!":** Sue Scattergood, "Famed Betty Crocker Meets Her Match in Sue Scattergood's Kitchen Here!", *Birmingham News*, May 6, 1949, Newspapers.com.

THE SISSY PROPHET OF ASPARAGUS

53   **His ass straight-up kicked ... "stunning and vivid pain":** Craig Claiborne, *Craig Claiborne's A Feast Made for Laughter* (Garden City, NY: Doubleday & Company, 1982), 37–38.

53   **best-selling American cookbooks:** Neuhaus, *Manly Meals*, 178.

55   **He's lost everything:** Thomas McNamee, *The Man Who Changed the Way We Eat: Craig Claiborne and the American Food Renaissance* (New York: Free Press, 2012), 12.

55   **take in boarders:** Claiborne, *A Feast*, 21.

55   **"Never forget ... ":** Claiborne, *A Feast*, 35.

55   **"Innocently":** Claiborne, *A Feast*, 38–39.

55   **a messy public confession:** Claiborne, *A Feast*, 19–21.

56   **"clandestine but common":** John Howard, "Gay Life," *Mississippi Encyclopedia* (website), Center for Study of Southern Culture and the Mississippi Humanities Council, July 11, 2017.

56   **"Fright. Fright":** Hubert Creekmore, *The Welcome* (Jackson: University Press of Mississippi, 2023), 180. Kindle.

57   **the bucket erupts:** Claiborne, *A Feast*, 3.

57   ***national terror of Black sexuality:*** Wesley Morris, "Last Taboo: Why Pop Culture Just Can't Deal with Black Sexuality," *New York Times Magazine*, Oct. 27, 2016.

58   **a double violation:** Claiborne, *A Feast*, 26.

58   **white asparagus from the can:** Claiborne, *A Feast*, 34.

59   **"Tinged with ultramarine":** Marcel Proust, *Swann's Way: Remembrance of Things Past, Volume One*, trans. by C. K. Scott Moncrieff (A Project Gutenberg ebook, 2020).

59   *des irisations qui ne sont pas de la terre:* Marcel Proust, *Du côté de chez Swann: À la recherche du temps perdu, Tome I,* (A Project Gutenberg ebook, 2001).

59   **three-layered salad:** Claiborne, *A Feast,* 34.

59   **Aunt Catherine works the plunger:** Claiborne, *A Feast,* 6–7.

60   *Peter at the gate:* Don Yoder, "Come, Butter, Come!", Smithsonian Folklife Festival Records: 1970 Festival of American Folklife, Ralph Rinzler Folklife Archives and Collections, Smithsonian Institution.

PAPER CHICKEN FOR DIVAS

61   **"Coatless, preoccupied men" . . . Hatless fetch boys:** Katherine Hill, "Putting on Chinese Play at Mandarin," *San Francisco Chronicle,* February 25, 1934.

61   **The sign out front:** CitySleuth, "The Lady from Shanghai–On the Lam–Mandarin Theatre 1," *Reel SF,* March 27, 2012.

62   **"They don't like sightseers . . . snatching a nap":** Hill, "Chinese Play."

62   **a public girls' academy:** "U.S., School Yearbooks, 1900–2016 for Esther Ng," Girls High School, San Francisco, 1934, Ancestry.com.

62   **landed a box office job . . . to meet the visiting actresses:** Gadd, "History of Esther Eng."

63   **"sleek boyish bob":** Quoted in *Golden Gate Girls,* directed. by S. Louisa Wei (2013, Women Make Movies), Kanopy, 20:34 mark.

63   **the beautiful Wai Kim-fong:** Wei, *Golden Gate Girls.*

63   **another San Franciscan, Dorothy Arzner:** S. Louisa Wei, " 'She Wears Slacks': Pioneer Women Directors Esther Eng and Dorothy Arzner," in *Early Cinematic Experience of Hong Kong,* Book III, ed. Winnie Fu (Hong Kong: Hong Kong Film Archive, 2014).

63   **Chinese resistance:** S. Louisa Wei, "Esther Eng," in *Women Film Pioneers Project,* ed. Jane Gaines, Radha Vatsal, and Monica Dall'Asta (New York: Columbia University Libraries, 2014).

64   **"First Cantonese Singing-Talking Picture":** Bren, "Blind Spot."

64   **"I just went ahead":** Betty Cornelius, "Esther Eng, Movie Maker, Visits Here," *Seattle Times,* June 9, 1946.

64   **Fountain Avenue:** Bren, "Blind Spot." See also Cornelius, "Esther Eng."

THE LONELINESS OF RHUBARB

65   **They moved on up:** Richard Orton, "Uncle Herman's World: HMK Smith Letters to Rena Harrell, 1930–1937," private family newsletter.

65   **She owns a circa-1810 farmhouse:** Turner, "Crack Christmas Recipes."

65   **"suavely conscious":** Emma Lou Fetta, "Daylight and Dark in New York," *The Observer* (New York), June 26, 1938.

66   **spoon bread, . . . creme brûlée:** Grace Turner, "Home-Cooked Dishes That Are Tops," *This Week in The Cincinnati Enquirer,* December 31, 1939, Newspapers.com.

66   **putters in his herb garden:** Orton, "Uncle Herman's World."

66   *The American Home* **magazine:** "Herman Smith, Menus and Recipes," *The Amer-*

ican Home, June–November 1941, vol. 26 index; and "Herman Smith, recipes and articles," *The American Home*, December 1941–May 1942, vol. 27 index.

66 **The Country Kitchen:** Della T. Lutes, *The Country Kitchen* (Boston: Little, Brown, and Company, 1936).

66 **"the best in every one who sees it":** Andre Sennwald, "The Screen," *New York Times*, March 22, 1935.

66 **Across the country:** "The Woman's Civic club . . . ," page 8, *Deuel County Herald* (Big Springs, NE), November 26, 1936; "I Cover the Shopping Front," *Burlington Daily News* (Burlington, NC), September 18, 1936; "D.A.R.'s Make Plans to Send Box to Island," *Modesto Bee* (Modesto, CA), November 25, 1936. Newspapers.com.

67 **A US at war decrees food rationing:** "Rationing," The National WWII Museum, New Orleans, nationalww2museum.org.

67 **"to a pleasant time and place":** Jane Holt, "News of Food," *New York Times*, November 28, 1942.

67 **worthy successor to Della Lutes:** Helen Bower, *Detroit Free Press*, quoted on the book jacket for *Stina: The Story of a Cook*.

67 **a French-speaking Alsatian refugee:** Herman Smith, *Stina: The Story of a Cook* (New York: M. Barrows & Company, 1942), 8.

68 **"Small, almost elfin":** Smith, *Stina*, 8.

68 **real-life queens Guilda and Lestra:** For Guilda, see Richard Burnett, "Remembering Guilda," *Xtra*, July 26, 2012. For Lestra, see "Lestra," Digital Transgender Archive.

68 **conjured resurrection:** B.C., " 'Stina' Lives Again in Charming Book," *Evening Star* (Washington, DC), November 20, 1942.

68 **goes on a quest:** Jacobs, "Did a Cook?"

69 **heaps of cookies, cakes, pains d'épices:** Smith, *Stina*, 17–25.

69 **With Stina's blessing:** Antic Hay Books, listing for signed copy of *Stina: The Story of a Cook*, accessed July 5, 2024, Antiquarian Booksellers' Association of America, ABAA.org. See also CorgiPack, listing for signed copy of *Stina: The Story of a Cook*, accessed July 5, 2024, AbeBooks.com.

70 **"Although this succulent plant":** Smith, *Stina*, 90.

70 **Māhū:** Outright Team, "The Meaning of Māhū," Outright International, March 22, 2023.

70 **"a lake of rhubarb":** Smith, *Stina*, 90.

BOOK OF SECRETS

72 **slight, brown-haired and brown-eyed:** See physical description of Richard in "U.S., World War II Draft Cards Young Men, 1940–1947," Iowa, Merrill-Orr, April 16, 1945, Ancestry.com.

72 **devoted to plants and flowers:** Spring, *Gourmands' Way*, 79.

72 **white-frame house . . . Marathon:** Jean Tallman, " 'The Greatest American Chef,'" *Des Moines Register*, June 17, 1973, Newspapers.com.

72 **a sober Christian tone:** Richard Olney, *Reflexions* (New York: Brick Tower Press, 1999), 120–21.

72 **three cents the bag:** Tallman, " 'Greatest American Chef.'"

72 **helps with the family cooking:** Tallman, " 'Greatest American Chef.'"

72   *Mohr's in Albert City:* Ad for Mohr's Cash Store in *Albert City Appeal* (Albert City, IA), October 17, 1940.

73   **In 1941 . . . Crown publishes:** Helen Robertson, " 'The Escoffier Cook Book' Is Designed for Culinary Artist Who Attempts French Cooking," *The Plain Dealer* (Cleveland, OH), October 13, 1941, Newspapers.com.

73   **Mousse of Crayfish . . . Poivrade Sauce for Venison:** A. Escoffier, *The Escoffier Cook Book: A Guide to the Fine Art of Cookery* (New York: Crown Publishers, 1941), 30, 336.

73   **Richard has seen the book:** I'm speculating that Richard sees the book in a shop. In the 1970s in Tallman, " 'Greatest American Chef,' " Richard's mother describes him "finding" a copy of the book when he's fourteen. She calls it "an old copy," but since the book was published in 1941, I suspect she's misremembering.

73   **Doris drops in:** Tallman, " 'Greatest American Chef.' "

74   **Then I'll never get married:** Judith Olney, email to the author, July 24, 2024.

"THE MAN AMONG THE WOMEN"

75   **"China's premier Movie Brat":** Bren, "Blind Spot."

75   **"gender rebel":** Gadd, "History of Esther Eng."

75   **an all-woman cast of thirty-six:** Bren, "Blind Spot."

76   **"secret parties or boat cruises":** Travis S. K. Kong, *Oral Histories of Older Gay Men in Hong Kong: Unspoken but Unforgotten* (Hong Kong: Hong Kong University Press, 2019), 8, Google Play.

76   **"the man among the women":** Wei, " 'She Wears Slacks,' " 132.

76   **"We used to call Fong":** Wei, " 'She Wears Slacks,' " 132.

76   **"the only woman directing":** Bren, "Blind Spot."

76   **a British Crown colony:** Kong, *Oral Histories*, 1.

77   **"the Chinese indigenous concept":** Tze-lan D. Sang, *The Emerging Lesbian: Female Same-Sex Desire in Modern China* (Chicago: The University of Chicago Press, 2003), 107–8.

77   **heeds her parents' warnings:** Meg Osman, "The Elegant Life of Esther Eng," *Forever a Pleasure* (blog), May 5, 2021.

77   **Lee Jun-fan, a.k.a Bruce Lee:** Bren, "Blind Spot."

78   **discovered by chance in a dumpster:** See note 3, S. Louisa Wei, "Finding Voices Through Her Images: Golden Gate Girls as an Attempt in Writing Women Filmmakers' History," *Feminist Media Histories* 2, no. 2 (April 2016): 45

INGREDIENT X

79   **The only photos I've seen of him:** Mary Hart, "Mystery Cake."

79   **"This is the story of 'Ingredient X'":** Mary Hart, "Mystery Cake."

80   **has been dubbed "chiffon":** General Mills, "Betty Crocker Presents 'Chiffon Cake,' The Cake Discovery of the Century with Gold Medal Flour," recipe booklet, 1949.

80   **the secret Harry's kept:** Mary Hart, "Mystery Cake."

81   **common salad oil:** Mary Hart, "Mystery Cake."

81   **"terrific popularity":** James Beard, *James Beard's American Cookery* (Boston: Little, Brown, 1972), 690.

81   **"Accidentally She Discovered It":** Ad for Mazzola, *Ladies' Home Journal*, June 1924.

82   **leaves a cake for you on his front porch:** Joseph Hart, "When Harry."

82   **Queen of the Nile:** Tennessee Williams, *A Streetcar Named Desire*, Scene 10, PBworks, 138.

83   **binarisms in a literature:** Eve Kosofsky Sedgwick, *Epistemology of the Closet* (Berkeley: University of California Press, 2008), 91–130.

83   **tangled in litigation:** Mary Hart, "Mystery Cake."

84   **creeping fear of memory loss:** Stephen Schmidt, "Secrets of Chiffon Cake," *Cook's Illustrated*, May/June 1996, 8.

84   **an out-of-work jewelry store clerk:** US Census Bureau, "1950 United States Federal Census for Albert R. McCarney," Los Angeles, Ancestry.com.

84   **trying to interest General Mills:** Mary Hart, "Mystery Cake."

84   **Christian Dior's New Look fashions:** Maddie Crisp, "Christian Dior and the New Look," *SMU Look*, November 9, 2021, Smulook.com.

85   **the company makes Harry an offer:** Mary Hart, "Mystery Cake."

85   **Some say twenty-five grand:** Joseph Hart, "When Harry."

86   **a rumor he's in South America:** Joseph Hart, "When Harry."

87   **South Flower Street:** US Census Bureau, "1950 United States Federal Census for Harry M. Baker," Los Angeles, Ancestry.com.

HUNGRY IN PARIS

91   **the latest flavor of derangement:** James Baldwin: "Paris, from across the ocean, looked like a refuge from the American madness . . . ," from "The New Lost Generation," *Esquire*, July 1, 1961.

91   **same old poverty of love:** "Love is at the heart of the Baldwin philosophy . . . ," David Leeming, *James Baldwin: A Biography* (New York: Arcade Publishing, 2015), 123. See also James Baldwin, *The Fire Next Time* (New York: Dell Publishing Co., Inc., 1964), 17: "To be loved baby, hard, at once, and forever, to strengthen you against the loveless world . . . "

91   **the last of the fellowship award money:** Leeming, *James Baldwin*, 54.

91   **He feels the guilt:** Leeming, *James Baldwin*, 55.

91   **expensive, shitty rooms in cold-water hotels:** Baldwin, "The New Lost Generation."

92   **just for standing:** Baldwin, "The New Lost Generation."

92   **killing themselves with booze or smack:** James Baldwin, "Here Be Dragons: James Baldwin's Critique of the American Ideal of Manhood," Beacon Broadside, July 7, 2022, beaconbroadside.com.

92   **Berdis's fried chicken back in Harlem:** James Baldwin, "Equal in Paris," in *James Baldwin: Collected Essays* (New York: The Library of America, 1998), 112.

92   **Chez Rafi:** Leeming, *James Baldwin*, 59.

92   **cheap tripe or onion soup at dawn:** James Baldwin, *Giovanni's Room* (New York: Vintage International, 2013), 47.

93   **Inez Cavanaugh's jangling club and soul food parlor:** Samuel Rutter, "Exploring James Baldwin's Old Haunts in New York and Paris," *T: The New York Times Style Magazine*, December 17, 2020.

93   **"the most terrifying personal anarchy":** Baldwin, "The New Lost Generation."

93   **They get drunk every night:** Inspired by Thomas Maltais, "Go Tell It at the Metro Bar," quoted in Leeming, *James Baldwin*, 60.

93   **"No thoughts of color in early Paris":** Maltais quoted in Leeming, *James Baldwin*, 60.

93   **Room No. 1 goes by the hour:** Olney, *Reflexions*, 15.

94   **"food, a room, a coat, a typewriter":** Leeming, *James Baldwin*, 58–59.

94   **American tourists swarming Paris:** John E. Booth, "The Whole of France Welcomes the Tourist," *New York Times*, February 19, 1950.

94   **"It's pork chops, baby":** Cecil Brown, "With James Baldwin at the Welcome Table," *The Common Reader*, September 23, 2019.

94   **Frank and Dorcas Neal's weekend salon:** David Hajdu, *Lush Life: A Biography of Billy Strayhorn* (London: Granta Books, 1996), 114–15.

94   **"For those in the group who were Black and gay":** Hajdu, *Lush Life*, 116.

95   **"a pot of chicken and rice":** Hajdu, *Lush Life*, 114–15.

95   **Billy calls the dish his "pot":** Hajdu, *Lush Life*, 193–94.

95   **A'Lelia Walker's Dark Tower:** Lauren Walser, "How A'Lelia Walker and The Dark Tower Shaped the Harlem Renaissance," *Saving Places*, The National Trust for Historic Preservation, March 29, 2017.

95   **homoerotic murals by Bruce Nugent:** Maya Wilson, "Before Baldwin: The Writings of Richard Bruce Nugent," *Off the Grid*, Village Preservation blog, September 21, 2023.

THE SHAPE OF BOHEMIA

96   **"STRICTLY FROM THE NEW BOHEMIA":** Rhea Talley, "They're Strictly from the New Bohemia," *Courier-Journal* (Louisville, KY), March 26, 1950.

97   **They mix with weathered scene queens:** Talley, "The New Bohemia."

97   **it meant dressing up deviant appetites:** See Gore Vidal, *The City and the Pillar* (New York: Vintage International, 2003), 203: "There was also the half-world where hetero- and homosexual mingled with a certain degree of frankness; this was particularly true of theatrical and literary groups . . ."

97   **the headquarters for this curious squad:** Talley, "The New Bohemia."

97   **operating without a license:** "Business Certificate for Partners" application, State of New York, September 30, 1949.

97   **"a canteen for the creative class":** John T. Edge, "Debts of Pleasure," *Oxford American*, September 15, 2013.

98   **who lives across the street:** Amanda Davis and Sarah Sargent, "Buffie Johnson Residence / Tennessee Williams Residence," NYC LGBT Historic Sites Project, November 2019, nyclgbtsites.org.

98   **listed as unmarried:** US Census Bureau, "1950 United States Federal Census for Virginia Reed," New York, NY, Ancestry.com.

98   **personal domestic of Spivy:** Johnny Nicholson quoted in Mary Cantwell, "A

Nightspot to Remember," *Vanity Fair*, January 1999: "Madame Spivy [a glory of New York / Paris nightlife] lent me her personal maid, Virginia Reed, for opening day. Virginia never went back."

98   **Madame Spivy. . . Bertha Levine:** "Madame Spivy," Queer Music Heritage (website).

98   **"a class picture of the young and the talented":** William Grimes, "Johnny Nicholson, Whose Midtown Cafe Drew the 'New Bohemians,' Dies at 99," *New York Times*, August 8, 2016.

99   **a world briefly at peace:** Gore Vidal, introduction to Karl Bissinger, *The Luminous Years: Portraits at Mid-Century by Karl Bissinger*, ed. Catherine Johnson (New York: Henry N. Abrams, Inc., 2003).

99   **Duffy's bar at the beach:** Esther Newton, *Cherry Grove, Fire Island: Sixty Years in America's First Gay and Lesbian Town* (Durham, NC: Duke University Press, 2014), 90.

99   **San Remo Café on Bleecker Street:** Jay Shockley, "San Remo Café," NYC LGBT Historic Sites Project, March 2017 (rev. January 2023), nyclgbtsites.org.

100   **"A dinner party":** Photo caption in a story by Charles J. Rolo, "The New Bohemia," *Flair*, February 1950.

THE BANQUETTE REVOLUTION

101   **The Paper Doll:** Information on the history and culture of The Paper Doll is from San Francisco Planning Department, "Landmark Designation Report," Paper Doll, 524 Union Street, San Francisco, 2018.

101   **"She just sort of turned it on":** Nan Alamilla Boyd, *Wide Open Town: A History of Queer San Francisco to 1965* (Berkeley: University of California Press, 2003), 82.

102   **"It offered sanctuary from the tourism":** San Francisco Planning Department, "Landmark Designation Report," 10.

102   **"all in men's clothes":** Susan Sontag, *Reborn: Early Diaries 1947–1963*, ed. David Rieff (New York: Penguin Books, 2009), 26.

102   **"They had these big booths":** Boyd, *Wide Open Town*, 82.

103   **"gay from the core outwards":** R. B. Read, "Subcultural Wonder," *San Francisco Examiner*, October 28, 1977, Newspapers.com.

RICHARD ~~FUCKS UP~~ TELLS THE TRUTH

104   **Do you like girls?:** See Allan Bérubé, *Coming Out Under Fire: The History of Gay Men and Women in World War Two* (New York: The Free Press, 1990), 8.

104   **occasionally guys do the unthinkable:** For the "unthinkable" act of admitting you're gay, see Ricardo Brown, *Evening Crowd at Kirmser's*, 11.

104   **He gets a letter from the Fulbright Commission:** Spring, *Gourmands' Way*, 77–78.

105   **an allowance of a hundred bucks a month:** Spring, *Gourmands' Way*, 77–78.

105   **He finds a room at Hôtel Verneuil:** Olney, *Reflexions*, 15.

105   **And everybody—*every*body:** Olney, *Reflexions*, 14–16.

THE SALVAGE QUEEN OF FIFTY-EIGHTH STREET

107 **Carroll Street in St. Louis:** Cantwell, "Nightspot to Remember."

107 **He leaves school after eighth grade:** US Census Bureau, "1930 United States Federal Census for John Bulica," St. Louis, MO, Ancestry.com.

107 **With seventy-five dollars in his wallet:** Cantwell, "Nightspot to Remember."

107 **Christmas-season work at Lord & Taylor:** Cantwell, "Nightspot to Remember."

108 **watches a man in the aisles cruising sailors:** Cantwell, "Nightspot to Remember."

108 **Karl and Johnny spend six months in Europe:** Cantwell, "Nightspot to Remember."

109 **shifting politically and culturally:** See Faderman, *Odd Girls*, 130.

109 **a massive purge:** Adkins, " 'These People Are Frightened to Death.' "

109 **"the dreariest place you can imagine":** Johnny Nicholson, quoted in Catherine Johnson, *Karl Bissinger*, documentary rough cut, private YouTube video, February 14, 2014, 15:54 mark.

109 **Daniel's on East Fifty-Fourth:** Clementine Paddleford, "New Discovery in Restaurants," *New York Herald*, March 24, 1951.

110 **Edna says forget about a café:** Cantwell, "Nightspot to Remember."

110 **"You're going to be the cook":** Edna Lewis, quoted in *Fried Chicken and Sweet Potato Pie*, directed by Bailey Barash (2006, Bbarash Productions), 7:19 mark.

THE QUEER EDUCATION OF MISS LEWIS

111 **"the self . . . at odds with everything around it":** bell hooks, quoted in Elyssa Goodman, "How bell hooks Paved the Way for Intersectional Feminism," *Them*, March 12, 2019.

112 **a tribute . . . to Edna's work and dedication:** Sarah Kirnon, Instagram direct message to the author, August 8, 2024.

112 **keen on living and cooking in Italy:** Edna Lewis and Scott Peacock, *The Gift of Southern Cooking: Recipes and Revelations from Two Great Southern Cooks* (New York: Alfred A. Knopf, 2003), xiii–xiv.

112 **"It was something I fought with":** Scott Peacock, quoted in Barash, *Fried Chicken*, 18:08.

113 **"It's a lot bigger than cooking":** Scott Peacock, quoted in Barash, *Fried Chicken*, 19:03.

113 **Amazon Best Sellers list:** Maura Judkis, "Edna Lewis' Classic Cookbook Zooms Up the Charts After 'Top Chef' Tribute," *Washington Post*, January 6, 2017.

113 **"Day-Glo pretty-in-pink":** Chang-Rae Lee, "The Quiet Cook," *Gourmet*, November 2001.

113 **Edna Regena Lewis:** Commonwealth of Virginia Bureau of Vital Statistics, "Certificate of Birth, Edna Regena Lewis," April 13, 1916, Ancestry.com.

113 **one of eight children:** Eric Asimov and Kim Severson, "Edna Lewis, 89, Dies; Wrote Cookbooks That Revived Refined Southern Cuisine," *New York Times*, February 14, 2006.

113 **a community founded by the formerly enslaved:** Francis Lam, "Edna Lewis and the Black Roots of American Cooking," *New York Times Magazine*, October 28, 2015.

114 **At fourteen she's already employed:** US Census Bureau, "1930 United States Federal Census for Edna E. *[sic]* Lewis," Taylor, Orange, VA, Ancestry.com.

114 **at fifteen leaves Virginia . . . two other young women:** Barash, *Fried Chicken*, 5:53.

114 **an ironing job at a Brooklyn laundry:** Lam, "Edna Lewis and the Black Roots."

114 **"the only ones who encouraged the Blacks":** Barash, *Fried Chicken*, 6:20.

114 **Jim Crow laws:** Chin Jou, "The Jim Crow North? Dining in New York City Before the Civil Rights Act of 1964," *Huffpost*, July 24, 2014 (updated September 23, 2014).

114 **Josephine Baker:** David Rosen, "The Night Josephine Baker Never Got Her Steak," *Black Star News*, blackstarnews.com.

115 **"Edna and Karl were both":** Phyllis Eckhaus, email to the author, August 24, 2023.

115 **"We were bohemians":** Karl Bissinger, quoted in Susanna Cuyler, *Jeanne Owens Pictorial Biography* (Highland Park, NJ: B. Rugged, 1985).

115 **"We all went to the same parties":** Edna Lewis, quoted in Cuyler, *Jeanne Owens*.

115 **"Sylvia's mother had a thrift shop":** Lewis, quoted in Cuyler, *Jeanne Owens*.

116 **a jar of gazpacho . . . whole pigs roasted:** Lewis, quoted in Cuyler, *Jeanne Owens*.

116 **different kinds of cookies:** Lewis, quoted in Cuyler, *Jeanne Owens*.

117 **mannequins in a 1947 Bonwit window:** Francine Snyder, "These 1947 Department Store Displays Paired Abstract Art and Fashion," Guggenheim.org, September 6, 2018.

117 **Edna marries Stephen Kingston:** "Marriage License Indexes, 1907–2018," Edna R. Lewis, New York, NY, Ancestry.com.

117 **ex–merchant seaman:** Asimov and Severson, "Edna Lewis."

117 **worked as a cook . . . in San Francisco:** "Marine Corps Muster Rolls, 1798–1958," Stephen Kingston, October 1945, Ancestry.com.

117 **vigorous defense of the Scottsboro Boys:** Lee, "The Quiet Cook."

117 **pamphlet . . . on Frederick Douglass:** Steve Kingston, *Frederick Douglass: Abolitionist, Liberator, Statesman* (New York: National Negro Congress, 1941).

118 **the American Communist Party:** Bettina Aptheker, *Communists in Closets: Queering the History 1930s–1990s* (New York: Routledge, 2023).

SOUFFLÉS IN SOUP CUPS

119 **"The entrance is a strip of hallway":** Paddleford, "New Discovery."

119 **"coming scented to glory":** Paddleford, "New Discovery."

120 **New York's front-line agency:** George Chauncey, *Gay New York: Gender, Urban Culture, and the Making of the Gay Male World 1890–1940* (New York: Basic Books, 1994), 336–37.

120 **"no legal right to assemble":** John D'Emilio, quoted in Newton, *Cherry Grove*, 82.

120 **"the moon and the stars and the rain":** Paddleford, "New Discovery."

121 **"I nearly fainted":** Charles Kaiser, *The Gay Metropolis 1940–1996* (New York: Houghton Mifflin Company, 1997), 108.

121 **"We were just who we were":** Karl Bissinger, quoted in Johnson, *Karl Bissinger*, 12:31 mark.

121 **"that's the word we used":** Karl Bissinger, quoted in Johnson, *Karl Bissinger*, 10:20 mark.

121 **"I think people felt safe":** Catherine Johnson, interview with the author, July 9, 2024.

121 **"Until Café Nicholson":** Babs Simpson, quoted in Cantwell, "Nightspot to Remember."

122 **"Just bold young people":** Edna Lewis, quoted in Cuyler, *Jeanne Owens*.

122 **"There's nobody *here* but us [n-word]s and fairies!":** Phyllis Eckhaus, email to the author, August 23, 2023.

122 **"We shopped on the Bowery":** Edna Lewis, quoted in Cantwell, "Nightspot to Remember."

122 **"an alchemy beyond money":** Newton, *Cherry Grove*, 88.

123 ***The first chocolate soufflé:*** Recipe quotes from Edna Lewis and Evangeline Peterson, *The Edna Lewis Cookbook* (Edinburg, VA: Axios Press, 2016), 72–73.

123 **a casserole with aspirations:** Irma S. Rombauer, *The Joy of Cooking* (self-published, 1931), 80–84.

123 **"only one to a meal, though, please":** Myra Waldo, quoted in Charlotte Turgeon, "Salads and Souffles," *New York Times*, October 17, 1954.

124 ***Jean Matlega:*** See the description of Matlega in Cantwell, "Nightspot to Remember."

BROTHER HA OF PELL STREET

125 **her father's movie distribution business:** Bren, "Blind Spot."

125 **"cropped in a mannish bob":** Cornelius, "Esther Eng, Movie Maker, Visits Here," *Seattle Times*, June 9, 1946.

125 **Esther's not done directing pictures:** Bren, "Blind Spot."

125 **families chowing on picnic lunches:** Edith Hills, "New Slant on Movies Ends Monroe Doctrine," *What Next!* syndicated column, February 3, 1954.

126 **sets it up for a family called Tan:** S. Louisa Wei, email to the author, January 11, 2024.

126 **"notably excellent":** Craig Claiborne, "Utensils and Edibles for Oriental Dishes Are in Abundance," *New York Times*, October 23, 1958.

126 **"It set a new standard for Chinese food":** Hungry Gerald, "Gone But Not Forgotten Restaurants: Bo-Bo," *Hungry Gerald* (blog), June 20, 2011.

127 **"People do remember Esther":** S. Louisa Wei, email to the author, January 11, 2024.

127 **"a niece who dressed up in man's suits":** Tze-lan D. Sang, email to author, January 10, 2024.

127 **"Gay culture, like everything else":** S. Louisa Wei, email to the author, January 11, 2024.

127 **she opens MongKok:** Osman, "Elegant Life."

127 **It's got swanky touches:** Betty Ryan, "Big Town Talk," *Holyoke Daily Transcript* (Holyoke, MA), August 6, 1959, Newspapers.com.

128 **deep-fried sausage-shaped dumplings:** Craig Claiborne, "Food: Oriental Fare," *New York Times*, June 19, 1959.

128 **Trader Vic's–style flexes:** John H. Kuhn, "Esther Eng's Features Many Chinese Treats," *Morning Call* (Paterson, NJ), July 23, 1965.

128 **"she is an outspoken lesbian":** Bruce Edward Hall, *Tea That Burns* (New York: The Free Press, 1998), 248.

128 **"known to gay people":** Wei, email to the author, January 11, 2024.

129 **It comes out of his mouth as *dikery*:** Gadd, "History of Esther Eng."

130 **Claiborne names it cellophane chicken:** Claiborne, "Oriental Fare."

130 **"a tender, pinkish morsel":** Ryan, "Big Town Talk."

130 **at least three pieces of clothing:** Audre Lorde, *Zami: A New Spelling of My Name* (Berkeley, CA: Crossing Press, 1982), 160.

130 **"a masculinized woman called Mulan":** Lei Qun, quoted in Wei, " 'She Wears Slacks,' " 133.

130 **When she dies from cancer:** "Esther Eng, Owned Restaurants Here," *New York Times*, January 27, 1970.

SATURDAY NIGHT FUNCTION

132 **a party of six or seven people:** Information about this party (these parties, this salon) is from two sources: David Leeming, *Amazing Grace: A Life of Beauford Delaney* (New York: Oxford University Press, 1998), Chapter 8, Kindle; Olney, *Reflexions*, 33.

133 **Jimmy's longtime mentor:** Leeming, *James Baldwin*, 93.

133 **a journalism apprenticeship:** "Bernard Hassell, Choreographer," *The Standard-Star* (New Rochelle, NY), September 26, 1991, Newspapers.com.

133 **Mary Painter:** See Olney, *Reflexions*, 31. Also Leeming, *James Baldwin*, 77. Also Leonard Silk, "Mary Painter Garin, 71, Innovator in Economic and Statistical Work," *New York Times*, October 24, 1991.

134 **were able to score:** Baldwin, "The New Lost Generation."

134 **earning his bread as a rent boy:** Leeming, *James Baldwin*, 74–75.

134 **Jimmy's the godfather:** Leeming, *James Baldwin*, 82.

134 **Arnold:** See Olney, *Reflexions*, 43. Also Leeming, *James Baldwin*, 106, 113–14, and 119–20.

134 **a picture of him . . . with Jimmy:** Leeming, *Amazing Grace*, Chapter 8, Kindle.

134 **"a gentle, sweet boy":** Olney, *Reflexions*, 43.

135 **It's Mary he calls:** Leeming, *James Baldwin*, 119–20.

135 **Elizabeth David's Poulet au Riz Basquaise:** Elizabeth David, *French Country Cooking* (London: Penguin Books, 1962), 121–22.

137 **"Kitchen Man":** Bessie Smith, "Kitchen Man," Genius, https://genius.com/Bessie-smith-kitchen-man-lyrics.

137 **"their faces . . . gray and damp":** James Baldwin, *Another Country* (New York: Vintage International, 1993), 228.

138 **an old Duke Ellington / Barney Bigard ditty:** Duke Ellington and Barney Bigard, "Saturday Night Function," first recording January 16, 1929, *SecondHandSongs*, https://secondhandsongs.com/work/149195.

138 **Richard's younger brother John:** Olney, *Reflexions*, 46.

138 **She returns in 1962:** Silk, "Mary Painter Garin."

138 **The last one unspools . . . in white wine:** Olney, *Reflexions*, 47.

139   **Yves and Eric let it sit on the table:** Baldwin, *Another Country*, 183–84.
140   **"grab Jimmy by those two dimples":** James Baldwin, *Just Above My Head* (New York: Dell Publishing Co., Inc., 1980), 29.

UP THE GOAT PATH

142   **from central Paris to Clamart:** Olney, *Reflexions*, 52.
142   **He tacks up white sheets:** Leeming, *Amazing Grace*, Chapter 8, Kindle.
142   **"Cherry orchards transformed the valley":** Olney, *Reflexions*, 128.

GEN AND LOU

147   **a thing designed for use:** Genevieve Callahan, *The California Cook Book for Indoor and Outdoor Eating* (New York: M. Barrows & Company, 1946).
147   **she "discovers" at Tommaso's restaurant:** Callahan, *California Cook Book*, 232.
147   **crab cioppino:** Callahan, *California Cook Book*, 124.
148   **"the sort of meals we like to serve our friends":** Callahan, *California Cook Book*, 6.
148   **"you can always balance a rich, glamorous dish":** Callahan, *California Cook Book*, 87.

PLEASURE EN FRANÇAIS

150   **the "spiritual revelation":** Claiborne, *A Feast*, 119.

WHEN COOKBOOKS LIE

151   **" 'Oh,' said Alice, 'I couldn't do that . . .' ":** Simon Michael Bessie, "A Happy Publisher's Note to the New Edition," in Alice B. Toklas, *The Alice B. Toklas Cook Book*, foreword by M. F. K. Fisher, publisher's note by Simon Michael Bessie (New York: Harper & Row, 1984), vii.
151   **But this origin story . . . is a lie:** Spring, *Gourmands' Way*, 449.
152   **"Suddenly it came to me":** Alice B. Toklas, in Edward Burns, ed., *Staying on Alone: Letters of Alice B. Toklas* (New York: Vintage Books, 1975), 78.
153   **"I wish all the men in OUR profession . . . were not *pedals*!":** Julia Child, quoted in Laura Shapiro, *Julia Child* (New York: Viking Penguin, 2007), 140–41.
153   **"a socially acceptable form of bigotry":** Shapiro, *Julia Child*, 135.
154   **an entire show on serving wine with cheese:** Julia Child, "Cheese and Wine Party," *The French Chef*, Season 6, ep. 13, December 30, 1970.
154   **a cookbook of shared voices:** Anna Linzie, *The True Story of Alice B. Toklas: A Study of Three Autobiographies* (Iowa City: University of Iowa Press, 2006), 198–99.
155   **"cruel enigma":** Toklas, *Cook Book* (1954), 30.
155   **"a carefully crafted textual persona":** Linzie, *True Story*, 12.
155   **"In the case of Gertrude Stein":** "Alice B. Toklas (1877–1967) The Bancroft

Library Interview," interview by Roland Duncan in 1952, Oral History Center, The Bancroft Library, University of California, Berkeley, 2012.

155 **"You will understand I hope"**: Toklas, quoted in Burns, *Staying on Alone*, 69.

156 **"sociopathic personality disturbance"**: Sara E. McHenry, "Gay Is Good": History of Homosexuality in the *DSM* and Modern Psychiatry," *American Journal of Psychiatry Residents' Journal* 18, no. 1, September 8, 2022.

FAREWELL TO FIRE ISLAND

157 **Henry yells *Dobey!***: McNamee, *The Man Who Changed*, 52.

158 **there's this entire gay world in Chicago**: McNamee, *The Man Who Changed*, 26.

158 **to give and take pleasure**: Craig Claiborne, quoted in a 1991 Dan Perlman interview transcript in McNamee, *The Man Who Changed*, 26.

158 **The boss shrugs**: McNamee, *The Man Who Changed*, 26.

158 **Grated Potato Pudding . . . Craig Wedding Punch**: Claiborne, *A Feast*, 26.

159 **"The palate would be . . . first day of spring"**: Craig Claiborne, "Asparagus Deserving of Title as Aristocratic Vegetable," *New York Times*, March 20, 1958.

159 **"A cultivated woman . . . Physical beauty is passing"**: Williams, *Streetcar*, Scene 10, PBworks, 136.

160 **cruising the streets for daddies in uniform**: Claiborne, *A Feast*, 106–7.

STRANGLING THE DOVES

161 **confessing her reluctance . . . "crime is inevitable"**: Toklas, *Cook Book* (1954), 37.

162 **"How are they all to say how do you do"**: Gertrude Stein, quoted in Jeanne Holland, "Uncovering Woman's Body in Gertrude Stein's 'Subject-Cases: The Background of a Detective Story,'" *College English* 52, no. 5 (1990): 540–51.

162 **"The mystery was held back"**: Alice B. Toklas, quoted in Duncan, "The Bancroft Library Interview," 69–70.

163 **"poor Mr. Carp"**: Toklas, *Cook Book* (1954), 39.

164 **"the sweet young corpses"**: Toklas, *Cook Book* (1954), 41.

164 **"pretty, dainty, and . . . elegant"**: Toklas, *Cook Book* (1954), 43.

164 **opacity of Alice and Gertrude's politics**: See Janet Malcolm, *Two Lives: Gertrude and Alice* (Melbourne: Melbourne University Press, 2007).

165 **the recipe Alice Waters reconfigured**: Alice Waters, *The Chez Panisse Menu Cookbook*, with Linda P. Guenzel (New York: Random House, 1982), 179–81.

165 **"In that case"**: Virgil Thomson, letter to the *New York Review*, in reply to Paul Padgette, "A Very Difficult Author," July 1, 1971.

166 **"one could become accustomed to murdering"**: Toklas, *Cook Book* (1954), 45.

166 **"your dove"**: Kay Turner, ed., *Baby Precious Always Shines: Selected Love Notes Between Gertrude Stein and Alice B. Toklas* (New York: St. Martin's Press, 1999), 157.

166 **"Fulfillment as a woman had only one definition"**: Betty Friedan, *The Feminine Mystique* (New York: W. W. Norton & Co., 2010), 92.

166 **would praise Feniger's visibility**: Camille Paglia, "Last Word: Sugar and Spice," *The Advocate*, April 30, 1996.

AN EDIBLE FOR SAINT TERESA

167 **A British-Canadian artist and writer:** "About Brion Gysin," briongysin.com, https://www.briongysin.com/about/.

167 **British and American writers and artists, many gay:** Richard Hamilton, "How Morocco Became a Haven for Gay Westerners in the 1950s," BBC World Service, October 12, 2014, BBC.com.

168 **"Miggles, mooters, reefers . . . ":** Dr. Richmond Barber, "The Parents' Corner," *San Bernardino Sun-Telegram* (San Bernardino, CA), May 7, 1950, Newspapers.com.

168 **"a willowy platinum blonde model":** "Seize Model in Shorts and Scented Marijuana," *Daily News* (New York), August 7, 1954, Newspapers.com.

169 **the Moroccan edible *majoun*:** Michael Rogers, "Conversations in Morocco: The *Rolling Stone* Interview [1974]," in *Conversations with Paul Bowles*, ed. by Gena Dagel Caponi (Jackson: University Press of Mississippi, 1993), 62–63.

169 **an all-white "heritage" organization:** "Eleanor Roosevelt and Marian Anderson," Franklin D. Roosevelt Presidential Library and Museum, fdrlibrary.org,

170 **"The pain was so great, that it made me moan":** Teresa of Ávila, *The Life of Teresa of Jesus*, trans. and ed. by E. Allison Peers (Scanned by Harry Plantinga, 1995), XXIX.17.

170 **they dash off a telegram:** John Birdsall, "Bohemian Rhapsody: How Alice B. Toklas Became the Accidental Godmother of Edibles," *Cannabis Now*, March 31, 2021.

170 **as beloved and ubiquitous:** Spring, *Gourmands' Way*, 133.

171 **"the best publicity stunt of the year":** Alice B. Toklas to Donald Gallup, October 1954, in Burns, *Staying on Alone*, 310.

CANNED CAMP

172 **Chef Lou Rand Hogan, a.k.a.:** Stephen Vider, " 'Oh Hell, May, Why Don't You People Have a Cookbook?': Camp Humor and Gay Domesticity," *American Quarterly* (Johns Hopkins University Press) 65, no. 4 (December 2013): 877–904.

172 **"The complete compendium of campy cuisine":** Lou Rand Hogan, *The Gay Cookbook* (Los Angeles: Sherbourne Press, 1965).

172 **Uncle Arthur to national TV:** "Ohio's Comedian: Paul Lynde," *Ohio Memory* (blog), The Ohio History Connection and the State Library of Ohio, July 28, 2023.

175 **"Homosexuality shears across the spectrum of American life":** Paul Welch, "Homosexuality in America," *Life*, June 26, 1964.

LES CHEF BROS

178 **"the composed and courtly gentleman":** McNamee, *The Man Who Changed*, 248–49.

178 **treats Pierre like a ghost contributor:** David Kamp, *The United States of Arugula: How We Became a Gourmet Nation* (New York: Broadway Books, 2006), 288.

179 **a house built from an architect's prefab kit:** McNamee, *The Man Who Changed*, 107.

179 **he had a "problem":** Kamp, *Arugula*, 99.

THE UNSHOWN BED

181   **"HERE BRIOCHE IS SHOWN"**: Craig Claiborne, *The New York Times Cook Book* (New York: Harper & Row, 1961), 473.

182   **The original story:** Craig Claiborne, "Brioche Add Elegance to Week-End Breakfast, Brunch," *New York Times*, June 18, 1959.

182   **awarding Liberace a libel settlement:** Roy Greenslade, "The Meaning of 'Fruit': How the *Daily Mirror* Libelled Liberace," *The Guardian*, May 26, 2009.

183   **"one of the ugliest people anyone had ever seen"**: M. F. K. Fisher in Toklas, *Cook Book* (1984), xii–xiii.

184   **"touched by the hands of her lover"**: Monique Truong, *The Book of Salt* (Boston: Mariner Books, 2004), 27.

RICHARD'S DIRTY SALAD

187   **Richard Olney is standing:** Undated snapshot [1973?] of Richard Olney serving lunch in Solliès-Toucas, in the author's collection.

187   **a "skimpy bathing suit"**: Alice Waters, "Introduction," in Olney, *Reflexions*, 17.

188   **"fresh, teased, surprised, excited"**: Richard Olney, *The French Menu Cookbook* (New York: Simon and Schuster, 1970), 22–23.

189   **"to respect and rejoice in the force of life"**: Baldwin, *Fire*, 61–63.

189   **considers it "dirty," low-class:** Richard Olney, *Simple French Food* (New York: Atheneum, 1974), 4–5.

190   **"Masons, carpenters, truck drivers . . . "**: Olney, *Simple*, 4.

190   **a paperback randomly pulled:** Craig Claiborne, "Tomato and Heart of Palm Salad," *Craig Claiborne's Favorites from the New York Times, Volume 3* (New York: Times Publishing, 1977), 42.

191   **"IMPROMPTU COMPOSED SALAD"**: For this and the quoted passages that follow, Olney, *Simple*, 50–55.

193   **its roots are savage:** "Canaille," *Larousse Langue Française*, larousse.fr.

194   **"I built my little house alone"**: Olaf, "Forest Folk," *RFD*, Winter Solstice 1974, 17.

195   **"the shape-shifting queerness of microorganisms"**: Stephanie Maroney, "Sandor Katz and the Possibilities of a Queer Fermentive Praxis," *Cuizine* 9, no. 2 (2018).

195   **the personal narrative they read in the dirt:** Iliana Regan, *Burn the Place: A Memoir* (Chicago: Agate Midway, 2019).

195   **"The formalization of gastro-sensory pleasure"**: Olney, *Simple*, 6.

THE WELCOME TABLE

197   **Harris sits at the outdoor table:** Jessica B. Harris, "Dining with James Baldwin," *Saveur*, May 15, 2017.

197   **sunglasses that were a gift from Miles:** Brown, "With James Baldwin." Brown refers to the cook as "Valérie Sordell."

197   *soupe au pistou*: Harris, "Dining with James Baldwin."
198   **He disidentifies with "gay"**: James Baldwin, *The Last Interview and Other Conversations* (New York: Melville House, 2014).

LEARNING TO COOK FROM MOTHER

199   **Lou Rand kicks off his new column**: Lou Rand, "The Golden Age of Queens," *Bay Area Reporter*, September 4, 1974.

FRESS, DARLING

201   **They name it Sha'ar Zahav**: Betty L. Kalis. "A Recipe for Success," in Congregation Sha'ar Zahav, *Out of Our Kitchen Closets: San Francisco Gay Jewish Cooking* (San Francisco: self-published, 1987), 8. Internet Archive.
201   **"Bless you, She"**: Garry Koenigsberg, quoted in Sha'ar Zahav, *Kitchen Closets*, 6.
202   *men* **handing round the gefilte fish**: John Birdsall, "Food and All Its Blessings," john-birdsall.com (originally published in *Crust*).

TRUMAN SERVES LUNCH

203   **lifts it for Andy Warhol's camera**: Andy Warhol, "[Truman Capote at his apartment with a quiche; Truman and Henry Geldzahler]," Stanford Libraries, Copyright © The Andy Warhol Foundation for the Visual Arts, Inc.
204   **tranquilizers or the anti-alcoholism drug Antabuse**: Anne Taylor Fleming, "The Private World of Truman Capote," *New York Times*, July 9, 1978.
204   **quiche is super-gay**: Kelly Alexander and Claire Bunschoten, "Crème de la Crème: How French Cuisine Became Beloved Among Status-Hungry Diners in the United States, from Thomas Jefferson to Kanye West," July 7, 2023, Aeon.
204   *Apicius gives a recipe for tyropatina*: "Tyropatina," Apicius VII, XIII, 301, romanbritain.org.
205   **"In the past a quiche was rolled out bread dough"**: Tante Ursule [Richard Olney], "Custard Tarts," *Petits Propos Culinaires*, no. 2 (August 1979): 18–19.
206   **cream, onions, and white poppy seeds**: Patrick Rambourg, "La Quiche Lorraine," *Historia*, no. 878 (February 2020).
207   **"the filling risen like a soufflé"**: Elizabeth David, "Eating Out in Provincial France 1965–1977," in *An Omelette and a Glass of Wine* (New York: Viking Penguin, 1985), 69.
207   **"Avenues of heavy-duty ranges"**: Harriet Cooke, "Kitchen Counsel," *Buffalo News* (Buffalo, NY), October 6, 1948, Newspapers.com.
207   **"something that most men would enjoy"**: Wilma Phillips Stewart, "Try Baking Lady Fingers the Waldorf-Astoria Way," *Des Moines Register*, October 11, 1948, Newspapers.com.
208   **appears for the first time in 1895**: Guy Beringer, "Brunch: A Plea," *Hunter's Weekly*, November 5, 1895. Internet Archive.

208 **first print sighting of "homosexual":** Jonathan Ned Katz, *The Invention of Heterosexuality* (New York: The Penguin Group, 1995), 19–20.

208 **"incelibate":** Charles A. Selden, "American Settles Great Wine Dispute," *New York Times*, July 7, 1931.

208 **"someone 'who lived alone'":** Susan Sheridan, "The Habit of Hospitality," *New York Times*, September 28, 1941.

209 **"fruitless pleasures":** Michel Foucault, *The History of Sexuality, Vol. 1: An Introduction*, trans. Robert Hurley (New York: Vintage Books, 1980), 36–37.

209 **"outside the linear progress of history":** Kevin Brazil, *Whatever Happened to Queer Happiness?* (London: Influx Press, 2022), 81–82.

A FRACTURED TIMELINE OF QUICHE

210 **the city's finest quiche Lorraine:** *Bay Area Reporter*, June 15, 1971.

210 **leather, cowboy, and hot pants:** *Bay Area Reporter*, November 1, 1972.

210 **bistro looks . . . an anthem for quiche:** *Bay Area Reporter*, January 18, 1979.

211 **hand-lettered illustrated recipe booklet:** Joni Gold, *Their Friends Were Young and Gay: A Fairy Tale in Food* (San Francisco: self-published, 1979).

211 **quiche and Champagne brunch:** *Bay Area Reporter*, December 20, 1979.

212 **bacon and chopped frozen spinach:** Rick Leed, *Dinner for Two* (San Francisco: Gay Sunshine Press, 1981), 5.

212 **the face of campy drag greeting cards:** Lynda Seaver, "The Secret of Her Excess," *Oakland Tribune*, August 13, 1987, Newspapers.com.

212 **sparks a protest:** Maureen Fan, "Greeting Card Line Pulled from Racks after Protest," *Los Angeles Times*, February 15, 1989.

212 **Quiche Lawanda:** Billi Gordon, *Billi Gordon's You've Had Worse Things in Your Mouth Cookbook* (San Francisco: West Graphics, 1985), 35.

213 **Wilson falls to:** Jim Sullivan, "Hero Worship: Remembering Ricky Wilson of The B-52's," *Rock and Roll Globe* (website), March 19, 2023.

213 **Gays Against Brunch:** *Bay Area Reporter*, July 3, 1980.

213 **"Let them eat quiche!":** *Bay Area Reporter*, February 4, 1982.

214 **It's a slim paperback:** Bruce Feirstein, *Real Men Don't Eat Quiche: A Guidebook to All That Is Truly Masculine* (New York: Pocket Books, 1982).

214 **a mob in the thousands riots:** Mikala Lugen, "The Day Disco Died: Remembering the Unbridled Chaos of 'Disco Demolition Night,'" EDM.com, July 12, 2021.

214 **fields a question about AIDS:** Ben Dreyfuss, "Flashback: The Reagan White House Thought AIDS Was Pretty Hilarious in 1982," *Mother Jones*, December 1, 2014.

215 **Phyllis Schlafly sends a quiche:** Paula Schwed, "Quiche Lobbed as ERA Battle Resumes," January 26, 1983, UPI Archives, upi.com.

215 **burning a huge cardboard effigy:** Dennis McMillan, "The Rolling Zoo," *Bay Area Reporter*, June 30, 1988.

216 **"Could that innocent-looking little lady . . . be poisoning our quiche?":** *Bay Area Reporter*, August 11, 1983.

216 **the Quiche of Peace:** "The Quiche of Peace: Lily Tomlin and Vito Russo," *Our Time*, episode 13, aired May 9, 1983, on WNYC-TV. YouTube, 3:13 mark.

217 **"Our promiscuity taught us many things":** Douglas Crimp, "How to Have Promiscuity in an Epidemic," *October* 43 (Winter 1987): 237–71, JSTOR.

A CULINARY EXTRAVAGANZA

219 **It's a gourmet jamboree:** Paul A. Camp [Paula Camp], "A Birthday Bash for Claiborne—and It's a Potluck Feast," *Chicago Tribune*, September 16, 1982, Newspapers.com.

219 **the lady in a bright pink dress:** Camp, "A Birthday Bash."

220 **"The more intense the taste":** Gael Greene, quoted in Marian Burros, "The Sweet Taste of Sin," *Washington Post*, February 7, 1979.

220 **"Have you tasted my turkey mole?" . . . A bit of conspicuous consumption":** Camp, "A Birthday Bash."

220 **"an element of enlightened self-interest":** Jeannette Ferrary, "36 Characters in Search of an Author," *San Francisco Chronicle*, October 3, 1982.

220 **"the guests drifted away from the party":** Camp, "A Birthday Bash."

221 **"when I had just achieved seminal flow":** This and the quotes that follow are from Claiborne, *A Feast*, 20.

223 **a mix of blanched asparagus, green beans, and sliced avocado:** Craig Claiborne with Pierre Franey, "Salad Days," *New York Times*, July 17, 1977.

223 **one-on-one with Craig Claiborne:** John F. Karr, "Come-Out Cookery," *Bay Area Reporter*, October 14, 1982.

ERNIE AND THE RAINBOW CAKE

226 **Mock Cooter Stew and Goldie's Yo-Yo Puddin:** Ernest Matthew Mickler, *White Trash Cooking* (Berkeley, CA: Ten Speed Press, 1986).

226 **Ernie was born in 1940 in Palm Valley:** Michael Adno, "The Short and Brilliant Life of Ernest Matthew Mickler," *The Bitter Southerner*, January 9, 2018.

228 **"flaunted their poverty":** bell hooks, "White Poverty: The Politics of Invisibility," in *Where We Stand: Class Matters* (New York: Routledge, 2000).

229 **"To be camp":** Mark W. Booth, *Camp* (London: Quartet, 1983), 18.

230 **"To make a good flour gravy":** Mickler, *White Trash*, 31.

231 **"Poor white trash I am for sure":** Dorothy Allison, "A Lesbian Appetite," in *Trash: Stories by Dorothy Allison* (Ithaca, NY: Firebrand Books, 1988), 151–65. Internet Archive.

231 **"The way we see ourselves":** Dorothy Allison, "A Question of Class," *History Is a Weapon* (website).

231 **Reba's Rainbow Ice-Box Cake:** Mickler, *White Trash*, 89–90.

MONDAY NIGHTS AT ZUNI

234 **"What has it been about male/male love":** Lou Sullivan in Ellis Martin and Zach Ozma, eds., *We Both Laughed in Pleasure: The Selected Diaries of Lou Sullivan 1961–1991* (New York: Nightboat Books, 2019), 303.

234 **the restaurant Billy West founded in San Francisco:** John Birdsall, "The For-gotten Queer Legacy of Billy West and Zuni Café," *New York Times*, May 28, 2021.

235 **"it wasn't even a discussion":** Jeffrey Fraenkel, interview with the author, May 9, 2021.

OPEN HOUSE

237 **"Sap-swollen tendrils":** Jim Powell, "Napoleon Reviendra," *Poetry*, January 1989.

239 **"a phrase I always thought was bullshit":** Thom Gunn, quoted in Colin Gillis, "Rethinking Sexuality in Thom Gunn's *The Man with Night Sweats*," *Contemporary Literature* 50, no. 1 (Spring 2009): 156–82.

239 **"a collective representation of itself":** Brazil, *Happiness*, 82

EPILOGUE: THE QUEEREST FOOD

243 **"We couldn't figure out any other way to live":** "Two Girls Who 'Wed' Must Face Court Today," *San Francisco Examiner*, November 28, 1947, Newspapers.com.

244 **glorious, pastel-yellow slices of lemon cake:** Ben Mims, "Sweet Southern Dreams," *Saveur*, February 27, 2012.

SOURCES

Abraham, Julie. *Are Girls Necessary? Lesbian Writing and Modern Histories*. Minneapolis: University of Minnesota Press, 2008. Scribd. First published 1996 by Routledge.

Adno, Michael. "The Short and Brilliant Life of Ernest Matthew Mickler." *The Bitter Southerner*, January 9, 2018.

Allison, Dorothy. "A Lesbian Appetite." In *Trash: Stories by Dorothy Allison*, 151–65. Ithaca, NY: Firebrand Books, 1988. Internet Archive.

Baldwin, James. *Another Country*. New York: Vintage International, 1993. First published 1962 by The Dial Press.

———. *The Fire Next Time*. New York: Dell Publishing Co., Inc., 1964. First published 1963 by The Dial Press.

———. *Giovanni's Room*. New York: Vintage International, 2013. First published 1956 by The Dial Press.

———. *Just Above My Head*. New York: Dell Publishing Co., Inc., 1980. First published 1978 by The Dial Press.

Barash, Bailey, dir. *Fried Chicken and Sweet Potato Pie*. Atlanta, GA: Bbarash Productions, 2006. Documentary video, 21:08 min.

Bérubé, Allan. *Coming Out Under Fire: The History of Gay Men and Women in World War Two*. New York: The Free Press, 1990.

Birdsall, John. *The Man Who Ate Too Much: The Life of James Beard*. New York: W. W. Norton & Company, 2020.

Bissinger, Karl. *The Luminous Years: Portraits at Mid-Century by Karl Bissinger*. Edited by Catherine Johnson. New York: Henry N. Abrams, 2003.

Boag, Peter. *Same-Sex Affairs: Constructing and Controlling Homosexuality in the Pacific Northwest*. Berkeley: University of California Press, 2003.

Boyd, Nan Alamilla. *Wide Open Town: A History of Queer San Francisco to 1965*. Berkeley: University of California Press, 2003.

Brazil, Kevin. *Whatever Happened to Queer Happiness?* London: Influx Press, 2022.

Bren, Frank. "Blind Spot: Looking for Esther Eng." *Metro* (Australian Teachers of Media) 145 (2005): 106–10.

Bridgman, Richard. *Gertrude Stein in Pieces*. New York: Oxford University Press, 1970.

Brown, Cecil. "With James Baldwin at the Welcome Table." *The Common Reader*, September 23, 2019.

The Brown Derby Service Organization. *The Brown Derby Cookbook.* Garden City, NY: Doubleday & Company, 1952.

Brown, Ricardo J. *The Evening Crowd at Kirmser's: A Gay Life in the 1940s.* Minneapolis: University of Minnesota Press, 2001.

Burns, Edward, ed. *Staying on Alone: Letters of Alice B. Toklas.* New York: Vintage Books, 1975.

Callahan, Genevieve. *The California Cook Book for Indoor and Outdoor Eating.* New York: M. Barrows & Company, 1946.

Cantwell, Mary. "A Nightspot to Remember." *Vanity Fair,* January 1999.

Chauncey, George. *Gay New York: Gender, Urban Culture, and the Making of the Gay Male World 1890–1940.* New York: Basic Books, 1994.

Choy, Wayson. "Paper Shadows," in *The Penguin Book of Canadian Short Stories,* edited by Jane Urquhart, 445–53. Toronto: Penguin Canada, 2007. Internet Archive.

Claiborne, Craig. *Craig Claiborne's A Feast Made for Laughter.* Garden City, NY: Doubleday & Company, 1982.

——. *The New York Times Cook Book.* New York: Harper & Row, 1961.

Claiborne, Craig, with Pierre Franey. *Craig Claiborne's The New New York Times Cookbook.* New York: Times Books, 1979.

Congregation Sha'ar Zahav. *Out of Our Kitchen Closets: San Francisco Gay Jewish Cooking.* San Francisco: self-published, 1987. Internet Archive.

Creekmore, Hubert. *The Welcome.* Jackson: University Press of Mississippi, 2023. Kindle. First published 1948 by Appleton-Century.

Crimp, Douglas. "How to Have Promiscuity in an Epidemic." *October,* vol. 43 (Winter 1987): 237–71. JSTOR.

Cuyler, Susanna. *Jeanne Owens Pictorial Biography.* Highland Park, NJ: B. Rugged, 1985.

David, Elizabeth. *An Omelette and a Glass of Wine.* New York: Viking Penguin, 1985.

——. *French Country Cooking.* London: Penguin Books, 1962. First published 1951 by John Lehmann.

——. *French Provincial Cooking.* London: Michael Joseph Ltd., 1960.

——. *Italian Food.* New York: Alfred A. Knopf, 1958. First published in the UK 1954 by MacDonald.

Escoffier, A. *The Escoffier Cook Book: A Guide to the Fine Art of Cookery.* New York: Crown Publishers, 1941.

Faderman, Lillian. *Odd Girls and Twilight Lovers: A History of Lesbian Life in Twentieth-Century America.* New York: Penguin Books, 1992. First published 1991 by Columbia University Press.

Feirstein, Bruce. *Real Men Don't Eat Quiche: A Guidebook to All That Is Truly Masculine.* New York: Pocket Books, 1982.

Foucault, Michel. *The History of Sexuality, Volume 1: An Introduction.* Translated by Robert Hurley. New York: Vintage Books, 1980. English translation first published 1978 by Random House.

Franklin, Sara B., "Introduction," in *Edna Lewis: At the Table with an American Original,* edited by Sara B. Franklin, 1–9. Chapel Hill: The University of North Carolina Press, 2018.

Gadd, Christianne A. "The History of Esther Eng." OutHistory. https://outhistory.org/exhibits/show/esther-eng/essay.

Gold, Joni. *Their Friends Were Young and Gay: A Fairy Tale in Food.* San Francisco: self-published, 1979.

Gordon, Billi. *Billi Gordon's You've Had Worse Things in Your Mouth Cookbook.* San Francisco: West Graphics, 1985.

Gunn, Thom. *The Man with Night Sweats.* New York: The Noonday Press, 1993. First published 1992 by Farrar, Straus and Giroux.

Hajdu, David. *Lush Life: A Biography of Billy Strayhorn.* London: Granta Books, 1996.

Hall, Radclyffe. *The Well of Loneliness.* A Project Gutenberg of Australia ebook, 2015. First published 1928 by Jonathan Cape.

Harris, Jessica B. "Dining with James Baldwin." *Saveur,* May 15, 2017.

Hart, Joseph. "When Harry Met Betty." *The Rake,* January 29, 2007.

Hart, Mary. "Mystery Cake: Secret 'Ingredient X' Revealed for Baking Mammoth 'Chiffon.'" *Star Tribune* (Minneapolis, MN), February 15, 1948. Newspapers.com.

Hogan, Lou Rand. *The Gay Cookbook.* Los Angeles: Sherbourne Press, 1965. Facsimile of the Bell Publishing Company edition by Last Century Media, 2020.

Jacobs, Craig. "Did a Cook Called 'Stina' Really Exist in Niles Back in the 1870s?" *Niles Daily Star* (Niles, MI), October 17, 2008.

James Beard Foundation. *The James Beard Celebration Cookbook: Memories and Recipes from His Friends,* edited by Barbara Kafka. New York: William Morrow, 1990.

James, Henry. "Florentine Notes" in *Italian Hours.* A Project Gutenberg ebook, August 2004. First US edition published 1909 by Houghton Mifflin.

Johnson, Catherine. *Karl Bissinger.* Documentary rough cut. Private YouTube video, February 14, 2014. 53:00.

Kaiser, Charles. *The Gay Metropolis 1940–1996.* New York: Houghton Mifflin Company, 1997.

Kamp, David. *The United States of Arugula: How We Became a Gourmet Nation.* New York: Broadway Books, 2006.

Katz, Jonathan [Ned]. *Gay American History: Lesbians and Gay Men in the U.S.A.* New York: Harper Colophon Books, 1976.

———. *The Invention of Heterosexuality.* New York: The Penguin Group, 1995.

Kong, Travis S. K. *Oral Histories of Older Gay Men in Hong Kong: Unspoken but Unforgotten.* Hong Kong: Hong Kong University Press, 2019. Google Play.

Leed, Rick. *Dinner for Two.* San Francisco: Gay Sunshine, 1981.

Leeming, David. *Amazing Grace: A Life of Beauford Delaney.* New York: Oxford University Press, 1998. Kindle.

———. *James Baldwin: A Biography.* New York: Arcade Publishing, 2015. First published 1994 by Alfred A. Knopf.

Lewis, Edna, and Evangeline Peterson. *The Edna Lewis Cookbook.* Edinburg, VA: Axios Press, 2016. First published 1972 by Bobbs-Merrill.

Lewis, Edna, and Scott Peacock. *The Gift of Southern Cooking: Recipes and Revelations from Two Great Southern Cooks.* New York: Alfred A. Knopf, 2003.

Lewis, Sasha Gregory. *Sunday's Women: A Report on Lesbian Life Today.* Boston: Beacon Press, 1979.

Li, Siu Leung. *Cross-Dressing in Chinese Opera.* Hong Kong: Hong Kong University Press, 2003. EBSCO Publishing: eBook Collection.

Linzie, Anna. *The True Story of Alice B. Toklas: A Study of Three Autobiographies.* Iowa City: University of Iowa Press, 2006.

Lorde, Audre. *Zami: A New Spelling of My Name.* Berkeley, CA: Crossing Press, 1982. Google Play. First published 1982 by Persephone Press.

Loughery, John. *The Other Side of Silence: Men's Lives and Gay Identities, a Twentieth-Century History.* New York: Henry Holt and Company, 1998.

Lutes, Della T. *The Country Kitchen.* Boston: Little, Brown, and Company, 1937.

Mann, William J. *Behind the Screen: How Gays and Lesbians Shaped Hollywood 1910–1969.* New York: Viking, 2001.

Marks, Susan. *Finding Betty Crocker: The Secret Life of America's First Lady of Food.* Minneapolis: University of Minnesota Press, 2007. First published 2005 by Simon and Schuster.

Martin, Ellis, and Zach Ozma, eds. *We Both Laughed in Pleasure: The Selected Diaries of Lou Sullivan 1961–1991.* New York: Nightboat Books, 2019.

McNamee, Thomas. *The Man Who Changed the Way We Eat: Craig Claiborne and the American Food Renaissance.* New York: Free Press, 2012.

Mickler, Ernest Matthew. *Sinkin Spells, Hot Flashes, Fits and Cravins.* Berkeley, CA: Ten Speed Press, 1988.

———. *White Trash Cooking.* Berkeley, CA: Ten Speed Press, 1986.

Mims, Ben. "Sweet Southern Dreams." *Saveur*, February 27, 2012.

Neuhaus, Jessamyn. *Manly Meals and Mom's Home Cooking: Cookbooks and Gender in Modern America.* Baltimore, MD: The Johns Hopkins University Press, 2003.

Newton, Esther. *Cherry Grove, Fire Island: Sixty Years in America's First Gay and Lesbian Town.* Durham, NC: Duke University Press, 2014. Google Play. First published 1993 by Beacon Press.

Olney, Richard. *Reflexions.* New York: Brick Tower Press, 1999.

———. *Simple French Food.* New York: Atheneum, 1974.

———. *The French Menu Cookbook.* New York: Simon and Schuster, 1970.

Osman, Meg. "The Elegant Life of Esther Eng." *Forever a Pleasure* (blog). May 5, 2021. Accessed February 17, 2022.

Paddleford, Clementine. "New Discovery in Restaurants." *New York Herald*, March 24, 1951.

Painter, George. *The Vice Clique: Portland's Great Sex Scandal.* Portland, OR: Espresso Book Machine at Powell's, 2013.

Perez-Gallardo, Carla Kaya; Hannah Black; and Wheeler. *Please Wait to Be Tasted: The Lil' Deb's Oasis Cookbook.* New York: Princeton Architectural Press, 2022.

Rao, Nancy Yunhwa. *Chinatown Opera Theater in North America.* Chicago: University of Illinois Press, 2017. Internet Archive.

Regan, Iliana. *Burn the Place: A Memoir.* Chicago: Agate Midway, 2019.

Rolo, Charles J. "The New Bohemia." *Flair*, February 1950.

Sang, Tze-lan D. *The Emerging Lesbian: Female Same-Sex Desire in Modern China.* Chicago: The University of Chicago Press, 2003.

Schmidt, Stephen. "Secrets of Chiffon Cake." *Cook's Illustrated*, June 1996.

Sedgwick, Eve Kosofsky. *Epistemology of the Closet.* Berkeley: University of California Press, 2008. First published 1990 by University of California Press.

Shapiro, Laura. *Julia Child.* New York: Viking Penguin, 2007.

Simon, Linda. *The Biography of Alice B. Toklas.* Garden City, NY: Doubleday & Company, 1977.

Smith, Herman. *Kitchens Near and Far.* New York: M. Barrows & Company, 1946.

———. *Stina: The Story of a Cook.* New York: M. Barrows & Company, 1942.

Sontag, Susan. *Reborn: Early Diaries 1947–1963*. Edited by David Rieff. New York: Penguin Books, 2009. First published 2008 by Farrar, Straus and Giroux.

Spring, Justin. *The Gourmands' Way: Six Americans in Paris and the Birth of a New Gastronomy*. New York: Farrar, Straus and Giroux, 2017. Google Play.

Stein, Gertrude. *As Fine as Melanctha (1914–1930)*. Freeport, NY: Books for Libraries Press, 1969. Internet Archive.

———. *The Autobiography of Alice B. Toklas*. New York: The Modern Library, 1993. First published 1933 by Harcourt, Brace and Company.

———. *The Making of Americans*. Strelbytskyy Multimedia Publishing, 2024. Google Play. First published in the US 1934 by Harcourt, Brace and Company.

Steward, Samuel M. *Chapters from an Autobiography*. San Francisco: Grey Fox Press, 1981.

Tallman, Jean. "The Greatest American Chef." *Des Moines Register*, June 17, 1973. Newspapers.com.

Tante Ursule [Richard Olney]. "Custard Tarts." *Petits Propos Culinaires* (London: Prospect Books), no. 2 (August 1979): 18–19.

The Kitchen Fairy. *The Gay of Cooking*. Laguna Beach, CA: Fairy Publications, 1982.

Toklas, Alice B. *The Alice B. Toklas Cook Book*. New York: Harper & Brothers, 1954.

———. *The Alice B. Toklas Cook Book*. Garden City, NY: Anchor Books, 1960.

———. *The Alice B. Toklas Cook Book*. Foreword by M. F. K. Fisher, publisher's note by Simon Michael Bessie. New York: Harper & Row, 1984.

———. *Aromas and Flavors of Past and Present*. Introduction and comments by Poppy Cannon. New York: Harper & Brothers, 1958.

———. *What Is Remembered*. New York: Holt, Rinehart and Winston, 1963.

Truong, Monique. *The Book of Salt*. Boston: Mariner Books, 2004. First published 2003 by Houghton Mifflin Company.

Vidal, Gore. *The City and the Pillar, A Novel*. New York: Vintage International, 2003. Google Play. First published 1948 by E. P. Dutton & Co.

Vider, Stephen. *The Queerness of Home: Gender, Sexuality, and the Politics of Domesticity after World War II*. Chicago: The University of Chicago Press, 2021.

Waters, Alice. *The Chez Panisse Menu Cookbook*. In collaboration with Linda P. Guenzel. New York: Random House, 1982.

Wei, S. Louisa. "Finding Voices Through Her Images: Golden Gate Girls as an Attempt in Writing Women Filmmakers' History." *Feminist Media Histories* 2, no. 2 (April 2016): 32–46.

———, dir. *Golden Gate Girls*. Hong Kong: Women Make Movies, 2013. Kanopy, 90 min.

———. " 'She Wears Slacks': Pioneer Women Directors Esther Eng and Dorothy Arzner." In *Early Cinematic Experience of Hong Kong*, Book III, edited by Winnie Fu, 110–50. Hong Kong: Hong Kong Film Archive, 2014.

Williams, Tennessee. *A Streetcar Named Desire*. PBworks. First published 1947 by New Directions.

INDEX